Library of
Davidson College

PAUL CAMBON
Master Diplomatist

PAUL CAMBON
Master Diplomatist

by KEITH EUBANK

GREENWOOD PRESS, PUBLISHERS
WESTPORT, CONNECTICUT

Library of Congress Cataloging in Publication Data
Eubank, Keith.
  Paul Cambon, master diplomatist.

    Reprint of the ed. published by the University of
Oklahoma Press, Norman.
    Bibliography: p.
    Includes index.
    1. Cambon, Paul, 1843-1924. 2. France--Foreign
relations--1870-1940. 3. Diplomats--France--Biography.
[DC342.8.C32E8 1978]   327'.2'0924 [B]   78-6089
ISBN 0-313-20502-7

The publication of this volume has been aided
by a grant from the Ford Foundation.

Copyright 1960 by the University of Oklahoma Press,
Publishing Division of the University.

Reprinted with the permission of University of Oklahoma Press

Reprinted in 1978 by Greenwood Press, Inc.
51 Riverside Avenue, Westport, CT. 06880

Printed in the United States of America

10 9 8 7 6 5 4 3 2 1

To Marilyn

PREFACE

MODERN NATIONS have systematized their relations by diplomacy. The professional practitioner of diplomacy serves as the official eyes and ears of his native land. The necessity for trained diplomats has been belittled in the past. In too many minds, the diplomat is a striped-pants devil or an effeminate parasite. Recently in the United States, the diplomat has appeared in the role of a target for Congressional investigating committees.

In past decades diplomacy and diplomats have fallen on evil days. In the first flush of peace after the world war of 1914–18, some idealists announced that the day of the diplomat had ended. Nations would deal with one another on the basis of reason in the parliament of man at Geneva. Open diplomacy openly practiced, without professional diplomats, would guarantee the safety of sovereign states. Politicians then engaged in what passed for open diplomacy; yet all too often the results were tragic. The counsel of professional diplomats was disregarded by the politicians; the advice of incompetent political appointees prevailed upon those who should have known better. Major diplomatic posts were filled by untrained or mediocre personnel because diplomatic staffs had been allowed to rot. When catastrophe broke on the world in 1939, the professional diplomat could not alone be blamed.

There is still much popular distrust of diplomats. Yet no adequate substitute for the diplomat has been found. Possibly a re-evaluation of diplomats and their profession is in order.

PAUL CAMBON

The pages that follow are offered as a case study of the value of a diplomat. The story is told necessarily through his eyes, and reflects the world as he saw it.

In 1870, France faced Germany alone and unaided. A short campaign brought her to a disgraceful defeat. When she faced Germany in 1914, France was no longer alone. Not only did she have friends and an ally, but Bismarck's network of alliances had been weakened. France had obtained a diplomatic victory. This is the story of Paul Cambon's role in achieving this victory. Perhaps it may illustrate the value of professional diplomats to the Western world, again beset by a time of troubles.

Keith Eubank

Denton, Texas
September 9, 1960

ACKNOWLEDGMENTS

IN MY INVESTIGATIONS of the career of Paul Cambon, I have had the aid of many persons, and it is a pleasure to acknowledge these obligations. Henri Cambon and Roger Cambon have been gracious with their help; however, this is not an authorized biography. I am deeply grateful for the advice and aid given by Professor Lynn M. Case of the University of Pennsylvania, who first suggested the subject. Professor Harry T. Taylor of Bloomfield College and Dean Frank H. Gafford of North Texas State College read parts of the manuscript and made useful suggestions. Professors Irby C. Nichols of the History Department of North Texas State College read the entire manuscript, and it benefited greatly from his advice. Sir Harold Nicolson, the late H. Wickham Steed, G. P. Gooch, and Paul Mantoux were kind enough to discuss Paul Cambon with me. Margaret I. Nichols and Vonie Jean Owens not only relieved me of the burden of typing the manuscript but also saved me from many errors in style.

For their kind assistance I must thank the Library of the University of Pennsylvania, the New York Public Library, Library of the American Philosophical Society in Philadelphia, Reading Room of the British Museum, Public Record Office in London, Foreign Office Library in London, National Archives in Washington, and the Library of North Texas State College, Denton, Texas.

The manuscript could not have been completed without the help of two research grants from the Faculty Research Committee of North Texas State College.

Also, I wish to express my gratitude to the following publishers for permission to quote from books published by them: Houghton Mifflin Company, J. A. Spender, *The Life of the Right Hon. Sir Henry Campbell-Bannerman;* J. B. Lippincott Company, Viscount Grey of Fallodon, *Twenty-five Years, 1892–1916;* Constable and Company, Ltd., Harold Nicolson, *Sir Arthur Nicolson, Bart., First Lord Carnock;* Council on Foreign Relations, André Giraud, "Diplomacy, Old and New," *Foreign Affairs;* Nicholson and Watson, Ltd., Reginald, Viscount Esher, *Journals and Letters;* J. B. Lippincott Company, J. A. Spender, *Life, Journalism and Politics;* Éditions Bernard Grasset, Paul Cambon, *Correspondance;* Oxford University Press, A. J. P. Taylor, *The Struggle for Mastery in Europe;* Longmans, Green and Company, G. P. Gooch, *Studies in Diplomacy and Statecraft;* Oxford University Press, Luigi Albertini, *The Origins of the War of 1914;* Odhams Press, W. S. Churchill, *The World Crisis, 1911–1918.*

Most of all I am indebted to my wife, Marilyn C. Eubank, for her help and encouragement.

KEITH EUBANK

CONTENTS

Preface		vii
Acknowledgments		ix
I.	The Training of a Diplomat	3
II.	Creation of the Tunisian Protectorate	16
III.	Madrid and Constantinople	34
IV.	Two Nightmares: Armenia and Crete	46
V.	Creation of the Entente Cordiale	61
VI.	Testing the Entente	90
VII.	Strengthening the Entente	109
VIII.	The Balkans and Morocco	126
IX.	Entente or Alliance?	143
X.	Prelude to Armageddon	156
XI.	War!	167
XII.	Peace and Retirement	191
XIII.	An Evaluation	201
Appendices:	A. Cambon's Discussion with Lansdowne on May 17, 1905	207
	B. Cambon's Inability to Speak English	209
Bibliography		210
Index		214

ILLUSTRATIONS

Paul Cambon	*facing page* 50
Seizing the Guns during the French Commune, 1871	51
"Au Revoir!" (Cartoon from *Punch*)	66
General Boulanger on his Way to the Chamber of Deputies, 1888	67
The Marquis of Salisbury Protesting the Armenian Massacres, 1895	98
Cartoon of Jules Cambon, 1902	99
The Visit of Edward VII to France, 1903	114
The Algeciras Seance	115
The French Diplomatic Team	146
Pierre Loti	147
Viscount Grey of Fallodon	162
Kaiser Wilhelm at the Height of his Glory, 1913	163

MAPS

The Ottoman Empire, circa 1890	*page* 37
Africa, 1914	93
The Balkan Peninsula, 1914	159

PAUL CAMBON
Master Diplomatist

I. THE TRAINING OF A DIPLOMAT

Louis phillipe maintained an uneasy hold on the throne of France in 1843. Louis Napoleon, a prisoner in the fortress of Ham, passed the hours reading, writing, making love to a cobbler's daughter, and planning for the day when he would seize that throne. A united Germany was only a figment of poets' imaginations, Otto von Bismarck was a young country squire, and Great Britain was settling down to the long reign of Victoria.

In this year Virginie Cambon, wife of Hippolyte Cambon, gave birth to their first child in Paris on January 20; he was baptized Pierre Paul. This baby grew to manhood during the Second Empire, watched the ignominious fall of Napoleon III, assisted in the administration of the young Third Republic, and helped in raising France to a diplomatic pinnacle unthought of by Louis Phillipe, only dreamed of by Napoleon III, and dreaded by Bismarck. Another baby was born into the Cambon family on April 4, 1845, and christened Jules Martin. He, like his elder brother, assisted in creating the diplomatic structure that crumbled with the death of the Third Republic in 1940.

Hippolyte Cambon died in 1849, and the rearing of his sons was left to his wife. Virginie Cambon was an attractive young mother with chestnut-brown hair, blue eyes, and a charming simplicity. To the day of her death in 1905 at the age of eighty-four, she maintained her interest in the latest books, the theater, politics, and painting. In politics she was a liberal, imparting her fervent anti-Bonapartist beliefs to her young sons. The Cambon home became a meeting place in Paris for many persons who were important in the political and intellectual life of the last years of the Second Empire and who made a lasting impression on the minds of the young Cambon boys.

During the boyhood of Paul, France underwent profound political changes. In February, 1848, the July Monarchy fell; the attempt at a Second Republic failed with the coup d'état of President Louis Napoleon on December 2, 1851. Eight-year-old Paul heard the excited announcement early on the morning of December 2 that the Chamber of Deputies had been occupied by troops of the Prince-President. From their home, Paul and his brother watched the troops galloping by. Six-year-old Jules thought it delightful, but not Paul, for he had been plying his grandparents with questions about the events. "If there is a revolution, they will cut the throat of the world," he announced grimly to his brother. "I was already nourishing some very conservative opinions," he later commented.[1]

Louis Napoleon established the Second Empire in 1852, capitalizing on the name of Napoleon and the dissatisfaction with the Second Republic. During the eighteen-year history of the Second Empire, the Cambon boys grew up and completed their education. They first attended a boarding school on the Left Bank and later were day students for some years at the Lycée Louis-le-Grand. Both boys made good records, but they could not be classed as extraordinary. Although Paul completed a leisurely study of law in three years, the prospect of a legal career did not excite him. He was not brokenhearted when he argued and lost his first and only case. For the next few years he worked as a law clerk, developing a clarity of thought and a precision of speech that proved to be invaluable in diplomacy.

Most of Cambon's friends were republican in thought and not at all happy with the reign of Napoleon III. Paul and his brother were welcomed in the homes of Charles and Jules Ferry, Adolphe Thiers,

---

[1] Henri Cambon, *Paul Cambon, ambassadeur de France*, 11–15; Geneviève Tabouis, *Jules Cambon par l'un des siens*, 7–15; Cambon to Henri Cambon, Dec. 2, 1911, Paul Cambon, *Correspondance, 1870–1924*, II, 305–307. Hereafter references to Paul Cambon do not include his given name. However, other members of the Cambon family will be identified by their given names.

and Jules Simon, all of whom became leaders in the Third Republic. These men influenced the thinking of the Cambon brothers and helped their careers in the service of the Third Republic, which followed the downfall of the Second Empire after the Franco-Prussian War in 1870.

A quarrel over the Hohenzollern candidacy for the throne of Spain precipitated the conflict. By July 15 war had been declared in Paris. France faced a German coalition without allies. Hostilities began on August 4 with a Prussian victory at Wissembourg. Defeated at Sedan on September 1, the French forces under Marshal MacMahon and the Emperor surrendered. By the evening of September 3, 1870, the news of Sedan was known throughout Paris; before the end of the next day, Paris had another revolution, ending the Second Empire and launching Paul Cambon on his career of government service.

Although a member of the National Guard, Paul was not called up for service as was his brother. Throughout the struggle, Paul remained in Paris following the war in the newspapers and impatiently awaiting orders for his unit of the National Guard. When Jules Ferry became mayor of Paris under the new regime, he remembered his young friend Paul Cambon and appointed him to his first position in the French government as secretary to the mayor, with his office in the Hôtel de Ville, the city hall of Paris.

The struggle with Prussia went on. By September 19, Paris had been invested. Despite attempts to carry on the war in the provinces, French resistance was crumbling. The fighting around Paris was desperate in December and January, 1871, but the situation was hopeless. By February 26 preliminary proposals for peace had been signed, and a final treaty was completed on May 10, 1871.

Cambon's work with Ferry lasted through the winter of 1870–71, while Paris was besieged by the Germans from without and wracked by turmoil from within. He emerged unscathed from the uprising of October 31, 1870, when a mob invaded the Hôtel de Ville demanding a new government. On January 22, 1871, he aided in the defense of the Hôtel de Ville when loyal troops dispersed a mob of National Guard who threatened to storm the seat of the Paris city government.

Although fighting around Paris ended in February, 1871, the situation was ugly and explosive. Many Parisians felt that France had betrayed them during the siege. The newly elected National Assembly was royalist and showed its royalism by meeting at Versailles, an insult to republican Paris. The Parisian mobs were antagonized by the announcement by the national government that the moratorium on the payment of commercial bills and house rents, which had been in effect since August 13, 1870, would be ended. Resentment increased when the pay of the National Guard was stopped before economic conditions had returned to normal; this pay was the only means of subsistence for many of the poorer classes in Paris. Only a spark was needed to set off civil war in a city where nerves were on edge after a long siege.

Early on March 18, 1871, regular troops were sent to seize some cannon held by the Paris National Guard on the Butte Montmartre because the Paris National Guard was now controlled by radicals and could no longer be trusted. Inexperienced troops, selected for the operation, easily captured the cannon. As they awaited the arrival of horses to draw the cannon away, a screaming mob closed around the young soldiers. The officers were captured by the mob, all discipline vanished, and the troops began to fraternize with the mob. The National Guard reoccupied the Butte Montmartre, and some of the captured officers were slain. The civil strife known to history as the Commune had begun.

Cambon, working in the Hôtel de Ville, followed these events by telegraph and kept Ferry fully informed while the latter was in a council meeting in the Ministry of Foreign Affairs. Soon after the disaster on the Butte Montmartre, a mob appeared in front of the Hôtel de Ville. A rifle shot scattered them, and they fled, expecting a volley to follow.

Ferry hurried back from the council meeting, where the members had agreed to defend the Hôtel de Ville. By early evening barricades were erected in the streets leading to the Place Hôtel de Ville. The defenders, who were now cut off from outside aid, blocked off the stairs, reinforced the doors, and curtained the windows to prevent any light from filtering through to help the marksmanship of the rebels.

The preparations were wasted, because an order came for the evacuation of all troops from the Hôtel de Ville. Adolphe Thiers, provisional president of the new republic, had decided to withdraw the regular army troops from the city, regroup them, and bring up reinforcements before quelling the Commune. The troops slipped out the back of the Hôtel de Ville, crossed the Notre Dame bridge to the left bank of the Seine, and made their way to the Champ de Mars. Only Jules Ferry, his brother Charles, a Dr. Worms, an engineer named Buette, and Paul and Jules Cambon were left in the building.

Jules Ferry announced that he intended to remain there. Paul Cambon spoke for the others—they too would remain with Ferry. Then, upon the advice of Charles Ferry, Jules decided that the six men should leave. Charles had reminded his brother that they would probably all be killed, and it would be useless to be responsible for the death of the sons of his old friend, Mme Cambon.

Before the group left, Paul Cambon persuaded Ferry to relieve himself of his responsibility toward the government. Ferry telegraphed his superiors that he was leaving because the troops had gone and the insurgents would soon seize the Hôtel de Ville. As soon as the telegram had been sent, the telegraph wires were cut. The six men slipped out a side door to the quay and made their way up the right bank of the Seine.

Jules Ferry, Buette, and Paul and Jules Cambon hurried to the *mairie*[2] of the first *arrondissement* in the Place Saint-Germain-l'Auxerois. Ferry made contact with the rest of the mayors, who were meeting in another *mairie,* and asked them to join him for a meeting.

Bored with waiting for the mayors to arrive, Paul Cambon slipped back along the quays to investigate the situation at the Hôtel de Ville. He found "the place swarming with armed members of the Paris National Guard, the building shone brightly with lights, the windows were open, but the doors were tightly closed." As he sauntered

---

[2] For administrative purposes, Paris was divided into districts or *arrondissements*. Each was administered by a mayor with his office in the *mairie* or town hall.

along the iron fence that bordered the building, a venerable member of the National Guard halted him with a demand to know what he wanted.

"Nothing," Cambon quickly replied.

Innocently he asked the significance of the lights and the troops.

"If you do not know," the old man snapped, "it's because you are a bad citizen!"

The young man said no more. He turned and hastily retraced his steps up the quay to the *mairie* of the first *arrondissement*, where he found Ferry meeting with the mayors and explaining the day's events. Then came a loud banging at the gate of the *mairie*. Voices screamed, "Death to Ferry! We want Ferry!"

In a moment the room was emptied as the mayors tried to escape the fury of the mob. At the gate of the *mairie,* armed men seeking Ferry inspected the mayors. Meline, the deputy mayor, abruptly stopped Ferry and his friends as they were about to leave by the front door and shoved them into a small room with a window that opened on a court separating the *mairie* from the church of Saint-Germain-l'Auxerois. Paul Cambon slipped out the window and motioned to Ferry and the others to follow him. All four men crept quietly along the wall surrounding the rectory of the church. A quick ring of the bell at the rectory door brought the concierge who admitted them. Arousing the curé from his bed, Ferry begged him to allow the fleeing men to pass through the church and out to the Rue de Prêtres, from which they could make their way to safety along the quays. Without asking any questions, the curé led the fugitives out of the rectory and across the court that separated church and rectory. In the distance the cries of the mob seeking Ferry echoed through the night.

Once inside the church, the men crept silently through the dark nave. At the front door of the church a hurried council took place. Had the mob thought to encircle the church? Paul Cambon scrambled up to a room in the tower, where he found a small stained-glass window. Cautiously, he opened it to reconnoiter. He returned to the others in a few minutes and whispered that the street was deserted except for an armed man who stood on the corner. A hurried consultation took place. Paul and Buette each had a revolver, and if the lone man gave them any trouble, Paul and Buette would hold him off long enough for Ferry to escape through an alley. Slowly they opened the church door. There was no move from the man on the corner, and they all slipped away safely to the Cambon home, where they woke Mme Cambon, recounted to her the history of the day, and obtained some food.

After he had eaten, Paul Cambon started out on a lone expedition to see how the mayors of the *arrondissements* were faring with the new rulers of Paris. He found them meeting at the *mairie* of the second *arrondissement* with delegates from the rebels, who sought some *modus vivendi* with the mayors in order that elections might be held to give the new Paris government some form of legality. Cambon walked quietly to the back of the room where the meeting was in progress. The mayor of the second *arrondissement* was presiding. Cambon slipped in behind him, identified himself, and the mayor explained the situation in a whisper. It was imperative that the mayors be given some mandate from the government in order to keep law and order. Cambon promised to bring the mandate later in the day or on March 20, as it was now about 3:00 A.M., March 19. He hurried out to report all of this to Jules Ferry.

Near daybreak Cambon slipped into a side door of the Gare Montparnasse, which was already occupied by the National Guard, and bought a railroad ticket to Versailles for Ferry. He took it to Ferry and begged him to leave the city at once while escape was still possible. Ferry seemed impervious to the dangers around him as he dawdled, leisurely seeking a book for the journey and pausing to ask Cambon for his revolver. At last the harassed young secretary shepherded Ferry into the railroad station unnoticed—so he thought. For a moment, they paused at the foot of the stairs leading up to the station platform.

"Look, Ferry!" someone shouted.

Armed men dashed through the waiting room. Ferry ran up the stairs four at a time and jumped on a train that was just leaving.

By the time his pursuers reached the platform, the train was well on its way, bearing Ferry to safety.

Cambon eluded his pursuers and later in the same day reached Versailles. There he found the remainder of the French national government crowded into the prefecture of Versailles. He informed Thiers, the chief executive of the new national government, of the mayors' desire for a mandate from the government to help in dealing with the Commune. It was granted, and once again Cambon entered the city and delivered the mandate to the mayors. After his return from Paris, he took up his work at Versailles. The government prepared to retake the city while the occupying Prussian troops watched.[3]

Thus the Commune began. It was the last gasp of the old street fighters of Paris, whose ancestors had raised the barricades in 1830 and 1848. The Communards fought to preserve the autonomy of Paris, for they envisioned a France composed of federated townships. Some were socialists and some favored co-operatives; yet all were republicans. The government completed its preparations, and its forces attacked the city on May 21. The last of the Communards died before a firing squad in the Père la Chaise cemetery on May 28.

The Franco-Prussian War, the siege of Paris, the Commune, and its tragic consequences all left an impression on the mind of Paul Cambon that stayed with him throughout his life. As an impressionable young man, intelligent and patriotic, he had watched the collapse of his country. At a time of crisis, France had been alienated from all her possible allies. To rebuild France and to strengthen her in order that this would never happen again became the passion and mission of Paul Cambon and many others of his generation. His later career can be understood only in the light of the humiliating days of the Franco-Prussian War and the Commune. Never again must France undergo such ignominy. He did not strive for a bloody revenge, but he sought to so bolster France that she would not again face a stronger foe, friendless and alone.

For the present, Paul Cambon helped repair the damage of war.

[3] "Souvenirs de 18 Mars 1871," *Correspondance,* I, 20–32. This is the only memoir that Paul Cambon ever wrote.

THE TRAINING OF A DIPLOMAT

In less than three weeks after his arrival at Versailles, he was appointed secretary-general to the prefect of the department of Alpes-Maritimes and took up his new duties in Nice on April 12, 1871. Cambon was transferred to Marseilles in August, 1871, where he became acting prefect of the department of Bouches-du-Rhône when his superior died unexpectedly. On February 5, 1872, he was appointed prefect of the department of Aube. His work in Aube was ended when Thiers resigned as president of the French Republic on May 24, 1873, in a battle with the National Assembly. Cambon, who was devoted to the Republic and a personal friend of Thiers, relinquished his position on July 1.

While Paul Cambon had been prefect of Aube, he had fallen in love with Anna Guépratte, whose father commanded a cavalry brigade in Troyes, where the prefecture was located. The young couple could not afford to get married until Cambon obtained a job as inspector of child welfare in the department of the Seine, through the help of Georges Clemenceau. They were married on January 7, 1875, by Paul's uncle, the Abbé Larue, in the cathedral of Meaux, afterwards setting up housekeeping in an apartment in Paris on the Rue de Clichy.

Anna was well suited to Paul in temperament and personality. She was warmhearted, devoted to her husband, and interested in all that went on around her. Unhappily, three years after their marriage, an unfortunate accident left her a semi-invalid for the remainder of her life. For Paul, her condition meant constant care and prolonged separation as Anna tried to improve her health by spending winters in less rigorous climates. Her poor health affected his career, also, for he could not accept posts in areas where the climate was harsh.

After the republican victories in the elections of February, 1876, Cambon returned to office in Besançon on March 22 as the prefect of the department of Doubs. Here his life was brightened by the birth of his only child, a son, on May 14, 1876. Little Henri became the center of all Paul Cambon's hopes, ambitions, and affections.[4]

[4] Cambon to Jules Cambon, April 11, 1871, March 27, 1876, *Correspondance,* I, 33, 72–73; H. Cambon, *Paul Cambon,* 20–24, 27–29.

The work of Cambon in the department of Doubs was ended by the crisis of May 16, 1877. President MacMahon forced Jules Simon and his cabinet to resign, although his party had a strong majority in the Chamber of Deputies. When the new premier, the Duke de Broglie, forced a dissolution of the Chamber, Cambon resigned on June 25.

Since his fifteen months in Besançon had strained his finances, Cambon took his family to Switzerland, where he could live more cheaply. At the end of the summer the Cambons moved into the home of Anna's family near Provins. Here, on September 24, Cambon broke his leg while riding a horse. Despite competent medical care, the accident resulted in a permanent shortening of the leg, and for the rest of his life, it was necessary for Cambon to wear a shoe with a built-up heel.

The injury forced him to remain in bed for many months cut off from the political battles being fought between the defenders of the Republic and MacMahon and his allies. The October elections were republican victories. In late November MacMahon began to lose the support of the Senate, on which he based his attempt to set up a conservative government. At last he surrendered and allowed the republicans to govern France. On December 13, Jules Dufaure constructed a cabinet from the Left Center with Émile Marcère, a friend of Cambon, as minister of the interior. Marcère offered Cambon the job of prefect in the department of Nord, which he accepted. At the end of December, Cambon, still on crutches, began his work in the prefecture at Lille.

The new republican government, secure in its position, determined to secularize the educational system. Jules Ferry, minister of public instruction, hoped to modernize the educational system of France and insure that the instruction would be less monarchist and more republican in tone. In March, 1880, the government issued decrees ordering the dissolution of the authorized religious orders that dominated French education. The most prominent of these was the Jesuit Order, which the republicans were seeking to destroy.

Although Cambon thought that extremists on both sides were using

THE TRAINING OF A DIPLOMAT

the struggle only for their own ends, he dispersed the Jesuits in his department without any undue disturbances on July 1, 1880. A legal battle over the right of Cambon as prefect to dissolve the orders followed; not until November did the courts declare in his favor. He promptly dissolved the remaining orders but not without violence. The affair so disgusted him that he considered resigning from the service of the Third Republic.[5] However, other events were to take Paul Cambon away from the battle between church and state.

In the spring of 1881 a French army had conquered Tunisia. Originally this army had been ordered to punish marauding tribesmen and to secure the Algerian frontier. The Bey of Tunis was forced to sign the Treaty of Bardo, which stated that France would control the Bey's foreign relations and guarantee his person and territory. French military forces were to occupy the country. France would reorganize the financial affairs of the Bey. Nowhere in this treaty was there mention of the methods to implement its provisions. There was no indication how France would control Tunisian affairs.

In Paris the government had no definite ideas about the control of Tunisia. The French could annex Tunisia as they had Algeria; most Frenchmen in 1881 would probably have thought such a procedure quite proper. In May, 1881, however, Jules Ferry, the premier, announced to the Chamber of Deputies that France had no intention of annexing Tunisia, although the Treaty of Bardo promised French protection for the territory of the Bey. This dilemma was solved by the development of the protectorate by Paul Cambon.

Early in 1882, Jules Herbette, the director of personnel in the Ministry of Foreign Affairs, asked Cambon if he would be willing to organize Tunisia. After first refusing the offer, Cambon accepted his new position on February 15. The *Journal Officiel* reported on February 23 that by the decree of February 18, "M. Cambon (Paul), prefect first class, and named in this rank to the duties of resident minister of the French Republic at Tunis, replacing M. Roustan."

[5] London *Times,* July 1, 2, 4, 5, Nov. 6, 10, 1880; Cambon to Mme Paul Cambon, Oct. 8 Nov. 6, 10, Dec. 29, 1880, Jan. 31, 1881, *Correspondance,* I, 122, 128–32, 135.

For the next month Cambon worked in Paris, participating in conferences about his work. He had to force Charles Freycinet, now premier, to make up his mind on the situation. What form of government would the former prefect set up? Should he exercise only diplomatic influence? Why 40,000 occupation troops, if he were to exercise only diplomatic influence? Would the Chamber of Deputies guarantee the debts of the Bey? Without a solution to these problems Cambon anticipated troubles in Tunisia.

By March 2, a preliminary report was drawn up covering the conferences on Tunisia. There would be no annexation—a completely new departure in French colonial history. The Bey's government would be maintained, and the country would be administered in the name of the Bey. The military authority would be subordinated to that of the resident minister, a Tunisian army would be created, and a French judicial system would be erected to replace the consular jurisdiction.[6] The financial system would be reorganized, and the international financial commission set up in 1869 to handle the Bey's debts would be suppressed.

From General Jean Billot, the minister of war, Cambon received the first inkling of the disagreement that would almost wreck his career. Billot warned him that "all the military are pessimistic because they are not allowed to treat Tunisia as a conquered country." Why should the glory of running the newest acquisition to the French empire be entrusted to a mere civilian? The attitude of the military did not trouble Cambon at the moment, but it would in the future.

Cambon left Paris for Tunisia on March 30. He could wait no longer for the government's decision on the policy for that country. A friend had already suggested that it would be better for him to go to Tunisia without definite instructions and look over the situation; then he would be in a better position to advise the government

---

[6] The consular jurisdiction resulted from the Capitulations—the system in force in some Moslem countries. The consuls tried cases involving their nationals who were accused of breaking local laws. Sometimes this system degenerated into semianarchy because the consuls would refuse to convict if they disapproved of the law in question.

about future policy. The procrastination of Freycinet forced him to do just this, although it was a procedure that he had sworn to reject. Paul Cambon left France without formal instructions because the French government did not know what to do with Tunisia. Indeed, he left France with no instructions at all other than a statement from his old friend Jules Ferry: "Go, look, propose!" The organization of Tunisia was now the concern of a thirty-nine-year-old prefect.

Freycinet may have allowed this situation to develop in order to protect himself from the wrath of the Chamber of Deputies if they did not like the Tunisian policy. He remembered the furor when the Chamber learned of the casualties suffered by the troops in Tunisia because of poor sanitation. When the dread day dawned on which Freycinet would have to answer for events in Tunisia, he could place all the blame on Cambon, who would be unable to produce any written instructions from his government to defend his actions.

In midafternoon of April 1, 1882, Cambon sailed from Toulon on the *Hirondelle,* a man-of-war placed at his disposal by the government.

II. CREATION OF
THE TUNISIAN PROTECTORATE

Tunisia was an economic ruin in 1882. Repeated invasions of Vandals, Arabs, Berbers, Spaniards, and Turks had laid waste the flourishing country that once had been the granary of the Roman Empire. Deforestation had injured the productivity of the land and increased the problem of water supply. Misrule in the government had only hastened the country's decay. Life and property were so insecure that natives registered as protected subjects of the European powers. Robbers roamed the countryside at will.

Ostensibly the Bey of Tunis, Mohammed es Sadok, ruled the country, but the real ruler was Mustapha Ben Ismail, the grand vizier, under whom corruption and favoritism flourished. Mustapha, a former collector of cigarette butts, had struck the Bey's fancy as a youth and had been brought into the palace.

The city of Tunis was a curious mixture of European and Moorish architecture, narrow, filthy streets, and noisy bazaars. From a distance the white stucco houses glared in the sun. The dusty streets thronged with a variety of racial and national types, who breathed in the sights and strange smells peculiar to a city in North Africa. Few of the streets were paved except in the European quarter. The city possessed only one hospital, the lower floor of which served as an insane asylum. The Bey's palace, Dar-el-Bey, dominated the better section of the city. The Kasba, or city fortress, was in ruins, although the Bey's ragged troops still guarded it with rusty matchlock rifles.

CREATION OF THE TUNISIAN PROTECTORATE

Paul Cambon caught sight of North Africa for the first time as the *Hirondelle* entered the Gulf of Tunis early in the morning of April 2, 1882. Cannon boomed a fifteen-gun salute that thundered around the white walls of La Goulette, the port town, until one wall collapsed. The ragged Tunisian soldiers presented arms as Cambon landed, and a crowd of Tunisians and Frenchmen were there to meet him.

On April 3, Cambon visited the Bey to assure him that his throne was secure. The Bey's horoscope had proclaimed his removal, and the roar of the cannon and the massing of troops for Cambon's arrival had seemed to verify the prediction. The next day Cambon visited Cardinal Lavigerie, the archbishop of Algiers and Carthage. In the afternoon, the French colony, the Moslem protégés, and the protected Jews called on their new defender. He assured the French colony of "his unremitting care" for their interest and of his desire to "second the government of the Bey and to show that France had not lost her renown as a civilizing nation."

On the same day, the call of the foreign consuls reminded Cambon of a musical comedy. The Russian consul was blind and deaf; the consulship had been in the same family for the last fifty years. The United States of America was represented by a consul who was a doctor, who was unable to speak French, and who dressed in the uniform of an American general whenever possible. The consul of Austria appeared wearing a helmet complete with white plumes. Cambon felt sorry for these men, who had nothing to occupy their time since very few of their nationals lived in Tunisia. All they did was "to decide questions of precedence and put on their uniforms, their epaulettes, and their sabers in order to pay calls on each other from time to time."[1]

When the official calls had been completed, Cambon and his staff drew up a report on Tunisia and the solution for her ills. The most important job for France was to obtain the abolition of the Capitulations. Under the Capitulations the consuls could paralyze the government by acquitting anyone who refused to obey the laws or pay taxes.

[1] Cambon to Mme Paul Cambon, April 3, 4, 1882, *Correspondance*, I, 167–68.

Cambon believed that a drastic remedy for the financial ills of the country was imperative, for the deficit that year would reach fifteen million francs. There seemed to be no way out of the financial quagmire except for France to assume the Bey's debts.

Cambon proposed to revitalize the economic life of Tunisia through the resources, institutions, and personnel of the country itself. France would assume the debts and intervene where necessary to maintain law and order. France need supply only a small staff to direct this job, and the foreign staff would not be conspicuous if native institutions and talent were used. The Tunisians would be satisfied, since they would still be ruled by their coreligionists, and they would have honesty and justice in their government. This program depended on two important conditions: first, the suppression of the international commission that handled the Bey's debts because it drained the economic life of the country, and, second, the suppression of the Capitulations. In place of the latter, Cambon wanted French courts to deal with cases involving Frenchmen. If the powers in Paris would not accept this minimum program, absolutely nothing could be accomplished in Tunisia.

Freycinet replied by letter on May 8 that he had been quite interested in reading Cambon's first report, yet nothing happened. Tired of waiting for action, Cambon left for Paris on May 20. He found the government suffering one of the frequent cabinet crises of the Third Republic; consequently, Freycinet was afraid to launch a bold policy in Tunisia. Eventually, Cambon obtained the assent of the parliamentary committee on Tunisian laws to the redemption of the debt and the suppression of the Capitulations.

On June 11, 1882, the massacres in Alexandria brought the Egyptian question to a boil. Through his friends in the Ministry of Foreign Affairs, Cambon learned that England was preparing to occupy Port Said "with or without us." As a price for French aid, the British proposed to suppress the Capitulations in Tunisia, but the Freycinet cabinet would have none of it, much to Cambon's disgust. He warned the Premier that they would awaken one morning to find the English occupying Port Said and their opportunity to settle the Capitulations lost. By September, British troops had entered Cairo after occupying the Suez Canal. The complete abandonment of Egypt by France to England was to Cambon "a moral defeat which will make us decline to the status of a second-rate power."[2]

Cambon returned to Tunis on July 6, bringing with him a saber from the President of the Republic for the Bey of Tunis. But more important, he brought a treaty for the Bey's signature, assuring him that France would observe his sovereign rights and administer justice in his name. He presented the saber to the Bey on July 8. Then they began to discuss each other's health. When the Bey complained of an eye disease, Cambon recommended Lingleton's patent medicine salve and promised to find some. Changing the topic, Cambon brought up the treaty; and with a little assurance, the Bey signed. The ground had been prepared by Mustapha ben Ismail, the former collector of cigarette butts, who hoped that Cambon would arrange to settle some of his outstanding debts. There remained only the job of obtaining the assent of the Chamber of Deputies, but that was never accomplished: this treaty was later superseded by more important treaties.

Cambon spent the remainder of the summer negotiating the submission of the dissident elements in Tunisia, who had fled across the border into Tripolitania rather than submit to the French. The rebels waited at the Tunisian border for aid and leadership from the Sultan of Turkey, whom they thought would produce a united Islamic force capable of driving the French from Tunisia. However, the Egyptian crisis diverted the Sultan's attention and efforts while the Tunisian refugees starved at the border. By the end of the summer some of the tribes and their leaders began to cross the border into Tunisia, where they surrendered to the Bey and the French. Cambon promised amnesty to those who returned peacefully and pleaded with them to submit because Allah distributed power as He saw fit. As the refugees returned, Cambon hurried to protect them against native robbers and French colonists, the latter being often worse than the robbers.

In the summer of 1882 the Bey designated Cambon as the "official

[2] Cambon to d'Estournelles, June 11, Oct. 8, 1882, Cambon to Mme Paul Cambon, Aug. 4, 5, 1882, *Correspondance,* I, 173–75, 180–81, 186–87.

intermediary in our relations with the representatives of friendly powers." When Bey Mohammed es Sadok died in October, Cambon invested Bey Sid Ali with power in the name of the French government. At the official reception that followed the investiture, Cambon introduced the new consuls to the new Bey, thus establishing himself as the Bey's intermediary.[3]

These developments helped Cambon's position in Tunisia, but they were an unconscious change in his original conception of the protectorate. Tunisian officials were being overshadowed by personnel from France. No longer did Cambon stand in the wings—he had advanced to the center of the stage. Under the conditions in Tunisia, this was perhaps inevitable.

As the representative of the French government, Cambon wanted a more legal basis for the protectorate. *De facto* recognition was not enough; he wanted it to be *de jure*. Only by ending the Capitulations could this be achieved. However, France alone could not abolish them, because other governments had to give their consent.

On March 10, 1883, Cambon left for Paris to confer on ways and means of reorganizing the Tunisian administration and abolishing the Capitulations. In Paris his pleas brought results, for he returned to Tunis on April 24 with the decree of March 27 that set up French tribunals in Tunisia and brought French citizens and protégés under French law. The new law was promulgated through beylical decrees, but the personnel of the courts came from Algeria. This new system was to replace gradually the consular courts and prepare the way for the ending of the Capitulations.

To the bureaucrats in the Ministry of Justice it was only logical to use personnel trained in Algeria because some day Tunisia would be annexed as Algeria had been. This was not the intention of Cambon, and the government's error almost ruined his career. The new judges knew only what had been done in Algeria, where French justice had

---

[3] Reade to Granville, July 3, Aug. 9, 23, Oct. 31, 1882, Cambon to Reade, Oct. 28, 1882, Public Record Office, London, MSS, Foreign Office, Tunisia, 102, vol. 140 (hereafter cited as PRO, FO, Tunisia, 102:140); Bey to Reade, Aug. 9, 1882, *ibid.*, 335:156, 2.

been imposed by force and the natives had been pushed back into the hinterland much as the white man had pushed back the Indians in America. By the imposition of French land laws the natives had been dispossessed, becoming practically serfs. Neither the judges from Algeria nor the Parisian bureaucrats realized that Cambon sought to create an entirely different regime in Tunisia. There the native was to have the same legal rights as Frenchmen and other Europeans.

On June 8, Cambon and the Bey signed the La Marsa Convention, drawn up in Paris during Cambon's recent trip. Under the terms of the Convention the Bey promised financial and administrative reforms desired by the French government, and, in turn, the French government agreed to guarantee his debts. The importance of the treaty came in the first article: "In order to help the French government in the accomplishment of its protectorate. . . ."[4] Cambon was in possession of a firm legal basis for his actions in Tunisia, and the guarantee of the Bey's debts would give him the necessary bargaining point in ending the Capitulations.

The Convention was necessary because the French Foreign Ministry began lengthy negotiations in September to obtain the assent of the major powers to the suppression of the Capitulations. Not until December 29 did Cambon receive the official dispatch announcing the end of the Capitulations on January 1, 1884. Thankfully he wrote his wife, "The success is complete and the new year begins well!"[5]

Early in 1884, Cambon traveled to Paris to help push through the Tunisian Law, as the La Marsa Convention was now called. He attended the meetings of the Chamber of Deputies to assist Ferry and to accustom himself to the parliamentary procedure if it became necessary for him to speak in behalf of the government. The sessions impressed him as "nonsense and balderdash."

The debate on the Tunisian bill began on March 31 with the oppo-

[4] P. H. X. (Paul, Baron de Constant d'Estournelles), *La politique Française en Tunisie, le protectorat et ses origines (1854–1891)*, 466–67.

[5] Duclerc to Tissot, Sept. 8, 1883, France, Ministère des Affaires Étrangères, *Documents diplomatiques français, 1871–1914* (hereafter cited as *DDF*), 1 ser., IV, 495–96; Cambon to d'Estournelles, Oct. 8, 1883, Cambon to Mme Paul Cambon, Dec. 30, 1883, Jan. 3, 1884, *Correspondance*, I, 186–87, 212–14.

sition claiming that France had been tricked, since the government had stated in 1881 that Tunisia could handle her financial affairs unaided. The opposition maintained that the bill would only produce more debts and higher taxes for a people who were already paying too much for their government. At least in the case of Algeria, said one of the opposition speakers, France had annexed that country and received some advantages; now she was obtaining only disadvantages in what amounted to annexation. Why should the French government guarantee debts which had been accumulated in the past under very doubtful conditions?

On April 1, Dubost and Ferry spoke for the government and announced that annexation was out of the question as it would be too expensive. Under the protectorate, the administration would be Tunisian and of a type which the Tunisians and the French could afford. This bill would reduce expenses because it would be possible to cut down on the servicing of the debt. Ferry wanted the cabinet as a whole to be responsible for Tunisia instead of the Chamber of Deputies, since control by the latter would amount to annexation.

Sometime before the debate began, the government had decided to use Cambon as a spokesman, and in the afternoon of April 1 one of the opposition speakers gave him his opening. He "climbed sedately those eight or nine fatal steps which have conducted so many people to a capitol or to a gallows." Speaking extemporaneously, he used the interruptions from both Right and Left to give him a chance to collect his thoughts.

The opposition speaker preceding him had stated that he had difficulty understanding the question, but Cambon claimed that this was the result of studying it from the old parliamentary debates. He thought that the problem should be examined from the official documents, which showed a debt of 350,000,000 francs in 1869 and of only 142,000,000 francs in 1884. The budget would not only service this debt but provide a surplus. The budget, he warned, must be regarded as a list of expenses, since a recent study had shown that many Tunisians were not paying their taxes. In spite of this difficulty, there was a surplus of 183,000 francs and expenses had been cut from 7,084,000 francs to 3,420,000 francs.

He listed the economies that had been achieved by reducing the Tunisian Army to one battalion and by selling the two ships that constituted the Tunisian Navy. He corrected the critics who had claimed that the favorable economic conditions in Tunisia would cease once the French Army had been withdrawn. That such had not been the case was proved by the fact that the army of occupation was now down to one division and prosperity continued.

When someone interrupted to ask why, then, did he want to guarantee the Bey's debts, Cambon replied that the guarantee would aid in the conversion of the debt and would result in a saving of 1,500,000 francs. Furthermore, the conversion would end the need for the International Debt Commission—a body that was interested only in the bondholders and not in improving the economy of the country. As he concluded, Cambon assured the Chamber that Tunisia would not mean any sacrifice on the part of France since the resources of Tunisia were sixteen million francs. He left the rostrum, and the professionals took over.

Compliments poured in the next day by mail and by telegraph. In the London *Times,* Henri Blowitz reported: "M. Cambon's maiden speech, as spokesman for the cabinet, showed a common sense and tact rarely met with nowadays at the Palais Bourbon, and the report today is that in the event of a separate Ministry of Colonies (now coupled with Marine) being created he would be the man to take it."[6]

On April 3 the Chamber of Deputies passed the completed bill, and five days later the Senate gave its approval by a show of hands. By early October the French protectorate was nearly complete. The international financial commission was gone, and in its place was a staff of French civilians.

Cambon was certain that all opposition to his administration was ended, for the effect of his triumph in Paris would give him the au-

[6] Cambon to Mme Paul Cambon, Jan. 21, April 2, 3, 1884, *Correspondance,* I, 215, 224–27; *Journal Officiel,* April 1, 2, 1884; London *Times,* April 3, 1884.

thority and prestige to complete the protectorate. Little did he realize the dangerous possibility in Ferry's statement, during the debate in the Chamber of Deputies, that Tunisia would be the responsibility of the cabinet. What could Cambon do if the cabinet were loath to support him? Such was the case in the Boulanger affair.

The joys of the work Cambon accomplished in 1884 were dissipated in the struggle with General Georges Boulanger during 1885. Before his appointment to Tunisia, Boulanger had had an outstanding career in the army. Graduated from St. Cyr in 1856, he served with distinction in Africa, Italy, and Indo-China and in the defense of Paris during the Franco-Prussian War. By 1871 he was a full colonel, but a demotion to lieutenant colonel because of the postwar reduction in the army followed, and it was not until 1874 that he was again a full colonel. Boulanger realized that under the Republic opportunities for rapid promotion would be few. The ambitious colonel must use his influence and cultivate connections to obtain promotion; military service would not be enough. Using his superficial charm and good looks, Boulanger sought to ingratiate himself with his superiors and with politicians in the Radical party. By 1884 he was a general of division at forty-seven years of age, and in the same year he was ordered to Tunisia to command the army of occupation.

In January, 1884, Cambon had learned that Boulanger would probably be appointed to Tunisia. He regarded the General as "an ambitious, unscrupulous man, and anything but trustworthy," having known him when he was stationed at Besançon. Boulanger had impressed himself on Cambon at a dinner for the Duke d'Aumale, whom he was cultivating for reasons of promotion, when, by sleight of hand, he had switched the place cards to move himself nearer to the guest of honor.[7]

By February 25 it was definite that Boulanger would receive the appointment. Cambon, then in Paris, hurried to discuss this development with Ferry. He insisted that Boulanger must not leave Paris

[7] Cambon to Mme Paul Cambon, Jan. 4, 1884, *"Lettres de Tunisie," Revue des deux mondes* (May 1, 1931), 381–82.

CREATION OF THE TUNISIAN PROTECTORATE

until he had been briefed regarding his future line of conduct. Cambon had lunch with the General on March 8 and found him "admirably clever, compliant, and charming." He explained his policy in Tunisia and Boulanger's status; he tried to impress on Boulanger that the civilian authority would be predominant. The General seemed to understand the gist of Cambon's remarks: Tunisia was not to be a military province. Cambon again saw Ferry, who assured him that he would keep Boulanger under control. Ferry kept his promise as long as he was premier; when he fell from power in 1885, there was no one strong enough to restrain the General.

Gradually Boulanger became aware of the dissatisfaction that Cambon's administration had produced. The army, the adventurers, the bureaucrats, and the judiciary all had concepts of French policy for Tunisia which differed from those held by Cambon. The army was too much infused with Algerian ideas to understand a government that protected local institutions. Tunisia was only another theater in which the army wanted to renew its exploits. The army found the protectorate humiliating and anti-French; incessantly army officers denounced Cambon's policy of "prudence and temperance," which nauseated them. Shortly after his arrival in Tunisia, he did everything possible to curtail the army's hegemony. He pleaded with Paris to give him the authority to quench the military's lust for power. Too often his requests were refused through the influence of General Jean Campenon, minister of war.

The chief block to a solution of the quarrel was the intelligence bureaus that the army employed to watch the natives. The bureaus constantly stirred up tumults among the natives to give the army reasons for glorious campaigns and to provide ambitious officers with opportunities to display courage and dash by marching troops hither and yon. These methods of gaining promotions did not aid in the establishment of a stable government. Campenon rejected civilian control over these bureaus, and Cambon finally reached a compromise: Campenon would be permitted to correspond directly with the officers in the bureaus, but Cambon would not permit the bureaus to become a means of provoking native uprisings.

Cambon was despised by those who wished to exploit the natives. The adventurers, who left all of their personal wealth in Algeria or in France, sought to make a fortune in Tunisia. When Cambon would not permit them to devour Tunisia, they accused him of ruining them. Believing that Tunisia should be theirs completely, some returned to France to stir up criticism of the protectorate, while others stayed, biding their time.

The bureaucrats complained that Cambon was being unfair because he did not open all jobs to Frenchmen. Those who did obtain positions were pained at the idea of such a simple form of government. To Cambon they seemed to idealize the complicated form of government exemplified by the elaborate Parisian system, and as a result they became the enemies of the protectorate.

The judiciary, influenced by their experience in Algeria, loathed the idea of dispensing justice in the name of the Bey of Tunis. They wanted to enforce French law just as it was enforced in Algeria and in France. They were like the military in that they could not visualize Algeria and Tunisia governed under different systems. To this Cambon asked only, "Why not?" He saw no reason why Tunisia must be another Algeria. In retaliation, the judiciary, he claimed, made common cause with all those who wanted "concessions, lush jobs, with the unemployed lawyers, starvelings from all nations who thought that annexation would satisfy their appetites." The judiciary claimed that Cambon would be a "potentate" if they did not curb his authority. They demanded the right to register the edicts of the Bey as the *parlements* had done in prerevolutionary France.[8]

Boulanger, who spoke for all of these malcontents, bided his time after the fall of Ferry's cabinet on March 30 since there were rumors that he might be taken into the cabinet as minister of war. He could strike whenever he pleased because there was no longer anyone in

[8] Cambon to d'Estournelles, Jan. 5, June 20, 1883, Cambon to Mme Paul Cambon, Nov. 7, 8, 15, 28, 30, 1883, July 26, 1884, Cambon to Ferry, Nov. 24, 1883, *Correspondance,* I, 189–90, 192, 195–200, 203–204, 234–37; Cambon to Freycinet, May 25, 1885, Henri Cambon, *Histoire de la régence de Tunis,* 300–303; Cambon to Mme Paul Cambon, Sept. 8, 1883, *"Lettres de Tunisie,"* 273–74.

CREATION OF THE TUNISIAN PROTECTORATE

the cabinet to curb him. He suddenly attacked Cambon's authority on June 5, 1885, in the Tisi affair.

Tisi, an Italian law clerk, became involved in an argument with a French officer in a café, and the usual insults followed. Tisi was arrested and given eight days' imprisonment, then the case was sent to a higher court in an effort to increase the sentence, and this seemed to satisfy Boulanger. On the evening of June 5, however, Cambon learned that Boulanger thought that justice was insufficient and intended to issue an order of the day instructing the soldiers to use their weapons "should an assault be committed on them without provocation being offered on their part" while they were in uniform. The troops were forbidden "to circulate alone and to go alone into public places." Cambon asked Boulanger to cancel the order, and he pretended he would accede to the request; but later in the evening Cambon was informed that the order had not been canceled and that it would be read at roll call on June 6. It was already posted in the cafés and public places, and the evening editions of the Paris newspapers had picked it up. To many persons in Tunis this meant that the army was preparing to take the law into its own hands. The consuls were frightened by the story in the Paris newspapers that the cabinet had approved of this step. The latent ill-feeling between Italians and Frenchmen flared up with recriminations and threats of demonstrations from both sides.

On June 15, Cambon defended his policy in a letter to Freycinet, now minister of foreign affairs. He admitted that he may have pushed the independence of the Bey too far in order to prevent a recurrence of past events when the Bey's government had been at the mercy of every comer. Too many Frenchmen wanted to use the system solely for the benefit of their own countrymen, for they hated the strength and independence of the Bey's government. Boulanger had become their spokesman, and, like many of his predecessors, he did not comprehend what Cambon was trying to accomplish in Tunisia. The General wanted to treat Tunisia like a conquered country, but his predecessors at least had been loyal and obedient to the civil government. "The idea of any subordination whatsoever to a civil official appeared insupportable to him," said Cambon. Boulanger wanted to show the world that he was the symbol and the guardian of the honor of the French Army. Cambon demanded that his long-standing request be fulfilled: the resident-general must have full political powers and Boulanger must be transferred.

Apparently in response to this demand, under the decree of June 23, 1885, the resident-general in Tunisia was made the "repository of the powers of the Republic in the Regency." All of the commanding officers of the naval and military units would be subject to his command, as well as all of the administrative services. He alone could correspond with the French government; exceptions would be made only in matters of a technical nature. Boulanger, however, would not obey this decree without orders from his superior, Campenon.[9]

Agitation began in Tunis for the recall of Cambon, with a meeting in a theater and the customary telegrams to the higher authorities in Paris. Cambon, determined to rid himself of Boulanger, obtained an order recalling the General from Tunisia. Boulanger announced as he left Tunis that he would carry on the fight for the officers of France in Paris.

Late in July the struggle shifted to Paris, whither Cambon hastened to lay his case before President Jules Grévy, who was angered by the conduct of Boulanger and M. Pontois, the chief judge; both of them, he felt, must go. Eugene Brisson, the premier, blamed Boulanger for all that had happened; Freycinet promised not to support Boulanger, but Cambon realized that Freycinet might prove unreliable since he was afraid of Campenon. When Cambon saw Campenon, the latter appeared to be sincerely angry at Boulanger's attitude and declared that Boulanger must not be sent back to Tunis because he may have sown seeds of discord that might be embarrassing for Cambon. Possibly it might be better to allow enough time to elapse for the matter to be forgotten. This appeared to be a subtle hint for Cambon to resign.

By August 23, Cambon was heartened by the news that Boulanger

[9] Arpa to Granville, June 8, 1885, PRO, FO, Tunisia, 102:163; London *Times*, June 8, 1885; Cambon to Freycinet, June 15, 1885, H. Cambon, *Histoire de la Régence*, 303–306; *Journal Officiel*, June 24, 1885.

would not be allowed to return to Tunisia, even to see his family. Freycinet assured Cambon, moreover, that he was doing everything possible to settle the affair, but he could not force Campenon to carry out his wishes because that was the prerogative of the Premier. Cambon talked with Brisson on September 12, but Brisson's political strength was too weak to fight both Campenon and the opposition; hence he wanted to settle for a nominal exercise of command by Boulanger. Dissatisfied with this proposal, Cambon sought out everyone who might have some influence. At Freycinet's request he prepared a lengthy report for Brisson to use in the discussions with Campenon, but Freycinet would do nothing more about the matter. It was now up to Brisson.

Boulanger and Pontois publicly accused Cambon of graft in connection with the waterworks of Tunis, but an inspector-general's investigation cleared him of all charges. These charges grew out of the complaints of many residents in Tunis about the high water rates. The newly installed water meters, made by a German firm, were the subject of most objections, actually because they were accurate. Persons who had received water free before their installation were vexed at the necessity of paying for water now.

To stop Pontois, Cambon demanded his removal, and the Ministry of Justice promised it in the future. In retaliation, Boulanger and Pontois prompted the publication of an article in *La Lanterne* demanding a trial to enable them to accuse Cambon of stealing. In the course of the trial they would probably accuse Cambon of intimidating the judiciary. If Cambon had brought suit against the paper for libel, the verdict would undoubtedly have been an acquittal for the newspaper, with Cambon damned as an embezzler. His predecessor, Theodore Roustan, had fallen into a similar trap. Cambon refused the bait.

Boulanger informed every officer by letter that he was available at the Hotel Louvre and would be happy to be of service to any of them. The newspapers took up the battle, with *La Lanterne* leading the Boulangist forces. Passions were so aroused that writers and editors in both camps fought a few duels, but there were no fatal consequences.

An approaching election caused the government to become frightened lest the Boulanger-Cambon quarrel aid the opposition. In order to extract both himself and the government from this dilemma, Freycinet proposed an investigation of the Tunisian administration. By a decree of November 23, 1885, a commission was directed to report on the Tunisian administration after hearing everyone who wished to give evidence. At first Cambon was furious. Such an investigation was a dangerous precedent because now a newspaper could make any charge whatsoever against a government official in order to obtain an investigation. Later, however, he welcomed the opportunity to tell the commission of his work in Tunisia and to reply to the attacks of Boulanger, Pontois, and *La Lanterne*.

Bonhoure, the editor of *La Lanterne,* rejected an invitation to testify, claiming that he had said everything in his paper. The manager of the newspaper also refused to appear. Boulanger declined to answer the request of the commission to appear unless ordered to do so by his superior, and the order was never given.

On December 24 the commission issued its report, to the effect that it found no grounds for questioning the integrity of the protectorate. The commission could only praise the economic reforms that Cambon had instituted in Tunisia. They warned that the conflict between the army and the civil power was injurious to French prestige, and that if it were prolonged, it might prove fatal. The commission disapproved of the attempt of the army to requisition any property that it desired. If the army wanted to regard Tunisia as an extension of Algeria, where property had been seized, the necessary legislation would have to come from the government, in which the army was only a minority.

The commission warned the judiciary not to establish a replica of the system of French justice in Tunisia because the cost to the French treasury would be prohibitive. The prosecutor must be placed under the authority of the resident-general in order not to embarrass the French government by his actions.

In the opinion of the commission, the root of the quarrel lay in Paris. The Ministries of War and Justice were following policies that would lead unconsciously to annexation. On the other hand, the Ministry of Foreign Affairs was following the policy of the protectorate. A decision must be made either to annex Tunisia and publicly confess that the protectorate had failed or to execute the decree of June 23 and insure that the judiciary and the army would obey it.[10]

Cambon debarked at Tunis on December 30, glad to be back with his honor intact. But his joy was dampened by the announcement on January 5, 1886, that Boulanger had been named minister of war in a new cabinet headed by Freycinet. At the same time, Cambon was awarded the Legion of Honor, and an official letter was published clearing his administration of all charges. Freycinet did not dare publish the report of the commission that had cleared Cambon because his cabinet represented a coalition of Moderate Republicans and Radicals, the latter of whom had taken Boulanger to their heart as the model of a republican general who would purge the army of royalism and clericalism and prepare for revenge against Germany.

Cambon's position in Tunisia was now impossible since the army took its orders from the very general who had defied him. Apparently, defiance of civil authority brought promotion. The news of Boulanger's appointment struck Cambon as "very funny, but very demoralizing." He asked, "What will officers say in seeing one of them who has done only foolish things arrive at the highest summit of the army?"[11]

As early as January 9 the London *Times* reported that "semi-official contradictions" had been given to the story that Cambon would be replaced. Trying to maintain his self-respect, Cambon left the initiative to the government and avoided asking for a transfer as long as he could. Freycinet attempted to prepare the way for the appointment of Cambon to Rome, but the retiring ambassador advised against this step on the grounds that Cambon's work in Tunisia had not

[10] "Rapport de le commission pour l'examen de la situation administrative en Tunisie," Dec. 24, 1885. Henri Cambon kindly lent the writer a copy of this unpublished report.

[11] Cambon to Mme Paul Cambon, Jan. 8, 11, 1886, *Correspondance*, I, 277–78.

been good preparation for Rome. In June, Freycinet offered Constantinople to Cambon, and he accepted the appointment gladly, only to have the Sultan object because he resented Cambon's success in tightening the hold of France on a country that the Sultan considered his vassal. When Cambon came to Paris in July, he begged Freycinet to transfer him anywhere outside of Tunisia. His work was finished there, he had accomplished his goal, and he knew that Boulanger would only cause trouble. In September, Freycinet offered the Vatican to Cambon, but he refused because he believed that this appointment might be offensive to the Italian government. On October 29 the official announcement was made that Cambon had been named "Ambassador of the Republic to His Majesty the King of Spain."

Cambon left Tunisia on November 15 with a feeling of sorrow, for, as he wrote to his wife, "It seems to me that I was here yesterday, it appears amazing to me that I will not be here tomorrow." In later years, he often said: "When I am no longer here, I want my name to remain engraved in some part of Tunis." He always looked on Tunis with a paternal air. On May 21, 1929, a statue to his memory was unveiled there.[12]

Paul Cambon left Tunisia with a record of efficiency and honesty, coupled with obstinacy in his dealings with men like Boulanger who opposed his policies. He longed to be remembered as the Lord Cromer of Tunisia, but Boulanger blocked that wish. He sincerely believed in the civilizing mission of France, but did not want to assimilate the native population as the American Indians had been assimilated because Tunisia was an old country with a high civilization of her own. He sought to repair the damage done to the country by her rulers, and to make his reforms more palatable, he used Tunisian officials. His adoption of the Torrens Act extracted property-holders from many legal quicksands. His example was followed in French colonial policy with the adoption of the act in Madagascar, the Congo, Morocco, and Indo-China.

Cambon wanted to maintain a close check on the army and judiciary in order to achieve these reforms and protect the natives from

[12] Cambon to Mme Paul Cambon, Nov. 10, 16, 1886, *ibid.*, 287–89.

exploitation. This policy helped to bring on an explosion in 1885, for it was inconceivable to Boulanger and those for whom he spoke that Cambon should place the interests of Tunisians before those of Frenchmen. Thus, there was less spoliation of the natives in Tunisia and more native participation in the Tunisian government than there had been in Algeria.

The brightest page of Cambon's work was the financial reforms in Tunisia. They were the result of a gradual process, beginning with honest tax collections. The only expense to France was the occupation army; Cambon cut the costs from 17,176,000 francs in 1884 to 7,498,901 francs in 1886. By 1888 the interest on the debt had been reduced to 3.5 per cent and a reserve of 11,000,000 francs had been accumulated.[13]

Cambon's trials during his years in Tunisia gave him valuable training in independent action. As a result of his work there, he was one of the few diplomats experienced in running a country by himself. In later years he was often forced to make decisions without help from Paris, for the constant succession of coalition cabinets gave little continuity to French foreign policy. He stood alone in Tunisia; he would stand alone again.

[13] Victor Serres, "Le protectorat Tunisie," *L'Afrique Française,* XL, 1932, 329–46; d'Estournelles, *La politique française,* 331–37, 390–94. The Torrens Act called for a commission to register all property titles after July 1, 1885. This was a great improvement over the hopelessly involved Moslem property laws then in existence.

III. MADRID AND CONSTANTINOPLE

ON DECEMBER 11, 1886, Cambon presented his credentials to Queen María, regent for the infant king, Alfonso XIII. The only ambassador then accredited to Madrid rode to the palace in an eighteenth-century carriage, escorted by an elaborate guard. The royal garrison received Cambon at the palace door used only by royalty and ambassadors presenting their credentials. Chamberlains and halberdiers escorted the new ambassador up the grand staircase and through the halls and salons of the palace. At last he reached the throne room, crowded with the great nobles and dignitaries of the realm. The Ambassador of the French Republic was announced. He bowed and moved into the room; then he stopped and bowed twice more as he advanced toward the throne. Cambon read a prepared speech, and the Queen replied with a speech written for her by the president of the council, Práxedes Sagasta. After she had finished her speech and descended from the throne, Cambon presented his credentials. A polite conversation followed about Tunis, the Madrid climate, and the French ministerial crisis. Cambon introduced his staff; the Queen curtsied and then left the throne room. With the same ceremony and pomp, Cambon was escorted to his waiting carriage. He completed the formalities by calling on Sagasta and Sigismond Moret, the minister of foreign affairs.[1]

Thus began Cambon's years in Madrid, a period of relaxation and quiet. Much of his time was devoted to reassuring the Spanish gov-

[1] Cambon to Mme Paul Cambon, Dec. 11, 1886, *Correspondance,* I, 293–97.

ernment about French plans in Morocco and in observing the unceasing protocol.

During his stay in Madrid, one of Cambon's major political problems was the question of Spanish membership in the Triple Alliance. In June, 1887, after investigating rumors that Spain was seeking to join this alliance, he decided that the rumors were the work of Moret, who desired to bring Spain into the Triple Alliance but could not overcome the pro-French tendencies of Sagasta, the premier. In February, 1888, when the Dual Alliance between Germany and Austria was revealed publicly, the story also appeared that Spain would obtain German diplomatic support if France sent troops to Morocco. This story provided Cambon with an opportunity to question Moret, who claimed that there had been no proposal from either Germany or Austria and that the Spanish government did not desire such an alliance. Cambon doubted this statement, for he was certain that Moret wanted an alliance with Germany and Austria but could not achieve it because important members of the Spanish government were pro-French.[2]

Cambon was correct in his conclusion that Spain was not a formal member of the Triple Alliance, although Moret had labored to reach this goal. Bismarck, possibly sensing that Moret was alone in his desire for membership in the Triple Alliance, had vetoed the idea and suggested an agreement between Spain and Italy. In an exchange of notes in 1887, Spain promised to refrain from joining France in any move in North Africa prejudicial to the interests of the Triple Alliance. Apparently France was now blocked from any further moves in the Mediterranean area, but Cambon would one day help to remove this block.

During the Barcelona exposition of 1888, Cambon begged his government to send as many ships to Spain as Italy and Austria were sending to impress the people. In response to his urgings, a French fleet appeared in all of its grandeur at the exposition. Cannon thundered daily; over 18,000 salvos were fired during the exposition.

A flock of doves was released at the opening of the exposition.

[2] Cambon to Flourens, Feb. 25, 1888, *DDF,* 1 ser., VI, 700–703.

One dove lighted on the feathered headdress of Count Giuseppe Tornielli, the Italian minister. Cambon gleefully shouted: "It's the Holy Ghost who has descended! Don't let it get away!"

The climax of the exposition for Cambon was the visit of the Queen Regent to the French fleet on May 25. He also presided at the banquet given by his government on May 26 for the important visitors. In his toast he voiced the desire of France for friendly relations with her neighbor across the Pyrenees. Throughout the exposition Cambon sought to impress the Spaniards with the might and power of their northern neighbor, who desired only Spain's friendship. There was no need for Spain to flirt with Germany, Austria, or Italy.[3]

In 1889, Cambon's old enemy, Boulanger, toyed with the idea of a coup d'état. At the crucial moment, however, he lost his nerve and fled to Belgium. A Senate investigation into his activities was held in Paris. Cambon was ordered to Paris to retell the tale of his struggle with Boulanger. He was amused to learn that the investigating committee knew no more about Boulanger than he did. He wrote his wife that the facts were beginning to accumulate. It was becoming apparent that Boulanger was "a conceited adventurer, audacious in his success, and contemptible before his bad luck." For the last time in his life, Cambon was glad to have done with Georges Boulanger.[4]

Because of the instability of the cabinets under the Third Republic, foreign ministers often had difficulty formulating policies; consequently they turned to career officials for advice. During Cambon's long career in the diplomatic service, the foreign ministers often sought his advice. As his career lengthened, he occasionally sent advice to new foreign ministers without their requesting it.

In 1889, Cambon found it best to advise the new minister of foreign affairs, Eugene Spuller. The Ambassador declared that Morocco was no longer a bone of contention, but rather it could become "an occasion of an entente and common action"; however, reassurances

---

[3] Cambon to Goblet, May 1, 1888, Cambon to Mme Paul Cambon, May 17, 18, 19, 21, 23, 27, 1888, *Correspondance,* I, 320–27.

[4] Cambon to Mme Paul Cambon, April 20, 21, 22, 1889, *ibid.,* 334–35. In 1891, Boulanger committed suicide over the grave of his mistress in Belgium.

over Morocco were not enough to attach Spain to France. An alignment must be found with appeal for the Spanish imagination. It might perhaps come through "the reconciliation of the Latin race." The first step was to entice Italy away from Berlin. He considered "the reconciliation of France and Italy and later the entente of these two powers with England as the obvious goal of French policy."

OTTOMAN EMPIRE, CIRCA 1890

France could not have her safety menaced on two frontiers at once; at present this was the case in the Vosges and the Alps. The argument with Italy meant that a sword would be pointed at the back of France whenever the duel might be taken up with Germany. Cambon believed that a reconciliation between France and Italy would even the balance of power with Germany; it might even help to obtain British good will.

He saw little value in the growing tendency toward an alliance with Russia. "The policy with Russia is an empirical policy, that with England and Italy is the only rational and profitable one." Instead of working out an alliance with Russia, it would have been better to use Egypt as a means of an entente with Britain and later with Italy.[5]

Cambon had proposed a difficult program that could not be achieved immediately; furthermore, its achievement involved definite changes in the foreign policies of all the nations involved. Circumstances were unfavorable for this program in 1889; the developments of the next fifteen years were needed before it could be put into effect. Little could be accomplished in view of the instability of the French cabinets and the consequent short periods of direction by the minister of foreign affairs. A term of office longer than usual was needed, and it did not occur until 1898. This program was uncompleted until 1904, when it involved ententes of France with Italy and England and an agreement with Spain concerning Morocco.

In May, 1891, the post at Constantinople had been offered to Cambon when the Count de Montebello was shifted to St. Petersburg. Cambon rejected the offer because he had received "one sour look" from the Sultan of Turkey and did not want another. Montebello assured him that all was forgotten about Tunisia. After renewed pressure from Montebello and Alexandre Ribot, the foreign minister, Cambon accepted the mission, although he knew that expenses in Constantinople would be heavy.

One feature of the new post frightened him. France was moving towards an alliance with Russia, and in Cambon's opinion this development affected his country's foreign policy to the detriment of her national interests. He complained:

> Our traditional policy in Constantinople has been agreement with England and opposition to the encroachments of Russia; but today we are cool towards England and we conduct a perfect love affair with the Russians. The diplomat who would sacrifice the true principles of our eastern policy and the true interests of France in Syria to the Russian illusion would be disgraced in the near future; the one who would attempt to keep himself independent of Russia would be accused by the thick heads in Paris of lacking patriotism and of selling his country to England. . . . You are no longer French

[5] Cambon to Spuller, March 11, 1889, *ibid.*, 331–33.

if you are not first a good Russian. A minister of foreign affairs who is not a dependent of the Russian ambassador would immediately become the target of the newspapers and of the interpelators of the Chamber. This worries me. I do not know what I am going to do later, and help will not reach me from Paris.

Cambon anticipated correctly his future difficulties.

On August 3, 1891, Paul Cambon was named ambassador to Constantinople and took leave of the Queen Regent. Somewhat sadly he ended his "stay in the country village of Madrid, to return to the busy life of the world."[6]

The Ottoman Empire was sick. The Turkish armies that besieged Vienna in the seventeenth century were no longer a threat to Western Europe. The Sultan's government maintained control over the subject peoples with ever increasing difficulties. By 1891, Serbia, Rumania, and Montenegro were independent. The uncertain future of the remainder of the empire plagued the foreign offices of the major European powers because a sudden breakup of the Ottoman Empire would drastically alter the balance of power in the Near East and Eastern Europe. Therefore, the peace of Europe demanded a solution to the problem of the "Sick Man of Europe," as the Ottoman Empire had often been called. Solutions for this problem were legion; prominent among them was the institution of Western reforms within the empire. Any list of reforms had to run the gauntlet of approval by the European powers who were interested in the future of the Ottoman Empire.

Great Britain feared Russian domination of the Straits of the Dardanelles and sought to bolster the Ottoman government as a buffer against Russian expansion. Austria-Hungary was interested in snatching Turkish territories, while Germany viewed the Ottoman Empire as a valuable field for economic expansion. The Russian government feared British control of the Straits of the Dardanelles and dreaded foreign intervention at Constantinople lest Russian influence there

[6] Cambon to Bompard, July 1, 1891, Cambon to d'Estournelles, Aug. 4, 1891, *ibid.*, 343-46.

be undermined. A strong desire developed among those influential in the Russian government to seize and occupy the Straits of the Dardanelles and Constantinople.

Over the tragic situation brooded the hunched, scraggy-bearded figure of Sultan Abdul-Hamid II. Secretive, cruel, shrewd, and eternally suspicious of everyone, he intrigued to keep his decaying empire together. Terrified by fears of assassination, Abdul built a rambling palace on the Yildiz, a hill outside the city. Here a strong cordon of blockhouses afforded protection from revolution, and a labyrinth of passages provided defense for a last-ditch stand. In this palace, surrounded by hordes of influential astrologers and soothsayers, eunuchs, dwarfs, and harem girls, the Sultan went through the motions of governing his empire by means of a vast network of spies, whose reports he studied with intense care. His ministers existed on his sufferance, and their fall from power could be swift, painful, and deadly. All administrative actions were subject to his approval, and all suggestions of reforms were considered proof of treason. Repression was the order of the day, and constructive policies were forbidden. This situation only made the Sultan less aware of the true conditions in his empire as he daily became more remote from reality.

The empire was in a state of internal decay: highwaymen made travel unsafe, ports and harbors were silting up, and the physical resources were unused. The civil service was stagnant, and bribery was widespread, even in the palace. The treasury was empty, and the army and bureaucrats were unpaid; only the spies received regular pay. Whatever monies could be collected by taxation were subject to control by an international financial commission whose main purpose was to protect the interests of the Sultan's foreign creditors. The history of the Ottoman Empire had much to do with her plight, for she had been conquered by a warrior nation and warriors did not work—there were subject peoples for such menial tasks. But many of the subject peoples were no longer interested in performing these tasks, and the descendants of the conquering warriors had forgotten their duty to rule the empire.

The Sultan blocked all attempts to reform the empire because reforms to him were European and Christian, and therefore to be avoided. They smacked of the Congress of Berlin of 1878, when the European powers had revised the Treaty of San Stefano after Russia's victory in the Russo-Turkish War and had taken away parts of Abdul's empire. Further, if he accepted any reforms, contrary to the Koran, religious opposition would endanger his throne.

Paul Cambon arrived in Constantinople on October 3, 1891, and moved into the French embassy on the shores of the Bosporus. It was a wooden Turkish palace painted brick red and bright yellow; the upper stories projected out over the blue waters of the Bosporus, giving the impression of floating in an ark.

His first audience with the Sultan was postponed twice in accordance with the Ottoman policy of treating Christians with disdain. Not until October 12 was he able to talk with the Sultan. Cambon announced that France had recovered her old power and influence in Europe, and the Sultan would err if he did not consider this fact in his foreign policy. The announcement indicated French determination to pursue an active policy in the Near East. Now it was only a question of finding the suitable opportunity to exert the power and influence of France, and Egypt seemed to provide such an opportunity.

Egypt had acquired a unique strategic value for the British Empire through the Suez Canal, for whoever controlled the canal could endanger imperial communications. The Egyptian government was bankrupt by 1876, and the British and French governments were under pressure to protect the interests of their nationals. In the spring of 1882 antiforeign riots in Egypt seemed to threaten the canal. An Anglo-French naval force appeared before Alexandria to stage a demonstration. The British admiral claimed that the fortifications around the harbor threatened his fleet; therefore, he ordered the bombardment of the forts after the French fleet had departed in protest. By September, Britain was the master of Egypt. The British government assured the powers that Egypt would be evacuated once public order was restored.

Freycinet, French premier during the occupation crisis, belatedly came around to the British position only to be overthrown on July

31, 1882. The Chamber of Deputies would not allow French forces to be swallowed up in Egypt, thus weakening the French position on the continent of Europe. At this time there was no official French objection to the British action.

Britain then found out how easy it was to occupy a country and how difficult it was to withdraw. There could be no withdrawal until the creditors were satisfied that their money would be safe and that anarchy would not descend on Egypt again. The canal also had to be secure. For the next twenty years, as the British occupation became more permanent, discord over the Egyptian question increased. France demanded the evacuation of British forces from Egypt. To French imperialists the continued occupation was a grievous blow to French influence in the Mediterranean area. The situation prevented an Anglo-French agreement and forced Britain to look to the Triple Alliance for support.

One way to weaken Britain's hold on Egypt might be through the Ottoman Empire; therefore, early in November, 1891, Cambon urged the Ottoman government to reassert Turkish control over its vassal, Egypt. He proposed that the Ottoman government renew its old protests against British control of Egypt. The British government must know that France and Turkey would not give up their respective claims in Egypt and that any "bloody resistance to their legitimate claims could lead to cataclysm." By this stratagem, Cambon sought to extract a British statement about the permanency of the occupation. If Britain's intention was to remain in Egypt forever, her promises to maintain the integrity of the Ottoman Empire under the Treaty of Berlin would appear false.

Cambon's policy of bringing pressure on the Sultan to oppose Britain in Egypt was little to the liking of Ribot, the minister of foreign affairs. He advised Cambon not to push the Turks too far, for they might make a representation in London that could fail and produce unpleasantness. Cambon retorted that if he went as slowly as Ribot desired, there would be an end to the policy of seeking a definite date for ending the occupation. By helping the Turks assert their sovereignty in Egypt, the way might be opened for talks between

Paris and London over the future of Egypt. But Nicholas Giers, the Russian foreign minister, advised Ribot that Russia had secondary interests in Egypt and would give France only moral support. With the Russian warning in mind, Ribot cautioned Cambon not to place France in an isolated position lest her new-found friend desert her.

In December, 1891, Cambon learned of a new British proposal to evacuate Egypt, provided Egypt could be reoccupied after giving the Turks forty-eight hours' notice. France was not invited to participate in the negotiations. Without French participation there would be no guarantee of an airtight arrangement to keep the British out of Egypt. Cambon informed Ribot of these developments and insisted that Russian help be utilized to bring a change in the Sultan's attitude. A frightened Ribot obtained Russian co-operation.

On January 18, 1892, Cambon and Alexander Nelidov, the Russian ambassador, presented identical notes to the Sultan demanding that he work to end the occupation of Egypt. Little help could be expected from the powers if the Sultan's government did not ask their advice. If the balance of power was upset in the Mediterranean, each nation would look after its own interests.

Early in February the Sultan agreed to consult France on the arrangements for the evacuation of Egypt. The Grand Vizier asked Cambon for the French views on the Egyptian question and for a proposal that could be the basis of talks with Britain. Cambon suggested that within a year of signing a provisional convention, the British and Ottoman governments would conclude a final agreement on the evacuation of Egypt. If some unforeseen factor held up the evacuation, Ottoman troops could occupy Egypt in conjunction with British forces. Once all danger had vanished, the Ottoman and British troops would depart simultaneously.

Cambon believed that the British wanted to withdraw from Egypt but did not want someone else to decide when the evacuation should begin. His proposal might succeed since any mention of a definite date for evacuation was omitted. Prolonging the occupation was dangerous because time worked against France. As he saw it, France could intervene in Constantinople and stop action from being completed, but positive action would have to come from London. Most of Europe was aligned against France and Russia, and the Sultan's word was not dependable; therefore, France must negotiate with Britain. Without this procedure, Great Britain would set up a protectorate in Egypt.[7]

Ribot hesitated at such a direct approach. He believed that the British government wanted the status quo kept in Egypt. As a result, Cambon was directed to avoid involving France officially in the negotiations. The final decision not to intervene was determined by the Russian government, whose attitude was that the negotiations would throw the Sultan into the arms of Britain and the Triple Alliance. Ribot was loath to antagonize St. Petersburg because negotiations were in progress for a Franco-Russian military agreement.

Ribot had failed to grasp the reality of the situation. The Egyptian question would be solved only by direct negotiations between France and Great Britain without Russia. It was apparent to Cambon that London and Paris must solve the problem between themselves since the Sultan and the British government could not.

By 1894 the British government had decided to make the occupation permanent. Both the Liberal and Conservative parties were agreed that the evacuation of Egypt would mean a return to anarchy with the Suez Canal endangered. British sacrifices in blood and money would be for naught. The Sultan was satisfied that the occupation should continue in order to play the French off against the British. But the French government would not fight for Egypt, and no one else would take up arms, not even the new ally, Russia. There was no Russian empire in North Africa to make St. Petersburg eager to take an active role in Egypt.

Cambon's first major assignment in Constantinople seemed a failure. In reality, he had reduced the problem to its essentials: the Sultan could not be depended upon to help evict the British, and a solution must be found by Britain and France. The French govern-

[7] Cambon to Ribot, Dec. 21, 27, 1891, Jan. 14, 16, 18, 23, 1892, Feb. 4, 8, 15, 18, 1892, *DDF,* 1 ser., IX, 168–71, 181–83, 209–11, 221–22, 225–28, 240, 262–63, 267–70, 281–86, 295–96, 306–308.

ment must decide what price it would pay the British government for the evacuation of Egypt, for it was obvious that none of those concerned would resort to war. For Cambon this was profitable knowledge which he could use when settling the problem in 1904. It had been a legal problem without bloodshed—the next problem of Armenia would indeed be bloody.

IV. TWO NIGHTMARES: ARMENIA AND CRETE

THE POLITICAL IDEAS of the nineteenth century had created a rebellious spirit in the subject peoples of the Ottoman Empire. Their revolts, when successful, often resulted in a loss of part of the empire. Abdul-Hamid II intended to retain all of his empire by employing every means at his command; thus, if revolution appeared imminent, he would crush it.

The Armenians were one of the subject peoples of the Empire who had endured oppressors for centuries. They lived, for the most part, in eastern Asia Minor within the Ottoman Empire and in the Russian Empire. The Armenians were not always predominant in the regions that they inhabited in the Ottoman Empire, for Turks and Kurds were mixed with them, and the latter, nomadic Moslem tribesmen, were often used to keep the Armenians in subjection. Since the Armenians were Christians, the Kurds fell to the slaughter with great joy.

Organized activity in behalf of the Armenians developed at the Congress of Berlin in 1878. Armenian lobbyists had caused a vague clause to be inserted in the Treaty of Berlin calling for Ottoman reforms in the Armenian regions. By the 1880's a definite revolutionary movement had developed among some of the Armenians, led chiefly by those who had studied in Western Europe and financed by Armenians who had left the Ottoman Empire to make their fortunes elsewhere. Although the bulk of the Armenian peasants de-

TWO NIGHTMARES: ARMENIA AND CRETE

sired to be left alone and to live as they always had under their conquerors if their conquerors would give them good government, by the 1890's outbreaks began to occur in the Armenian provinces. The Sultan was cognizant of these activities and was eager to suppress them for he feared they would lead to intervention by the European powers.

Cambon was not especially alarmed until 1893, when he alerted Paris that the Armenian question might become a source of European conflict some day because the country was strategically located near British and Russian interests in the Mediterranean and Persian Gulf areas. As Cambon viewed the situation, "The interests of Russia and of England in this region are so evident and so divergent that a conflict will result from this intervention.... In a word, the two powers wish an independent Armenia, Russia in order to dominate it or annex it, England in order to bar the road to Russia." France should watch and wait and obtain all possible information.

Cambon's analysis was wrong in one fatal respect, which he discovered after much Armenian blood had been shed: Russia did not want an independent Armenia because she feared that Armenians within the Russian Empire might develop similar ideas. The Russian government could not approve any measures in Turkish Armenia that might encourage political independence in Russian Armenia.

As the incidents involving Armenians increased in 1893 and 1894, Cambon saw the problem in a different light. It was time to make a definite study of the situation and all the diplomatic factors involved, yet he could not reach any workable solution. Independence was out of the question because the Armenians were mixed with the Turks. Semi-autonomy would require pressure on the Sultan, and the agreement of all the powers to such a measure was doubtful. Any attempt to move the Armenians to one section of the country would cause an insurrection, bringing in Great Britain and Russia. Reforms were of little value because Turkish promises were worthless. There seemed to be no possible solution.[1]

[1] Cambon to Develle, April 18, 1893, Cambon to Casimir-Périer, Feb. 20, 1894, *DDF,* 1 ser., X, 300–305, XI, 71–76.

On November 14, 1894, Cambon learned of massacres in the province of Bittis in Asia Minor. The slaughter occurred in August and September, with some accounts placing the casualties as high as 8,000. The Kurds had attacked the Armenians and were repulsed. Turkish troops completed the massacres—men were bound and burned alive, in addition to the usual raping and murdering.

When the Sultan asked Cambon for advice, he replied that there would be nothing to worry about if the Sultan instituted his own investigation of the massacres, appointing respected men to carry out the task. The guilty must be punished and the Sultan's authority must be restored in Bittis. Cambon knew that there was slight chance that his advice would be followed, but he hoped that the Sultan would try to do something to forestall the British, who demanded an inquiry. They might invoke the Treaty of Berlin, and such an action could mean intervention and war.

The Sultan finally ordered an investigation, and early in December, Sir Philip Currie, the British ambassador, suggested that the British, Russian, and French governments also take part. Cambon, acting on the orders of Gabriel Hanotaux, the French foreign minister, gave Currie the impression that France would be unwilling to assume any responsibility in the investigation unless Russia also took part. When the British prepared to enter the investigation alone, France and Russia ordered their consuls in Erzurum to participate. Throughout the weeks that followed, the Sultan impeded the work of the commission of inquiry wherever possible.[2]

By April, 1895, it was apparent that the commission was failing to obtain results. The three ambassadors presented the Sultan with a list of reforms on May 11. They amounted to an enforcement of the existing legislation, and advocated nothing the Turks could denounce as innovations. The Sultan delayed his answer until June 3, and replied then only under pressure from Cambon and Currie. He re-

[2] Hanotaux to Cambon, Nov. 27, 1894, Cambon to Hanotaux, Dec. 8, 13, 14, 19, 1894, *ibid.*, 439, 473–75, 482–83, 492–93; Currie to Kimberley, Nov. 26, Dec. 5, 13, 17, 18, 19, 21, 26, 29, 1894, May 31, 1895, PRO, FO, Turkey, 78:4544, 4546, 4612.

TWO NIGHTMARES: ARMENIA AND CRETE

jected practically all of the reforms because he did not believe that the entente between France, Britain, and Russia would last. When the ambassadors pressed him to explain his refusal, he answered that the government of the Asiatic provinces left nothing to be desired, and that the existing laws were perfectly satisfactory as far as the reforms were concerned, for all of the outrages were punishable by law. However, he said nothing about enforcing the laws.

The discussions of reforms took a terrifying turn on September 30, when some Armenians demonstrated in Constantinople. A police agent was killed by the demonstrators; then the police attacked the crowd and dispersed it. Mass arrests followed. More rioting erupted during the night, but by the morning of October 1 troops had entered the city and all seemed calm. Later the riots broke out anew and continued throughout the night. On October 2 the police armed the *softas,* Moslem theological students, and wholesale massacres began. The Armenians took refuge in the churches, while crowds, screaming for vengeance, paraded through the streets with the body of the dead police agent. At last the crazed mob satisfied its blood lust with a slaughter of Armenian prisoners who had been arrested by the police. Cambon telegraphed Hanotaux to speed up the Russians, who had delayed the negotiations, and he begged for agreement among the foreign offices on the demands that were to be made of the Ottoman government.[3]

The ambassadors protested to the Sultan about the failure of the police (who appeared to encourage the mass murders) to maintain law and order. The ambassadors thought that the Sultan would take the necessary action to protect the Christians and end the disorders, but he accused the Armenians of causing the violence and hiding in the churches in order to continue their troublemaking. The Ottoman government was doing all in its power to restore peace, but first the Armenians had to cease their attempts to incite a revolution.

[3] Cambon to Hanotaux, Sept. 28, 30, Oct. 1, 2, 1895, France, Ministère, des Affaires Étrangères, *Documents diplomatiques. Affaires Arméniennes, projets de reformes dans l'empire Ottoman, 1893–1897,* 139–42; Cambon to Hanotaux, Oct. 1, 2, 1895, *DDF,* 1 ser., XII, 223–27; Cambon to Mme Hippolyte Cambon, Oct. 3, 1895, *Correspondance,* I, 393.

The Sultan, alarmed by the attitude of the ambassadors, who seemed united at last, agreed to certain reforms on October 17. These included the admittance of Christians into the administration of the empire wherever they formed a minority. Within two days the Sultan actually gave orders for the reforms. Nevertheless, massacres continued in the provinces although they had ceased in Constantinople. By November the killing and rioting had increased to such an extent in Diarbekir, a town in southeastern Asia Minor, that Cambon warned the Ottoman government to restore peace. If anything happened to the French consul there, the French government would use force. The rioters soon quieted down. On November 6, in a note to the Sultan, the ambassadors of France, Great Britain, Russia, Austria-Hungary, Germany, and Italy warned that their respective governments would take forceful action if the outrages in the provinces did not cease.

Fearful that they might be going too far, the Russian ambassador announced that he saw no danger of an imminent revolution despite the anarchy. Because of the Russian alliance and the pro-Russian policies of Hanotaux, Cambon had to agree publicly with this statement. Privately, he thought otherwise.[4]

The ambassadors agreed on measures for their own protection if the massacres broke out again. Ammunition and arms were to be brought up to the embassies from gunboats; the firing of the guns on the Russian gunboat would signal fresh trouble. The crews were to land and make their way to the embassies, where they would take up defensive positions.

When the ambassadors announced their intention to call for additional naval protection, Abdul-Hamid attempted to stop them. He demanded that they rescind their orders, but Cambon saw no reason to accede and so advised Marcellin Berthelot, now minister for foreign affairs. Eventually the Sultan agreed that the warships could pass the Dardanelles unmolested. British warships would now be able to threaten Russia with a surprise attack through the Black Sea—such was the opinion of St. Petersburg.

[4] Herbert to Salisbury, Nov. 6, 1895, PRO, FO, Turkey, 78:4629.

Courtesy United Press International, Inc.

PAUL CAMBON

Courtesy Culver Service

A contemporary drawing of the insurgent Communists seizing the guns during the French Commune, 1871.

TWO NIGHTMARES: ARMENIA AND CRETE

The split in the powers, long desired by Abdul-Hamid, appeared at the meeting of the ambassadors on December 10. The British, Austrian, and Italian ambassadors wanted forceful action. Nelidov did not, and he let it be known that any further action was up to their governments; that he would protect only Russian nationals. He rejected the proposal for an international commission to study the problem on the spot. Cambon was in a dilemma. His instructions were to co-operate with Nelidov, yet personally he wanted action. To salve his conscience, he suggested that the ambassadors pool their information as the basis for a new ultimatum to the Sultan. Currie rejected this proposal, and nothing definite could be decided by the ambassadors. The prospects for a future agreement over Armenia seemed dim.[5]

There were more alarms and excursions as the massacres continued in the provinces throughout 1896. The ambassadors intervened to negotiate a cease-fire in Zeitoun, where some embattled Armenians held out against increasing odds. The Armenians finally laid down their arms in February on the promise of the Sultan that there would be a general amnesty, tax reductions, and other reforms, including the appointment of a Christian governor. By June, when the Christian governor had not been appointed, the Sultan asked the ambassadors to stop bothering him with their requests for this reform. Cambon reminded Hanotaux, again minister for foreign affairs, that France must not go back on her word, for, if France were to give in to the Sultan, "we would lose every consideration among the Christian population." Hanotaux supported Cambon, and the ambassadors continued their requests until the dilatory Sultan complied by appointing a Christian governor on June 16.[6]

In western Asia Minor, the threat of a massacre next appeared in the town of Van when the Kurds began to close in. Even the Otto-

---

[5] Currie to Salisbury, Dec. 11, 1895, *ibid.,* vol. 4624.

[6] Cambon to Berthelot, Dec. 24, 1895, Jan. 3, 10, Feb. 11, 1896, Cambon to Hanotaux, June 15, 16, 1896, Hanotaux to Cambon, June 7, 1896, *Affaires Arméniennes,* 192–95, 214, 233–34, 239; Herbert to Salisbury, June 15, 1896, PRO, FO, Turkey, 78:4709.

man troops wanted to flee. Cambon demanded that additional troops be sent with orders to fire on their coreligionists. After the usual procrastination, the Sultan agreed. Alarming news arrived that the governor of Diarbekir was permitting the Moslems to sell arms openly and threats were being made against the Christians. Cambon and Michael Herbert, the British chargé d'affaires, both warned the Porte of its responsibility should the governor stay in power and violence occur. It was not until November, 1896, that they were successful in forcing the governor's removal.

Massacres broke out again in Constantinople on August 28, and the Turks shed Christian blood with even greater vigor. The massacres started when a group of Armenian revolutionaries seized a bank in Constantinople to dramatize their plight and to win world sympathy. Cambon was in France when these massacres occurred. He returned in September to find that they had stopped, but the diplomatic colony expected them to start again momentarily. When Cambon saw Abdul-Hamid on September 26, he cautioned him that the European governments did not like the pillaging and murders; a renewal of trouble might bring intervention. The French government felt that only the Sultan could maintain law and order and that he must use all of his power, both religious and political, to restore peace. Cambon urged the usual reforms and the release of the innocent from prison. The Sultan thanked Cambon for his advice and promised to put it into effect, but Cambon believed that none of these promises would be kept because the Sultan did not think that there was any solidarity in the concert of the powers. Whatever the ambassadors might say, the Sultan did not worry.[7]

In September, Cambon informed Hanotaux that his colleagues were agreed that nothing could be obtained from Abdul-Hamid without an entente of the powers. The ambassadors had exhausted all of

[7] Herbert to Salisbury, Aug. 31, Sept. 2, 1896, PRO, FO, Turkey 78:4713; Currie to Salisbury, Sept. 16, 27, 1896, *ibid.,* 78:4712, 4724; Cambon to Hanotaux, Sept. 26, 1896, *DDF,* 1 ser., XII, 755–56; Cambon to Mme Paul Cambon, Sept. 24, 1896, *Correspondance,* I, 411–13.

their resources, and now the governments must arrive at a definite policy on Turkey and the Armenians.

Cambon realized that it was useless for him to work on this problem unless his government decided on a more forceful policy. Because of the Franco-Russian alliance, the Paris government would not oppose the desires of its ally, which plotted to end the Ottoman Empire. French interests in the Near East were subordinated to Russian, a policy which Cambon bitterly resented. Russia would not join with Great Britain in stopping the slaughter of the Armenians because such action might be the salvation of the Ottoman Empire. Russia joined in the collective notes to the Sultan only to prevent the British from working alone in Asia Minor.[8]

Massacres erupted once more in 1898, and again Cambon and his colleagues made prompt representations to the Sultan. This time he removed two governors in whose provinces the outbreaks had occurred. There the problem rested because of the jealousy of Russia and Great Britain. Massacres would take place again, and again Armenians would die.

By the fall of 1896, Cambon turned his attention to another problem of the Ottoman Empire. The peoples of Crete were beginning a struggle to free themselves of their Ottoman overlords. The Armenian nightmare had ended for Cambon and a new one in Crete had begun.

For centuries the island of Crete had suffered from misrule by the Turks. Then a powerful movement for annexation by Greece developed late in the nineteenth century. By June, 1896, fear of the growing unrest moved Cambon to warn the Sultan that clemency and appeasement were mandatory to prevent a revolution. Privately he thought that his advice had gone for naught and that those in the Sultan's entourage who wanted repression would win out, creating "a second edition of Armenia." This time there would be a

---

[8] Cambon to Hanotaux, Sept. 31, 1896, *DDF,* 1 ser., XII, 762-63; Saurma to Hohenlohe, Oct. 25, 1896, *Die grosse Politik der europäischen Kabinette 1871-1914* (hereafter cited as *GP*), XII, 37-38.

difference—the "Cretans will defend themselves; the Greeks will take part."⁹

At a meeting of the ambassadors on June 9, Cambon reported his discussions of Cretan affairs with the Sultan, stressing that the Ottoman government would not be influenced by any representations unless the European powers were willing to support their ambassadors with force. The Turks were convinced that they could slaughter the Cretans with impunity as they had the Armenians. "They want a lesson," Cambon informed the ambassadors, "and we shall never get anything out of them until they receive one." If their governments asked their advice, there was only one answer: "Turkey must be forced by the joint action of the six powers to hold her hand in Crete." After a discussion, the ambassadors agreed that the Sultan must come to terms peacefully with the Cretans.

The European powers were more frightened of the consequences of the revolt to themselves than to the Cretans. A successful revolt might start a partition of the Ottoman Empire, followed by a struggle over the spoils. Support for the Cretans could open the door to a general war. European public opinion, however, was strongly pro-Cretan. Greece supported the rebels because she wished to annex the island. The dilemma was both puzzling and dangerous for the governments.

On June 13, 1896, the Ottoman foreign minister asked Cambon's opinion regarding Crete. This time Cambon was more forceful and urged the convocation of an assembly at once, the revival of the Pact of Halepa, a general amnesty, the withdrawal of Turkish troops, a cease-fire, and a guarantee from the powers to the Cretans that the Porte would observe the conditions laid down.¹⁰

By August 10 the ambassadors had drawn up a series of detailed

⁹ Cambon to Mme Hippolyte Cambon, June 8, 1896, *Correspondance*, I, 405–406.
¹⁰ Herbert to Salisbury, June 14, 1896, PRO, FO, Turkey 78:4723. The Pact of Halepa, issued by the Sultan in 1878, granted Crete an assembly in which Christians predominated, gave preference to natives for official posts, and permitted part of the taxes to be used for local needs. Most of the provisions were withdrawn in 1889.

TWO NIGHTMARES: ARMENIA AND CRETE

reforms for Crete, much along the lines that Cambon had suggested on June 13, and the Sultan accepted them on August 29. He agreed to the request of the powers for Cretan autonomy, but the Greeks were not interested. The Sultan renewed an order to his troops merely to push the Greeks back across the border of Thessaly, which they had been violating. War finally came, and the Greek minister was handed his passport on April 18, 1897.

The war went badly for Greece, whose ineffective army could avail little against the Prussian-trained Turkish troops. By May the powers were asked to mediate. An armistice was signed on May 19; Greece had been defeated. Throughout the long summer the ambassadors argued and sweated as they negotiated a peace. It reminded Cambon of the torture sometimes given in the past to prisoners: after arduous work the prisoner's finished article was destroyed before his eyes. The ambassadors, Cambon moaned, were in a worse position because they knew that "all the negotiations in the world would change nothing." Six weary ambassadors signed the peace preliminaries on September 18, 1897. Greece had to pay an indemnity and agree to a rectification of the frontier in favor of Turkey. Crete was lost to Turkey because the powers continued their control. By 1913, Crete had been formally annexed by Greece, and one more step had been taken in the partition of the Ottoman Empire.

Looking back on the Cretan problem, Cambon found the powers guilty of permitting themselves to be led by events. Warnings had been useless. If the powers had been firm with the Sultan and secured the re-establishment of the Pact of Halepa, Cambon was certain that the Cretans might have been quieted for some years; however, the Sultan profited from the irresolution of the powers. Cambon wished that the powers had followed the suggestion of the ambassadors and set up some form of autonomy from the beginning of the crisis. The cabinets, far from the scene, paid slight attention to the ambassadors' proposals, hoping that the crisis would somehow dissipate. Cambon believed that they were responsible for much of the bloodshed in Crete.[11]

[11] Cambon to Admiral Pottier, Feb. 9, 1898, *Correspondance*, I, 433-36.

The Armenian and Cretan nightmares intensified Cambon's doubts about the value of the Russian alliance. French interests were being sacrificed to Russian. Although France badly needed an ally after 1870, Cambon wondered whether Russia was the best one.

The Russian foreign office was interested in breaking up the Ottoman Empire. Cambon fought this policy, hoping through the concert of powers to maintain the empire's territorial integrity and avoid a general war. He would have the powers force reforms on Turkey to save herself, and it galled him when the ally of France blocked all attempts to put force into the warning to the Sultan.

Cambon decided that Russia was afraid that the desire for independence among the Armenians would spread to those within Russian frontiers. To avoid such a situation, Russia hoped and worked for the collapse of the Ottoman Empire by joining every negotiation, conversation, and proposal that had "the appearance of advancing the Armenian question without resolving it." Russia backed away when it became necessary to impress on the Sultan that the European entente was a serious affair and rejected the type of language that would stop the Sultan's evasive tactics. Why, Cambon wondered, should French policies in the Ottoman Empire be subject to a Russian veto? France counted enough in the world and she gave Russia enough help that she did not have to follow blindly the directions of St. Petersburg.

Russian policies convinced Abdul-Hamid that the reality of a European agreement was fictitious. The Tsar's diplomats sabotaged united action, Cambon complained, because the Russian government saw only English intrigues in the Armenian troubles. Refusing to recognize that the methods of the Sultan's government caused the unrest, the Russian government encouraged the Sultan in his resistance to European advice.[12]

By December, 1896, Cambon's bitter complaints about the Russian alliance had increased. In his judgment Russia had obtained the better part of the bargain. Those in France who practiced the alliance

[12] Cambon to Félix Faure, Jan. 19, 1896, *Revue d'histoire diplomatique* (July–Sept., 1954), 191–95; Cambon to Hanotaux, Oct. 29, 1896, *Correspondance,* I, 419–20.

often forgot that if France were to be taken seriously, she must remain her own master. They neglected the fact that in this alliance there were two parties, and, in the opinion of Cambon, they had forgotten that "since they speak with the French Army behind them and in the name of a people whose history does not date from yesterday, they have the right to treat on equal terms with the autocrat of all the Russians." He was disgusted with the French politicians who acted like subalterns because they were dazzled by the prospects of meeting crowned heads and exchanging notes with princes. "The original vice of the entente," in his opinion, was that France had offered Russia everything and Russia had promised nothing in return. France appeared so honored in rendering services to Russia that Russia believed this to be sufficient payment and forgot to render any services in return.

Cambon was infuriated by the failure of the French government to point out to Russia where French interests in the Near East differed from Russian interests. Russia closed her eyes to these differences and tried to ignore them.

Cambon wanted to follow a policy in which France could work for a *rapprochement* between Russia and Great Britain. Through their alliance she would influence Russia, and through her financial interests, Great Britain. United thus to these powers, France could play an important role in the Near East; and at the same time, she could prevent clashes between Britain and Russia over Turkey. But the French ministers did not realize the value of this kind of policy and continued to subordinate French interests to Russian. Cambon believed it was necessary to recognize the differences between Russia and France. Much tact would have to be used to prevent Russian coolness, but the abandonment of French interests now might endanger the alliance in the future. He wanted to see the alliance well defined and rendered profitable for both members; otherwise, if France gave away too much because of the alliance, she would "lose not only the respect of her enemies but the consideration of her friends."[13]

[13] Cambon to Henri Cambon, Dec. 16, 1896, *ibid.*, 421–23.

The crisis between the allies over the Ottoman Empire reached its height during the winter of 1896–97 when the Russian government prepared to seize the Straits of the Dardanelles, but the plans were never put into operation. In March, 1897, Nelidov revealed the story to Cambon and alleged that Russia was ready to use force—her troops were only awaiting the signal before launching the attack. Cambon in his report noted ironically that, thanks to the powers of Europe, Russia had prevented collective action in Constantinople and had obtained the prime role for herself in the Turkish capital. Turko-Russian relations had never been better, and part of the Turkish fleet had even been sent away to make the occupation easier.[14]

Cambon's bitterness increased when, after President Félix Faure visited Russia in 1897, extensive preparations were made to celebrate his return, just as if "he had come from winning an unexpected victory." This would only harm France's position in the world and place her more and more in the pockets of the Tsar. Unfortunately these actions made it appear "to all the world, and to the Russians in particular, that we consider their friendship as our only plank of safety." Worst of all, France appeared to be nothing and made herself subservient in order to please Russia.[15]

Cambon's disgust with the Russian alliance made him more aware of the interests common to France and Great Britain. He found himself attracted more towards British than Russian policy. His later work of settling the mutual colonial problems of France and Great Britain may have originated in Constantinople; there he realized how much these two countries had in common. Cambon was now ready for the ambassadorship in London.

As early as 1893, Jules Develle, the foreign minister, had suggested the post in London to Cambon. He refused partly because of his wife's poor health, partly because he felt it poor policy to change ambassadors in Constantinople often. In Paris governments could be changed easily, but in Constantinople it was a matter of tradition and

[14] Hanotaux to Montebello, Jan. 12, 31, 1897, Cambon to Hanotaux, March 24, 1897, *DDF,* 1 ser., XIII, 108–110, 159, 282–84.
[15] Cambon to Mme Paul Cambon, Sept. 1, 2, 1897, *Correspondance,* I, 428–29.

habit to change ambassadors only when it was absolutely necessary. Death alone removed Sir William White from his post as Her Majesty's ambassador in 1891, and most of Cambon's colleagues had been there ten or fifteen years. In Cambon's opinion, much of the weakness of French policy in the Near East was the result of the continual change in ambassadors. Although he confessed that "I am not here on a bed of roses," yet his departure from Constantinople would ruin the last sixteen months' work, and he urged Develle "as minister of foreign affairs you ought then to refuse absolutely to move me."

By 1898, Cambon's situation was different. Anna Cambon had died after years of poor health, and he could accede to the request of Théophile Delcassé, now French foreign minister, to transfer him to London, where Baron Alphonse de Courcel had asked for a replacement.

Cambon knew that Delcassé was embarrassed to find a successor for Courcel. His sense of duty led him to accept the post, although it would be a difficult one. "London," he wrote, "is an unknown theater for me; I do not know the English society; my mourning prevents me from making contact with it for some long months, and in England, more than anywhere else, policy is made through daily relations." Delcassé must not be surprised if his mission remained "colorless."[16]

Amid Cambon's preparations for departure from Constantinople, Kaiser William II appeared in the city on a visit to cement relations between his nation and Turkey. In his first talk with Cambon, William spoke at length on archaeology, Cicero, Demosthenes, Greek sarcophagi, and Turkey. In a private audience later, the Emperor's chief topic of conversation was Jules Cambon, who was then governor-general of Algeria. In Cambon's opinion, William II was only a "very sharp traveling salesman who tries to dazzle the gallery with the air of knowing everything."[17]

[16] Cambon to Develle, May 27, 1893, Cambon to Delcassé, Sept. 29, 1898, *ibid.*, 358–61, 439–41; Monson to Salisbury, July 20, 1898, PRO, FO, France, 27:3400; H. Cambon, *Paul Cambon,* 162.

[17] Cambon to Mme Hippolyte Cambon, Oct. 24, Nov. 1, 1898, *Correspondance,* I, 442–46.

After a last audience with the Sultan and a round of the customary farewell receptions, Cambon left Constantinople for Paris on November 10, 1898. Despite the apparent failure of much of his work in Constantinople, he was saddened at the thought of leaving. He was going to a country whose language he did not know and where some were discussing the possibility of war with France. It was not a pleasant prospect.

Cambon failed to a certain degree in Turkey because she joined the Central Powers in World War I and lost her empire. His failure was not of his own making. The alliance with Russia damned the French in the eyes of the Sultan and rendered impossible any policy that Cambon might advance. He and his colleagues were handicapped because public opinion favored freedom for the subject peoples of the Ottoman Empire. Freedom for these peoples only hastened the disintegration of the empire and this threatened European peace.

Cambon's policies in Constantinople suffered because French and Russian foreign policies did not seek the same goal in the East. France looked with longing at Egypt, where Russia was of little help. The Russian foreign office looked only at the Straits of the Dardanelles. It was the nightmare of the Russians that Great Britain alone, or in a combination, might seize the Straits under the guise of using force to bring reforms to the Ottoman Empire. France would not make war over the Dardanelles but rather over Alsace-Lorraine.

The years Cambon spent in Constantinople served to prepare him for his new post. In his struggles with the Sultan, Cambon had been forced to co-operate with the British. He came to realize that the future of French diplomacy lay in some understanding with Great Britain. France was not an equal partner in the Russian alliance; French interests were often spurned to advance the different views of St. Petersburg. A friend was needed with similar views.

In Constantinople, Cambon saw how much France and Great Britain had in common. Delcassé undoubtedly knew Cambon's feelings about French relations with Russia and with Britain. There was no one else in the French diplomatic service better fitted to bring about the diplomatic revolution with Great Britain that Delcassé contemplated.

V. CREATION OF THE ENTENTE CORDIALE

ANGLO-FRENCH relations were at their worst when Cambon left Constantinople for London. On September 19, 1898, the forces of British and French imperialism in the persons of Captain Jean Marchand and Lord Kitchener had met at Fashoda, a swampy half-ruined outpost of the Upper Nile in an area of the Sudan.

Captain Marchand had led an expedition from the French Congo in an effort to establish a foothold on the upper Nile and thus force the British to negotiate over the control of Egypt. At the same time, a French expedition from Ethiopia had made an unsuccessful attempt to join Marchand at Fashoda. It must be recalled that at the time Marchand started out, the Sudan was not under Anglo-Egyptian control, having been conquered by the Mahdi, a religious fanatic, in 1885.

The British government, as was to be expected, kept a close check on Marchand's courageous trek, which had been widely reported in the French press. Repeated warnings from the British Foreign Office that no European power other than Great Britain had any claim to the Nile Valley were ignored, and by August, British military intelligence had drafted a tentative plan for an attack on Brest if war broke out. Marchand had reached Fashoda on July 10, 1898, with a small force of 120 native troops and a few officers.

In 1896, the British government had decided to reconquer the Sudan, and in pursuance of that objective, Lord Kitchener, commanding an Anglo-Egyptian force, defeated the Khalifa, the successor of the Mahdi, on September 2, 1898. When Kitchener received information that the French were entrenched on the Nile, he pushed on south with his victorious forces. On September 19, he and Marchand met with great politeness, each requesting the other to withdraw. Neither would retreat.[1]

Although there was a comic-opera air about the whole affair, it was treated as tinder for war in France and Britain, where newspapers played up the meeting for all its headline value and where fleets readied for war. Hostilities could break out at any moment.

In the midst of the crisis, Delcassé proposed Paul Cambon to the British government to replace Courcel as ambassador. "In making this selection of the most eminent and capable member of the French diplomatic service," emphasized Delcassé, "the French Republic is also choosing an ambassador notoriously most friendly and inspired with the best disposition towards England." Sir Edmund Monson, British ambassador in Paris, informed Delcassé on September 19 that Queen Victoria would be happy to receive Cambon as ambassador to the Court of St. James.[2]

The London *Times* of December 8, 1898, reported: "M. Cambon, the new French ambassador to the Court of St. James arrived in London last night, reaching Victoria at 8:15. His excellency, who was accompanied by his son, was delayed somewhat by the dislocation of the cross-channel service. Baron de Courcel, the retiring ambassador, went in person to meet M. Cambon and greeted him with great cordiality. He also presented Mr. W. Green, the station superintendent, who was present on behalf of the railway company." Thus Paul Cambon arrived in London, where he was to live and work for the next twenty-two years.

In 1898, Paul Cambon was fifty-five years of age. His hair was

[1] Ardagh to Sanderson, July 23, 1897, PRO, FO, GD 40:14; draft plan for attack, Aug. 12, 1898, PRO, GD, 40:2; Keith Eubank, "The Fashoda Crisis Re-examined," *The Historian,* XXII, Feb., 1960, 145–62.

[2] Monson to Salisbury, Sept. 18, 1898, PRO, FO, France 27:3400; Monson to Delcassé, Sept. 19, 1898, *ibid.,* 146:3551; Gosselin to Monson, Sept. 19, 1898, *ibid.,* 27:3399.

white and thinning; his beard and mustaches were full, neat, and well trimmed. Of medium height and frame, he always dressed conservatively in clothes from good Parisian tailors. His distinguished appearance fulfilled the popular conception of a French ambassador. His manner was quiet and assured, undoubtedly because of the confidence he had acquired through long experience.

In London his mornings were devoted to routine work of the embassy, such as reading reports and telegrams and receiving visitors. After a late midday dinner, he took a daily walk in Hyde Park, often ending it with a call at the Foreign Office in Whitehall. "A small but distinguished figure, with startlingly white hair and beard, with prominent glaucous eyes, he would enter the room slowly, place his grey top hat upon its accustomed table, sink into his accustomed leather chair, and exclaim, as he drew off first one kid glove and then the other, *'Eh bien, mon cher, voici encore votre pain quotidien!'* "[3]

After returning to the embassy, he usually wrote a dispatch or telegram describing events at the Foreign Office. The remainder of the afternoon was devoted to his voluminous correspondence. After supper, if it was not necessary for him to attend an official function and the London weather permitted, he often went for an evening stroll. He finished the evening with more work or perhaps a game of chess with one of his assistants.

In 1898, when Cambon arrived, London was the nerve center of an empire whose power appeared limitless. The British Empire still enjoyed world economic prominence; her currency was sound; and one could accumulate wealth without suffering drastic taxation. Her merchant fleet was still the greatest carrier of the world's goods.

Robert Cecil, third Marquis of Salisbury, was the leader of the Conservatives, as well as prime minister and foreign secretary. Since the reign of Elizabeth I, his family had played a prominent role in British politics. His own career in foreign affairs included participation in the Berlin Congress of 1878, which he had attended as foreign secretary in Disraeli's cabinet. He was tall and broad shouldered, with a huge beard that reminded Cambon of Moses. Salisbury was

[3] Harold Nicolson, *Sir Arthur Nicolson, bart., first Lord Carnock*, 415.

loath to commit Britain to either of the power blocs. He distrusted the constant turnover in French cabinets and objected to France's crossing Britain's path in Africa. He spurned German attempts to inveigle Britain into the Triple Alliance because he believed that the rewards for an ally were not worth the cost.

Except for the Mediterranean Agreements in 1887,[4] Britain had remained generally aloof from Continental alliances, but in 1898 powerful voices were heard calling for the end of British isolation. Chief among them was the voice of Joseph Chamberlain, the tall, dynamic colonial secretary who was one of the leading imperialists. It was to be Cambon's job to help effect the end of British isolation and lay the groundwork for the allied efforts of 1914–18.

After settling himself at Albert Gate House, the French embassy, Cambon called on Salisbury on December 9. The conversation was general in nature; Cambon gave Salisbury "a full explanation of the differences between the principles of French and English colonial administration." The Prime Minister informed Cambon that the Queen wanted to see him that day. This led to a comparison of the length of the reigns of Louis XIV and Victoria. There was no contrasting of morals, but Cambon remarked that when Louis died, he lamented his love for war. Salisbury replied that the Queen had no love for war at all, and this, Cambon noted to Delcassé, "was the only allusion to the possibility of a conflict between France and England."

By five-thirty that afternoon Cambon had arrived at Windsor Castle, where he was joined by Salisbury, whom Cambon described as having "the bearing and the manner of a patriarch." Cambon lectured Salisbury on French philosophy until a servant led them to the apartment of the Queen. The Prime Minister made the necessary introductions; the Queen was happy to know Cambon and asked about President Faure. Cambon presented his credentials, naming

---

[4] The Mediterranean Agreements called for a maintenance of the status quo, previous agreement before any changes, and mutual support for the interests of the signatory powers. Italy and Britain signed it in January, 1887, and Austria adhered in March. In general, it was supposed to curtail French expansion.

him "Ambassador Extraordinary and Plenipotentiary," and when the customary remarks had been made, he withdrew. As he conversed with the Queen during the state dinner that followed, Cambon was impressed by her mental vigor. He was unimpressed by the meal: "The cooking was detestable and I would not tolerate such a dinner at my home."[5]

The reception given to the new French ambassador seemed sincere, but Cambon warned Delcassé that despite the cordiality of his reception the basic problem of Anglo-French relations was still unsolved. Both the Queen and Salisbury were trying to soften the wrath that had been aroused in Britain by recent events, and Cambon regretted the absence of any counterweight to the widespread bellicose attitude. He wondered whether Salisbury's influence could head off disaster. It was dangerous business; the slightest slip by the French ambassador could be fatal for the cause of peace.

Cambon made a few public statements to calm tempers. At the reception for the French colony in December, 1898, he told his guests that he hoped they could be depended upon to help with his difficult task. "The interests of France and England," he said, "are not incompatible, and they ought always to be in accord with those of civilization and progress."

At the French Chamber of Commerce banquet on January 31, 1899, he declared that nations should regulate their activities in accordance with the rights of their neighbors, for such a policy would tend to produce harmony. Those to whom he spoke could do much towards maintaining peaceful relations between France and England, "whose enterprise and energy were the marvel of all those who studied the country." By such statements Cambon hoped to reduce British antipathy for France and to lay the foundations for future negotiations.

Realizing the untenable position of Marchand, Delcassé ordered his recall, and on January 11, 1899, Cambon announced officially that Fashoda had been evacuated. Seizing his opportunity, he also sug-

[5] Cambon to Mme Guépratte, Dec. 9, 1898, Cambon to Delcassé, Dec. 12, 1898, *Correspondance,* II, 9–13.

gested to Salisbury that the moment had come to talk frankly, reminding him of his promise to Courcel, that talks towards a settlement of the question of the Bahr el Ghazal, where Fashoda was located, could begin once the disputed outpost was evacuated. While not denying his promise, Salisbury claimed that the trouble resulted from a French attempt to stake out political claims and at the same time to seek a commercial outlet in the valley of the Nile. A commercial outlet would be allowed, but not a political one—that was out of the question. Instantly Cambon suggested a line of demarcation skirting the Bahr el Ghazal while giving the French a commercial outlet to the tributaries of the Nile. Salisbury promised to consider such a move after obtaining some idea of the geography of the area.

Next Cambon mentioned Newfoundland, where French fishing rights were in dispute, but Salisbury would not take up the question; it had been discussed for sixty years and could go on for a long time. If there were any other Anglo-French differences, concluded Cambon, he would place himself at Salisbury's disposal to improve relations between the two nations. As he finished, he begged Salisbury to inform him at once if there were any misunderstandings.

On January 20, Cambon returned to Whitehall, bringing Delcassé's approval of the line of demarcation. Salisbury accepted the proposal as a possible basis for settlement, but the cabinet must first give it detailed study.

Negotiations continued through January and February. Much to Cambon's regret, the newspapers reported that official talks were in progress over the Fashoda crisis. By February 22, Cambon and Salisbury were discussing the details of the agreement, and on March 21 they signed the formal document. Cambon's first task in his new post had been accomplished successfully; war had been averted. His line of demarcation became the western boundary of the Sudan.

Cambon believed that the best possible solution had been found. He advised his son, who was beginning a diplomatic career, that the policy of seeking only what was possible would save France from many vexations. France had lost Bahr el Ghazal, but Cambon at-

Courtesy Historical Pictures Service

"AU REVOIR!"

Germany: *"Farewell, Madame, and if . . ."*
France: *"Ha! We shall meet again!"*

Cartoon from *Punch*, September 27, 1873.

Courtesy Culver Service

A contemporary drawing of General Boulanger passing through the Place de la Concorde, Paris, on his way to the Chamber of Deputies, 1888.

CREATION OF THE ENTENTE CORDIALE

tached little importance to this swamp. He believed, however, that the agreement with Great Britain would compensate for the loss because it would bring West Africa into the French sphere of influence.[6]

With the outbreak of the Boer War in the summer of 1899, Cambon was caught between a rising tide of anti-British feeling in France and the mounting indignation of Great Britain at the French attitude. In desperation he begged Delcassé to quiet the French newspapers, which seemed intent on destroying all prospects for peace. In October, after two days in Paris, Cambon was appalled by the violence of the "hate Britain" campaign. On all sides he was asked why France did not seek a quarrel with Britain, now that she was occupied in the Transvaal.

The climax came when a Paris newspaper published a cartoon revealing the exposed limbs of Queen Victoria as she hid Joseph Chamberlain under her skirts. Sir Edward Monson, the British ambassador, left Paris for Cannes. The Minister of Fine Arts gave the cartoonist a decoration. Cambon breathed freely again when he heard no immediate repercussions. He was afraid that such episodes might lead the British government to believe that the French people wanted war, in which case Britain would finish off the Boers and then fall on France, using a new Fashoda as a pretext to start the war. The arrogant attitude of the British people only made the situation more deadly. Fascinated and alarmed, Cambon found the British arrogance somehow admirable. Their coolness was amazing and terrifying.

By the end of March, 1900, the affair of the cartoon had died down. Matters had been worse than Cambon imagined because the Queen had seen the cartoon and had been greatly incensed. She had ordered

[6] Salisbury to Monson, Jan. 11, 20, 21, Feb. 22, 1899, PRO, FO, France, 27: 3463, 3461, 3454, 146:3612; Cambon to Delcassé, Jan. 12, 21, 1899, Delcassé to Cambon, Jan. 24, 1899, France, Ministère des Affaires Étrangères, *Documents diplomatiques français, correspondence concernant la declaration additionelle du Mars 1899 à la convention franco-anglaise du Juin 1899*, 7-9; Cambon to Delcassé, Feb. 1, 1899, Cambon to Henri Cambon, March 23, 1899, *Correspondance*, I, 23-24; Salisbury to Monson, March 15, 1899, *British Documents on the Origin of the War 1898-1914* (hereafter cited as *BD*), I, 201-202.

Salisbury to send Monson from Paris for his health, and when he resisted her demands, she raised a great cry. Cambon rather grimly noted: "This old woman has a head of iron; no one has any influence over her."[7]

Britain received sympathy from her foreign critics when Queen Victoria died on January 22, 1901. An era in British history had ended. Enormous confusion developed over the funeral, and Cambon was much amused at the chaos. The funeral preparations were hopelessly snarled because Britain had not buried a sovereign for sixty-four years and no one knew what to do. Thirty-six hours before the funeral Cambon reported: "They do and undo; everything is mixed up, and it is impossible to obtain precise information. The funniest thing is that this disorder is not causing any trouble. The secretary of Lord Lansdowne has only just told me very quietly, 'We are very stupid.' But the superiority of the British is that it is a matter of complete indifference to them if they appear to be stupid."

Victoria was laid to rest in the crypt of St. George's Chapel, Windsor, while Cambon sat in a stall of a Knight of the Order of the Garter shivering in the cold. A buffet and reception followed for the diplomatic missions and the distinguished guests, including Victoria's grandson, Emperor William II. As Cambon was leaving, William II stopped him.

"My dear Cambon," said the Emperor, "I am very happy to see you and to tell you that I have spoken about you here; you will be aware of it."

Cambon kept his silence. William continued: "You know already my sentiments for your country. I consider France indispensable for the equilibrium of Europe; a strong France is necessary for me, and if you have some difficulty, count on me; I will lend you my help."

Cambon replied: "I am deeply touched by the sentiments of your majesty, and I will transmit them to Paris. But France asks only to live in peace, and I hope and I believe that she will never have need of the help of your majesty."

[7] Cambon to Mme Hippolyte Cambon, Nov. 28, 1899, Cambon to d'Estournelles, Oct. 28, 1899, Cambon to Jules Cambon, Feb. 20, March 22, 1900, *Correspondance*, II, 29–40.

"Yes, yes," William rejoined, "but some event could present itself where I would be in a position to render service to you. I would not fail. I love your country. I have been very grateful for the fashion in which she received my subjects last year at the exposition. You realize yourself that I know how to practice being grateful."

The conversation turned to the topic of Jules Cambon. Finally the Ambassador presented the members of his mission to William, who seemed genuinely eager to meet them.[8]

Despite the efforts of William II, a change was taking place in British foreign policy. During the few years that Cambon had been in London, Joseph Chamberlain, the energetic colonial secretary, had attempted twice to reach an agreement with Germany—first in 1899 and later in 1901. Both times his efforts had come to naught. Salisbury finally quashed any agreement with his famous memorandum of 1901 declaring that the dangers of isolation were not as great as those inherent in a military alliance that might drag Britain into a war not of her own making.

The differences preventing agreement were fundamental: Germany wanted explicit guarantees of British support in sections of the world where British interests were few, particularly in Central Europe. Likewise, Britain sought German support in the Far East, where Germany had few pressing interests. The Germans, however, did not comprehend the importance of the attitude of the British. An agreement over areas where British interests were deeply involved was possible, but not a military alliance over Central Europe because any threat that would necessitate such an alliance was lacking.

Since uneasy conditions did exist in the Far East, the relations between Britain and Japan produced the Anglo-Japanese Alliance of 1902, which was aimed at Russia. Both members guaranteed the possessions of the other and pledged neutrality if one were attacked by a single power; both pledged aid if one member were attacked by more than one power.

[8] Cambon to Delcassé, Jan., Feb. 6, 1901, *DDF,* 2 ser., I, 75, 86–87; Eckardstein to the Foreign Office, Feb. 2, 1901, *GP,* XVI, 290–92; Cambon to Jules Cambon, Feb. 14, 1901, Cambon to Mme Hippolyte Cambon, Jan. 28, 30, 1901, *Correspondance,* II, 52–57.

The news of this alliance shook Cambon. He damned it as unnecessary and as an instrument limiting British freedom of action. He cautioned Lord Lansdowne, the secretary of state for foreign affairs, "The Japanese are the most cunning of the Asiatics. They will hide behind the British at the slightest disturbance and eventually involve Britain in quarrels which are not of her making."

The Anglo-Japanese Alliance opened a new era in British foreign policy, for already in January, 1902, Count Paul von Metternich, the German ambassador, reported on good authority that Cambon and Chamberlain were discussing the solution of the outstanding problems between the two countries. The next month Baron von Eckardstein, the German chargé d'affaires, sensed a change in British foreign policy when he saw Cambon and Chamberlain, after a dinner at Marlborough House, go off to the billiard room, where they talked "exactly twenty-eight minutes in the most animated manner." Eckardstein's eavesdropping rewarded him with hearing the pair mention two very interesting words, "Morocco" and "Egypt." When Cambon left, Chamberlain berated Eckardstein for the attitude of the German newspapers toward Britain during the Boer War.[9] A diplomatic revolution was in the making, but the making would be long and arduous.

Delcassé wanted to end the eternal quarrels with Britain over colonies, spheres of influence, treaties, and those pinpricks that embittered relations. He therefore empowered Cambon to propose settlement of "all outstanding questions in dispute between England and France" at the time of his appointment as ambassador. A barrier to this settlement had been Lord Salisbury, who feared to commit Britain to any one of the rival camps on the Continent. The Prime Minister believed that the government in which Delcassé was foreign

[9] Cambon to Delcassé, Feb. 12, 1902, *DDF,* 2 ser., II, 88–91; Metternich to the Foreign Office, Jan. 30, 1902, *GP,* XVII, 342–43; Baron von Eckardstein, *Ten Years at the Court of St. James 1896–1905,* 228–29; Julian Amery, *The Life of Joseph Chamberlain,* IV, 179–82. Cambon omitted any reference to this talk in his dispatches; probably he did not take Chamberlain seriously at this time. To Cambon he was too much the opportunistic politician. The author cannot agree with Amery that Chamberlain initiated the Entente Cordiale.

CREATION OF THE ENTENTE CORDIALE

minister could not last long, that, as a result, any official French friendship for Britain would be short lived. On July 12, 1902, Salisbury retired from the cabinet, and Arthur Balfour took his place. Lord Lansdowne, secretary of state for foreign affairs since 1901, would now be free to pursue a more friendly policy towards France. There was no longer anyone of importance in the cabinet to insist on an aloof position toward affairs on the Continent. Now it might be possible for Cambon to achieve the diplomatic revolution desired by Delcassé.

The forebears of the Secretary of State for Foreign Affairs, Henry Petty-Fitzmaurice, fifth Marquis of Lansdowne, included twelfth-century Normans on his father's side and a French grandfather on the maternal side who fought under Napoleon I. Lord Lansdowne had served his country as governor-general of Canada, viceroy of India, and secretary for war. His tall, thin figure, bald head, and side whiskers delighted the cartoonists. He was quiet by nature, and lacked the vigorous drive and glamour that would arouse the masses. His practical sense made him ideally suited for the job of settling Anglo-French misunderstandings.

The problems facing Cambon and Lansdowne were colonial in nature. They involved Newfoundland, New Hebrides, Madagascar, Siam, Egypt, and Morocco. None were finally settled until the agreement of April 8, 1904.

In Newfoundland, France claimed ill-defined fishing rights under the Treaty of Utrecht. These related to French fishermen along the "treaty shore." Salisbury had seen no need to settle these troubles, preferring a makeshift arrangement whereby British and French naval officers attempted to maintain law and order among the fishermen. It could only be hoped that there would not be an outbreak of violence over the placing of nets or the wandering of a fishing schooner into foreign waters. Salisbury saw little point in Britain's approaching France because attempts at a settlement in 1890 and 1892 had failed. He knew that the French legislature would not sanction any agreement and that the compensation demanded by the French would be too high.

Cambon brought up the question of Newfoundland on his own initiative in November, 1900; however, Salisbury was not interested in an agreement. When Lansdowne became foreign secretary, Cambon broached the subject again. Vainly the pair sought a basis for agreement. Three problems stopped them: the subsidies paid to the French fishermen by the French government, places for the French fishermen to purchase bait, and the proper compensation for the abandonment of French rights in Newfoundland.

Another problem was the Anglo-French dispute in the New Hebrides. As early as October, 1899, Cambon had proposed to Salisbury that partitioning might reduce the friction, but Salisbury was cool towards the idea because British and French citizens were scattered unevenly over the islands. In February, 1901, Cambon suggested to Lansdowne that a commission be appointed to deal with native affairs on the spot and to handle troublesome cases involving the property of British and French nationals in the New Hebrides. Although Lansdowne accepted the substance of Cambon's suggestion, they could not agree on the personnel of the commission.

When Madagascar became a French colony in 1896, trade treaties between the island and Great Britain had been cancelled immediately. New preferential tariffs between the new colony and France worked a particular hardship on Lancashire cotton interests. In Siam, Britain and France were at odds over spheres of influence.

Moreover, Egypt still separated Great Britain and France. How could a graceful and final exit be arranged for the British? Fashoda had revealed the weakness of France and the strength of Great Britain. To the British, the security of imperial communications required that they control the canal zone. Cambon believed that agreement was possible if the French government would decide on a satisfactory price.

France wanted a definite settlement in Morocco. It not only controlled the Atlantic approaches to the Straits of Gibraltar, but also dominated the western portion of the Mediterranean Sea. Internal dissensions made it a political vacuum into which any interested power could step, thereby threatening the British base at Gibraltar and the French African empire. Britain controlled more than 50 per cent of Moroccan trade. An English entourage, headed by Harry Maclean, surrounded the Sultan of Morocco and gave the Quai d'Orsay no peace of mind. A former noncommissioned officer in the British Army, Maclean was training the Sultan's army. Despite the assurances of the French embassy in Madrid that Maclean's importance was exaggerated, he was dangerous to Cambon. Some of Cambon's suspicions were legitimate, for Maclean was in communication with the Intelligence Division of the War Office.[10]

By January, 1902, Cambon was certain that the time was fast approaching when some settlement had to be reached in connection with Morocco. It would be dangerous for French interests if any other single power became a predominant force there. Already the British had the monopoly of the telegraph system, and Maclean had control of the army. France must reach an agreement with Britain and Spain over Morocco in which the status quo would be maintained. This accord would be "precise, clear, and limited and could not frighten anyone and would constitute a line for the future upon which other accords could be hung."

Cambon used the annual chamber of commerce banquet to enunciate his desire for a mutual agreement between France and Britain. He urged: "Every reasonable man, every good Frenchman, and every good Englishman ought to desire between the two countries relations characterized by as much confidence and cordiality as possible."[11] He had set the stage for serious negotiations.

After Salisbury's resignation, Cambon and Lansdowne met in Whitehall on July 23, 1902, for a momentous talk. It began with a discussion of Morocco. Lansdowne assured Cambon that he understood the special interests of France in the area along the Moroccan-Algerian frontier, where there was political unrest. Cambon was

[10] Patenotre to Delcassé, Nov. 18, 1902, Cambon to Delcassé, June 28, 1901, *DDF*, 2 ser., II, 611–12, I, 354–55; Intelligence Division, War Office to Foreign Office, Jan. 11, 1902, PRO, FO, Morocco, 99:400.

[11] Cambon to Henri Cambon, Jan. 4, 1902, Cambon to Delcassé, Jan. 13, 1902, Cambon to Jules Cambon, Jan. 16, 1902, *Correspondance*, II, 66–72.

uneasy about the future because the Moroccan tribes were restless and the Sultan of Morocco was weak. Maclean's being there did not help because his presence was contrary to the policy of maintaining the status quo. Lansdowne replied that the British government wanted to continue the status quo and had refused a request for a regular military mission to be sent to the Sultan. Maclean was only an instructor, and the Sultan could dismiss him tomorrow.

Cambon begged that they speak frankly to avoid misunderstanding. He knew that Britain was interested in Morocco only because she did not want any single power to control Tangiers, but Europe would not permit Britain to control both sides of the Straits of Gibraltar. Why not internationalize Tangiers? In exchange, France could be given some influence and, if necessary, police power in southern Morocco. They must exchange views in order that there should be no misunderstanding. All of this was unofficial, and he would have to obtain the permission of Delcassé to make it official. Lansdowne was silent for a moment and then remarked, "I will talk with you when you are ready."

In all probability Delcassé knew of this conversation in advance, and Cambon described his proposals as "unofficial" in order to discover whether the proposed measure would be acceptable. If he met rebuff, he could withdraw his proposal and relations would still be amicable.

On August 6, Cambon came to the Foreign Office with definite proposals from Delcassé. The disagreement over Siam could be settled on the basis of an earlier agreement, made in 1896. The two governments should discuss the necessary action "in the event of Morocco's passing into liquidation." Like Cambon, Delcassé proposed that Tangiers be internationalized. Britain and France had colonial disagreements only in Siam and Morocco, Cambon stated. Morocco was merely an "elongation" of Algeria; it was an open gate to the French Empire; therefore, France could not allow a force to be established in Morocco that might evade her influence. Delcassé promised to protect British interests in Morocco and indicated that Spain would be given a sufficient sphere in the hinterland in the event of the general liquidation of the country. Lansdowne feared an international crisis in the event of a premature liquidation of Morocco, because countries other than Britain and France were interested. Cambon did not dispute this, but he found no harm in discussing the subject. Lansdowne promised to consider what had been said and to consult the cabinet; he would be unable to tell Cambon anything definite until after the parliamentary vacation.[12]

Cambon believed that Lansdowne was receptive to all he had said. Lansdowne, however, was annoyed at one word: "liquidation." It cannot be determined whether the word was the result of Cambon's eagerness for an agreement or the product of Delcassé's instructions. This one word would make the work of Cambon harder and prolong the negotiations into 1904.

During the parliamentary vacation a leak occurred. On September 1, Walter B. Harris of the London *Times* by letter informed Sir Arthur Nicolson, British minister in Tangiers, that a Moorish official had shown him the draft of a document of French origin containing an account of the negotiations over Morocco calling for the neutralization of the Straits and a guarantee of commercial freedom for Britain in Morocco. Harris claimed that his informant was in the pay of the French, but had shown the document to him in the hope that he could stop the negotiations. Describing the negotiations as "a low game," Harris implied that he might reveal the details if he were not awarded a decoration. Nicolson denied everything and threatened Harris with an official denial if he published the story.

The Moroccan minister of war informed the German vice-consul in Fez that talks aimed at giving France a free hand in Morocco were in progress in London between France and Britain. Harris told the same vice-consul that he was the source of this information and urged inquiries in London to break up the negotiations.[13] The

[12] Lansdowne to Monson, July 23, Aug. 6, 1902, *BD,* II, 263–64, 294–96; Cambon to Delcassé, Aug. 9, 1902, *DDF,* 2 ser., II, 437–43; Cambon to Henri Cambon, Aug. 6, 1902, *Correspondance,* II, 75–76.

[13] Harris to Nicolson, Sept. 1, 1902, PRO, FO, Morocco, 99:396; Mentzingen to the Foreign Office, Sept. 14, 1902, Maenss to Mentzingen, Sept. 29, 1902, *GP,* XVII, 344, 347; Nicolson to Villiers, Nov. 30, 1902, Foreign Office Library,

Austrian chargé d'affaires in Paris hastened to ask Monson about the negotiations. In London, von Eckardstein extracted a carefully guarded statement from Lansdowne that France had made certain propositions.

Harry Maclean decided that it was time to visit his oculist in London. His eyes bothered him so much, Cambon noted, that he covered the caravan route from Fez to Tangiers in three days—this trip ordinarily took from eight to ten days. Upon his arrival in London, Maclean apparently forgot to visit the oculist but hurried to Balmoral Castle to see Edward VII, thus substantiating Cambon's opinion of Maclean.

When Cambon and Lansdowne next met, on October 15, Harris had done his work well. Lansdowne claimed that the cabinet was too busy to take up the matters discussed in August because of an education bill. Cambon brought up the subject of Maclean: "Is he an ambassador extraordinary? Does he have any powers? What does he come to negotiate?" Lansdowne insisted that Maclean only sought a loan for Morocco.[14]

An agent of the French general staff who checked on Maclean's movements during his stay in Britain reported that Maclean had visited Edward VII at Balmoral; he had seen Lansdowne in Ireland and stayed with the Balfour family; twice he had conferred with Sir Thomas Sanderson, the permanent undersecretary in the Foreign Office; and he had visited Lord Roberts, the commander in chief of the British Army during the Boer War. According to the report there was no alliance between Britain and Morocco, yet Maclean had been permitted to come to Britain and recruit officers for the army of the Sultan.

Cambon believed that Maclean had been using the Moroccan treasury to buy arms and that with his commissions from the arms companies he had bribed members of the Sultan's court in order to

---

Nicolson MSS, FO, 321:1. Nicolson never found out the source of Harris' information. Nicolson forbade Harris to set foot again in the legation.

[14] Cambon to Delcassé, Oct. 23, 1902, *DDF*, 2 ser., II, 559–60; Lansdowne to Monson, Oct. 15, 1902, *BD*, II, 268–70.

maintain his position. Now the money was gone and he had come to London for a loan. France, Cambon felt, must take this opportunity to rid herself of "one of the most active official agents of the British government."

Cambon's theories about Maclean's trip were not accurate. French intelligence agents had done a better job. Maclean's trip to the oculist was indeed a subterfuge; he was an agent for the Sultan. During his stay in London, Maclean told Nicolson, who was now in London also, the reason for his trip. The Sultan had instructed him to ascertain the truth of the rumors about the establishment of a French protectorate in Morocco. If the rumors were true, Maclean was to proceed to Berlin with a letter for William II asking him to place Morocco under his protection. Nicolson declared that the rumors were not true. Then, Maclean continued, the Sultan wanted a guarantee that the status quo would not be disturbed and that Britain would support him in any crisis. For his part the Sultan guaranteed stable government for seven years, in which time he promised to develop the resources of the country, Britain to be released from her part of the bargain if he failed. Further, he wanted a personal guarantee from Edward VII for his life and property should he lose his throne. Finally, Maclean announced, the Sultan needed a loan of 300,000 pounds and British help in order to build railroads.

Lansdowne informed Maclean in writing that Britain was a firm adherent of the status quo and could not agree to his proposition, but would not permit "any one power being given a free hand in that country." Edward VII promised his friendship to the Sultan in a a letter, countersigned by Lansdowne, in which it was also stated that the reports about the protectorate were unfounded. Nicolson advised the government against the loan since the French might be antagonized.

British military intelligence regarded Tangiers as the danger spot in Morocco because of its strategic importance. The status quo in Morocco must be prolonged as long as possible in order to keep any one power out of Tangiers, particularly France or Germany. In time, France would probably absorb Morocco, but if Maclean were to take his offer to Berlin and obtain German protection and help, it might mean German control of Tangiers. With her growing fleet based at Tangiers, Germany would be very dangerous to Britain's interests in the Mediterranean.[15]

Harris and Maclean had planted good seed and it bore good fruit—for a while. There were those who did not want the French tricolor planted in Morocco; others wanted to maintain the independence of Morocco because the present seemed more secure than the future.

By December, British activities in connection with the negotiations ground to a halt. Cambon sensed that this was so while discussing the Moroccan question with Lansdowne on a visit to his country place. He warned Lansdowne of the dangers accruing from the lack of accord among the powers over Morocco, but Lansdowne was silent. Cambon tried another opening: they did not need a formal treaty, but could discuss the present situation and prepare for future eventualities. Lansdowne finally spoke. Possibly he and Delcassé might not always be in office. Would their successors feel the same way? Cambon countered that it was exactly because Lansdowne, Delcassé, and Cambon would not be there always that they must prepare for unexpected events in the future. This could be done by the exchange of views. After telling Cambon that it would perhaps be better if their governments merely talked unofficially about the matter, Lansdowne pointedly changed the subject.

For the time, any hope for a definite settlement was dead. There was little that Cambon could do to revive the discussion even though at the next meeting on December 31 he preached the gospel of the status quo and did all he could to destroy any thought in Lansdowne's mind that he had ever flirted with the heresy of the liquidation of Morocco. Cambon admitted to Lansdowne that there was danger

[15] Report from the Intelligence Division of the French General Staff, Oct. 7, 1902, Cambon to Delcassé, Oct. 23, 1902, *DDF,* 2 ser., II, 522–23, 559–61; Memoranda of Nicolson's talks with Maclean, Sept. 24, 25, Oct. 3, 8, 1902, Edward VII to the Sultan, Oct. 21, 1902, Memorandum for Maclean from Lansdowne, Oct. 30, 1902, "Memorandum Respecting the Present Situation in Morocco," Intelligence Division, Sept. 25, 1902, PRO, FO, Morocco, 99:400; Memorandum for Maclean from Lansdowne, Oct. 24, 1902, *BD,* II, 272–73.

that the Kaiser might step in as the champion of the Europeans should the revolts in Morocco increase; therefore, they must prevent such intervention. Lansdowne suddenly showed interest; what was this about Germany? It was true, said Cambon, although the Germans denied it, that they had attempted earlier to obtain a coaling station in Morocco near the Algerian border. Cambon was certain that the Kaiser wanted to establish Germany in the Mediterranean and to push out French trade by flooding the area with German products. Lansdowne wanted further study; any division such as liquidation might cause trouble and bring in the Kaiser. Cambon now saw the cause of the hesitation on the part of the British—they were afraid of German interference.

The sad truth was that the diplomats had moved too fast. Public opinion and diplomatic repercussions had affected the British cabinet. Cambon would have to wait until the way for the accord had been prepared by propaganda and an exchange of cordialities in order to offset Harris' disclosures. The fear of German interference, revealed by Maclean's trip, had probably frightened the British cabinet. There is the possibility that Lansdowne, who was opposed to partition in 1902, hoped that the Sultan would keep his promise and seriously undertake to reform Morocco. Part of the trouble, Cambon admitted later, was that Delcassé had not offered the British enough compensation for the neutralization of the Straits of Gibraltar. Sufficient compensation for Britain would be the settlement of the Egyptian question, but Delcassé still avoided so dangerous a political problem. He would have to offer more before the diplomatic revolution could be accomplished.

The task now facing Delcassé and Cambon was to prepare public opinion for an accord and to create conditions in Britain and in France that would make the agreement possible. Newspapers, magazines, and the British and French chambers of commerce began to play up the need of some formal understanding between the erstwhile rivals of Fashoda.

Cambon and Lansdowne came to an agreement over one aspect of the Moroccan question in February, 1903, when a joint loan to the

Sultan of Morocco was negotiated among British, French, and Spanish banks. The loan was to be a private affair, and the governments would do nothing unless the Moroccan government defaulted. This was a faltering step; yet it showed that France and Britain could agree when the occasion demanded it.

Cambon's work was aided by worsening relations between Germany and Britain. By October, 1902, the Admiralty was certain that the enlarged German Navy was being built to fight the British Navy. More articles appeared in the British press warning of the German menace, and in Germany articles were printed dealing with an invasion of England.

In his annual speech at the chamber of commerce banquet, Cambon pointedly thanked the chamber for helping to create the *rapprochement* that was now taking place between Britain and France. The Paris correspondent of the London *Times* reported that Cambon's speech "will act as a powerful stimulus to a movement which is already on foot" on both sides of the Channel. Personally, Cambon did not feel that he had said anything out of the ordinary. He had been saying much the same thing for years. Why the excitement? He believed that it was because public opinion was turning against Germany and toward France. However, he warned Delcassé not to think that the British would be any less exacting when the time came for bargaining, for they would not be influenced by sentiment.[16]

A new factor appeared when Cambon notified Delcassé on March 14 of an impending state visit of Edward VII to France. Although the idea of the visit was Edward's, Cambon urged him to make a speech as soon as possible after his arrival in Paris. He must tell the French people of his feeling for France—that he had always felt at home in their country. Cambon also suggested a quiet dinner with Émile Loubet, the president of France.

He watched the papers for any discordant note on the coming visit, and was relieved when they devoted more space to Algeria and even praised the French administration. To him the British seemed very

[16] London *Times,* March 3, 6, 1903; Cambon to Delcassé, March 13, 1903, *DDF,* 2 ser., III, 183–85.

happy because the visit showed that the international quarantine resulting from the Boer War had now been lifted.

In May, 1903, Edward visited Paris. The only discordant notes were a few *"Vivent les Boers! Vive la Russie! Vive Marchand!"* The King's conduct during the visit produced an excellent effect on French public opinion. At the end of his visit, as he drove to the railroad station, the crowds shouted, *"Vive notre roi!"* The trip had indeed been successful, although Cambon was unable to take part in the festivities because of the illness of his mother and uncle.

Even before the visit of the King, preparations were begun for the state visit of Loubet to Britain. By the end of April, Cambon reported that arrangements were being made for the official welcome of the President of the Republic to the city of London by the Lord Mayor. With this in mind, Cambon implored Delcassé not to let anything disrupt the preparations or the ensuing uproar would be unbearable.

Although the plan of a visit by the President of the French Republic was admirable for Anglo-French relations, Cambon thought it might set a bad precedent. The president was not a "sovereign; he is only an elected, temporary magistrate." If this visit were permitted, "he will always be en route during the seven years of his term in office."

This seemed a minor annoyance, however, when Edward VII horrified Cambon by asking if the French officials would wear *culottes* when they paid their official calls. *Culottes* were the knee breeches that had been considered aristocratic dress during the French Revolution; the working-class republicans refused to wear them and so became known as *sans culottes*. The ambassador had a problem: how should he advise the government of the nation of the *sans culottes* on the wearing of these silken knee breeches that were then considered the official dress for ambassadors at state functions? First he announced that the descendants of the men of 1789 would appear just as they were accustomed to dress in Paris. Then the King reminded him that the United States representatives, who were from an older republic, wore the *culottes*. But Cambon held such attire to be impossible. He complained, "All Paris will laugh at it, and the press will throw itself into an orgy of puns." London finally decided that President Loubet might appear without the *culottes,* but not Delcassé, to which the latter replied that they would either receive "a minister without *culottes* or *culottes* without a minister!" Finally Edward acquiesced in the affair. Cambon believed that the King had caused all this commotion for his own amusement, "at our expense and sought to *culotter* a government which considered itself as a government of *sans culottes.*"[17]

By July, 1903, Cambon was perfecting the final preparations for the visit of Loubet and Delcassé while trying to keep up with the latest changes in the program conceived by Edward VII. Cambon also warned Delcassé that the entire trip would be of little value unless there was an exchange of views between the two foreign ministers. For this purpose he arranged a meeting on July 7, of the foreign ministers. He decided that it was "necessary to sacrifice protocol to politics," and at the dinner at the French embassy for the visiting French dignitaries, he seated Delcassé between Lansdowne and Chamberlain because he believed that "Chamberlain is at present the actual government of England, and I know that, disgusted with the Germans, he desires to turn to our side."

The visit of Loubet was a glorious success. Cambon observed that never in fifty years had such enthusiasm been aroused in Britain for the ruler of another country. This enthusiasm had penetrated even to the smallest hamlet. The dinner at the French embassy on June 7 was perfect, and "the departure of the King after the dinner was a sight worthy of the fifth act of a grand opera." Bright lights illuminated the embassy, and the Life Guards delighted the cheering throngs as they passed with their helmets reflecting the lights.

At the meeting on July 7, Lansdowne and Delcassé were in general agreement on the outstanding problems. To Delcassé the main problem was Morocco. With the waning of the Sultan's authority, France was the natural power to regenerate the country. Delcassé made no

[17] Cambon to Delcassé, April 27, 1903, Cambon to Henri Cambon, June 6, 18, 1903, *Correspondance,* II, 92–94.

objection when Lansdowne mentioned the Egyptian question. However, he wished that question to be considered after the difficulties in Morocco had been settled. Lansdowne accepted Delcassé's idea of compensation for French rights in Newfoundland.

With the departure of Delcassé and Loubet on June 9, Cambon now took up the talks. At the first meeting Lansdowne brought up three things that Britain wanted: "commercial liberty in Morocco, freedom of the Straits, and an accord with Spain." Cambon accepted them and proposed the French desire: economic dominance in Morocco, since this territory bordered on Algeria for 1,800 kilometers. Lansdowne concurred, and the entente seemed agreed on in principle. But, on July 29, Cambon dejectedly reported, "I thought the negotiations were under way in the most satisfactory manner when Lord Lansdowne observed to me that you had not made any allusion to the question of Egypt." Cambon conceded that Egypt might have to be discussed, but this was not the proper time and there were other powers that would have to be acquainted with Britain's demands. Lansdowne disagreed; he thought it was time to discuss Egypt.

Cambon warned Delcassé that Lansdowne had raised this question only after lengthy consideration on the part of the entire British government, but the French ambassador would not have France give up easily her rights in Egypt. He said, "It is necessary for us to show ourselves more exacting in Morocco or elsewhere." Delcassé confessed that Lansdowne had spoken of financial matters in Egypt. He agreed with Cambon that France would only give up her rights in Egypt for equivalent concessions.[18]

On October 1, Lansdowne presented Cambon with the British government's proposals covering affairs in Morocco, Egypt, Newfoundland, New Hebrides, Nigeria, Zanzibar, and Madagascar. To Cambon and Delcassé the important matters were Morocco and Egypt. In Morocco, Britain wanted freedom of trade, neutralization

[18] Lansdowne to Monson, July 7, 29, 1903, *BD*, II, 294–307, 304–305; Cambon to Delcassé, July 22, 31, 1903, Delcassé to Cambon, July 21, Aug. 2, 1903, *DDF*, 2 ser., III, 471–76, 497–99, 510–11.

of the Straits of Gibraltar, and the inclusion of Spain in the negotiations. As for Egypt, Britain would not change the form of the government, the occupation would be permanent, the *Caisse de la Dette* would be ended, the debt would be converted, the railway system would be reorganized, the Capitulations would be abolished, and Britain would examine similar proposals in regard to Morocco.

To Cambon the proposal was preposterous, for Britain was to give up what she did not possess in Morocco, while France was to give up much that she held firmly in Egypt. If Britain would not grant France concessions outright, Cambon suggested that, as France extended her hold over Morocco, she would give up an equivalent amount of control in Egypt. Lansdowne would have none of it. He wanted an immediate "yes" or "no" to the permanency of the British occupation.

When Cambon saw Lansdowne on October 21, he reminded him that French public opinion would not permit the surrender of French advantages in the Valley of the Nile without adequate compensation. If there would be no compensation, there must be a gradual abandonment of the French position in Egypt. He then brought up the question of Newfoundland. If France were to give up her rights in Newfoundland, she must have some compensation—perhaps Gambia? Lansdowne was definitely opposed because the Colonial Office would object.

When they met later in the month, Lansdowne was still against Gambia and progressive abandonment in Egypt. Cambon urged him to reflect further on the matter. If France abandoned Egypt without compensation for Newfoundland and with only a hope in Morocco, Britain would get by far the best of the bargain.

By November, Cambon saw no alternative but to be frank with Lansdowne. Britain was in a rather bad position. At the mercy of French public opinion, she was forced to negotiate with only those Frenchmen who had the nerve to attempt it, and if these men left the government, there was no indication what the future might bring. What could Britain do if France were to refuse everything and call on Russia and Germany for help? Lansdowne exclaimed quickly that there might be some way of settling the difficulties.

At the same time, Cambon restrained Delcassé from agreeing too hastily to the arrangements. He cautioned: "It is my advice not to cede anything, to take our time; *we must not show ourselves pressed. We have the right to be difficult.*" The British were more eager to settle the Egyptian question than the French were to conclude an agreement over Morocco. Delcassé wanted to conclude the accord just to be done with it, but Cambon wanted to wait for a better British offer.

By December these tactics paid dividends. Lansdowne and Cambon agreed on reciprocal commercial freedom for France and Britain in Morocco and Egypt. Difficulties over the neutralization of the Straits were ironed out, but they were still faced with the problem of a suitable compensation for the ceding of French rights in Newfoundland.[19]

At the beginning of 1904, Cambon asked Lansdowne for territory on the Niger River in Africa as compensation for those rights that France would give up in Newfoundland, since the Colonial Office would not permit Gambia to be ceded. Lansdowne curtly refused. It was British territory! "This is admirable," Cambon wrote. "They imply that they will only concede to us territory that does not belong to England!"

He believed that the trouble lay in the fact that Delcassé's request for compensation sounded like an adjustment of frontiers. Tactics must be altered. On January 14, he gave Lansdowne an ultimatum. France must have some territorial compensation for the fisheries that she would give up in Newfoundland. As requested, France had formulated two demands for compensation—Gambia and territory on the Niger River—and both had been rejected. Now France would

---

[19] Cambon to Delcassé, Oct. 11, 22, 28, Nov. 4, 22, 1903, Cambon to Cogardon, Nov. 18, 1903, *DDF,* 2 ser., IV, 15–16, 42–45, 69, 83–84, 115–16, 127–31; Lansdowne to Monson, Oct. 7, 1903, *BD,* II, 311–18; Cambon to Delcassé, Oct. 23, Cambon to Henri Cambon, Dec. 10, 1903, *Correspondance,* II, 98–101.

await Britain's offer. Until the compensation for Newfoundland was agreed on, it was useless to talk about Egypt. The French people attached great importance to these negotiations, for France had enjoyed rights in Newfoundland since the time of Louis XIV. Until there was a British offer of some kind of compensation for French rights and privileges in Newfoundland, France would proceed no farther in the talks. Cambon reminded Lansdowne that although Britain might continue to occupy Egypt under the present arrangement, she could do nothing without French permission. Now it was up to the Foreign Secretary to make the next move. Spreading out a map of Africa, he pointed to the region of Sokoto in northern Nigeria, and suggested an arrangement over this territory. Cambon was not overjoyed, for the area seemed to have little value, and the interview came to an end.

In his report to Delcassé, Cambon revealed his intention in the ultimatum. He believed that the British cabinet was blocking the settlement and must be shaken out of its obstinacy. Delcassé must not make any new offers. They would wait until Lord Cromer, the British consul-general in Egypt, heard about the near breakdown in the negotiations. Then a change could be expected in the attitude of the British.

The Earl of Cromer, the British consul-general in Cairo, who controlled the British occupation of Egypt, had consistently pushed Lansdowne to speed up the negotiations. When the news of Cambon's ultimatum reached Cromer through the French consul in Cairo (at Cambon's suggestion), Cromer telegraphed Lansdowne that they should satisfy France with anything for Newfoundland, because the French "can hamper us greatly here, whereas, if they choose, they can carry out their Morocco policy without our help." The Egyptian question, left unsolved, would always be a source of danger for the two nations.[20]

The Russo-Japanese War, which began on February 8, 1904, helped

[20] Cambon to Cogardon, Jan. 7, 1904, Cambon to Delcassé, Jan. 14, 1904, *DDF*, 2 ser., IV, 225–26, 248–51; Cambon to Henri Cambon, Dec. 26, 1903, Jan. 9, 1904, *Correspondance*, II, 101–107.

CREATION OF THE ENTENTE CORDIALE

to speed the negotiations. France and Britain were each allied to one of the belligerents, but neither wanted to become embroiled in the conflict. Many persons in influential positions feared that if the negotiations were broken off now, the two countries might soon become involved in the war.

By February, Lansdowne implored Cambon to accept nine thousand square kilometers in Sokoto and seven thousand square kilometers in the neighborhood of Lake Tchad. Lansdowne begged him to resume his demands about Newfoundland. Realizing that time was running out, the British cabinet gave in on February 25. France would obtain a free hand in Morocco, the territory around Sokoto, and the Los Islands off the coast of French Guinea.

In the final wording of the accord Cambon suggested a compromise to Balfour over the recognition of the permanency of the British occupation in Egypt. Balfour wanted an outright statement of French backing in the accord, but Cambon objected because it might cause trouble during the passage of the accord through the Chamber of Deputies. His proposal for a phrase stating merely that France would not "fix a term to the British occupation" was accepted for the final version.

On April 8, 1904, Cambon and Lansdowne signed the agreement. Delcassé had instructed Cambon to inform him immediately by telephone of the signing. The Ambassador was none too familiar with the new method of communication. Returning to the embassy, he entered the telephone booth that was the pride of the establishment. Connections were made with Paris, and finally with Delcassé. The elderly ambassador filled his lungs and yelled, *"It's Signed!"* Everyone in the embassy heard the glad tidings at the same time as Delcassé.[21]

The accord gave Britain a free hand in Egypt with no time limit placed on the occupation. France renounced all her rights in Newfoundland under the Treaty of Utrecht. A specific area was designated where French fishermen could ply their trade, subject to local regulations. As compensation for this concession, France received

[21] François Charles-Roux, *Souvenirs diplomatiques d'un age revolu*, 247–48.

territory in Nigeria and Gambia as well as the Los Islands.

France pledged not to alter the political status of Morocco. Britain agreed that France should preserve order in Morocco and assist in all necessary reforms. Britain would not obstruct France in this country, provided British treaty rights were left intact. Both nations promised to give each other diplomatic support in executing the clauses relative to Egypt and Morocco. In the future this became the most important clause in the accord. In secret clauses they agreed on the area that Spain would control when the Sultan ceased to exercise his authority. Other clauses called for a delimitation of French and British spheres of influence in Siam and the adjustment of mutual grievances in Madagascar and New Hebrides.

The accord, Cambon wrote his son, could not have been accomplished except for the Boer War, which weakened Britain, the Russo-Japanese War, which frightened both countries, the willingness of both foreign ministers to talk and to compromise, and the desire on the part of everyone to avoid any chance of war between France and Great Britain. The accord was a happy agreement, he added, but one must always be ready for such occasions and not just wish for them. Both sides were ready because the negotiations had been going on for such a long time. The meetings ended successfully because circumstances had been favorable, but even circumstances could not have brought a satisfactory conclusion if affairs had not been prepared for a long time. "This only proves," Cambon wrote, "that nothing is improvised either in war or in politics."[22]

The accord was an attempt to remove the causes of war between France and Great Britain. Basically it was a settlement of colonial differences in an age when governments fostered the development of empires and colonies with righteous zeal. The two areas potentially most dangerous were Morocco and Egypt; both were strategic areas and power vacuums whose rule could not be left to chance lest war result. It was hoped that through the accord these problems would be finally solved.

The fear of Germany did not occupy a particularly prominent

[22] Cambon to Henri Cambon, April 9, 1904, *Correspondance*, II, 133–34.

CREATION OF THE ENTENTE CORDIALE

place in the reasons for an agreement. If an accord were not achieved, there was a far greater danger of an Anglo-French war over a colonial crisis. The Entente Cordiale, as the accord of April 8, 1904, has been called, was an attempt to wipe out all sources of Anglo-French colonial conflicts. In the long run, the Entente affected Anglo-French relations with Germany, for it produced common interests and created unity in the crises of 1905 and 1911. It did not bring Britain into the war in 1914, but as a result of this understanding, each government knew where the sympathies of the other lay. The accord was not an alliance, but tactless German diplomacy was to make it one.

In the study of the creation of the Entente Cordiale it is difficult to determine exactly what Cambon did on his own initiative, because he visited Delcassé almost weekly and there is no written record of their conferences. Certainly he did not lay out the strategy of the diplomatic campaign, for that was the task of Delcassé, but he did conduct the campaign on the tactical level. From the moment of his arrival in London, he tried to show himself ever willing and anxious to meet with the leaders of the British government and to discuss the problems that might effect peace or war. He strove to show them that he was ready whenever they wanted to negotiate.

In the Entente Cordiale, Cambon helped to create a diplomatic revolution. The German statesmen who hoped to keep France isolated never dreamed that she would make up her differences with Great Britain. They felt that Britain and France could be counted on to dislike each other and to quarrel incessantly everywhere. With the large number of colonial incidents and problems, continual bad feelings between the two nations seemed a foregone conclusion. Thus the Entente Cordiale was a shock to the German Foreign Office. The prognostications of the wily Baron Friedrich von Holstein had gone awry. Probably the most influential career official in the German Foreign Office, Holstein maintained that Britain and France could never come to an agreement. Germany had time on her side, and she needed only to wait until Britain would accept her price. This was no longer the case. A step had been taken in undoing 1870, and Paul Cambon was happy to have had a part in such a task.

VI. TESTING THE ENTENTE

BEFORE THE ENTENTE CORDIALE was completed, it was tested by the Russo-Japanese War, which began on February 8, 1904. That same day Cambon met with Lansdowne, and they agreed that the conflict must be limited to Russia and Japan, for the allies had little desire to join the belligerents.

By mid-February, Cambon was acting as peacemaker between Lansdowne and Count Alexander Benckendorff, the Russian ambassador. The latter was bitter towards the British, alleging that Japanese torpedo boats had attacked Port Arthur from British-controlled Wei-hai-wei on February 9. Since relations between the Russian and British ambassadors were, not unnaturally, strained on account of the international situation, would Cambon, asked Benckendorff, speak with Lansdowne on his behalf? Cambon complied and begged Lansdowne to avoid any move that might be viewed as suspicious by the Russians and to speak frankly with the Russian ambassador. After a conference with Lansdowne, Benckendorff once again asked Cambon's help—this time urging him to get Delcassé to use his influence in St. Petersburg, a rather odd request, but made in the belief that no one in St. Petersburg read his dispatches. Cambon agreed gladly because "the situation is very perilous."

Cambon repeatedly implored Lansdowne to give Benckendorff a clear and unequivocal statement of Britain's intentions—in writing. Although Lansdowne promised to do so, by early May he had made only vague statements. Such faulty diplomacy caused Cambon to

TESTING THE ENTENTE

lament his difficulties in preventing "misunderstandings between a minister who remembers everything he hears and an ambassador who does not attach any importance to what he says." Eventually Lansdowne talked enough and Benckendorff listened enough to clear up some of the misunderstanding. By mid-April there was even talk of an Anglo-Russian understanding.

Any hopes for an agreement between Russia and Britain were ended in July, however, when two Russian men-of-war disguised as freighters seized the British ship *Molacca* in the Red Sea. Through French intervention the incident was settled by early August, but a loud outburst of anti-Russian sentiment from British newspapers alarmed Cambon. He sensed that if Russia did not prevent such occurrences, France might find herself engulfed by a wave of anti-Russian feeling sweeping across Britain.

In the wake of the *Molacca* incident came that of the Dogger Bank. During the night of October 21–22, the Russian Baltic fleet was steaming through the North Sea on the way to the Pacific Ocean, when it ran into a British fishing fleet on the Dogger Bank. The Russian officers imagined they were being attacked by Japanese torpedo boats that had put out from British ports. The fleet opened fire, sank one of the fishing boats, killed two fishermen, wounded others, and steamed on without stopping to pick up survivors. The British newspapers blazoned forth the story on the morning of October 25, after the surviving fishing boats had limped into port. Benckendorff, who had been on the Continent for a vacation, was met by a police escort and hostile crowds in London.

Immediately the British government demanded an investigation. Benckendorff could promise nothing because he lacked instructions from his government and begged for time in order to communicate with St. Petersburg.

Fear of such a situation had long haunted Cambon. At once he met with Benckendorff, and they agreed that the incident could be settled on the basis of an expression of regret from the Russians, a promise of indemnity, and an investigation to determine the officers responsible, with British representation in the investigation. Speed was essential; everything must be done not later than the next day—October 26. Cambon dreaded the procrastination of the Russian government.

On October 26, despite the procedure agreed upon at the meeting between Cambon and Benckendorff, the Russian ambassador appeared at the Foreign Office in Whitehall only to express his regret for the unfortunate incident. Lansdowne insisted that the Russian fleet be stopped at the next port of call and the implicated officers removed for investigation.

Benckendorff was desperate. He implored Cambon to have Paris increase the pressure on St. Petersburg. In his dispatch to Paris, Cambon, in turn, warned that the British newspapers had aroused the public more than ever. Further, he understood that the British fleet had received orders to stop the Russian fleet by force if St. Petersburg delayed too long, although this might mean only that orders had been drawn up. But the British Navy was very much excited. It could be dangerous.

On the afternoon of October 26, while Lansdowne was explaining to Cambon what he had said to Benckendorff earlier in the day, a telegram arrived from Sir Charles Hardinge, the British ambassador in St. Petersburg, stating that the Russian government had ordered the fleet to stop at Vigo. The pressure exerted by Cambon and Delcassé seemed to be having some effect. Later the same day, the British government expressed its wish that the responsible Russian officers be taken off the ships at Vigo and sent to St. Petersburg for investigation. Cambon viewed such action as an honorable basis for settlement and thought that the situation was improving.

When he spoke with Lansdowne on October 28, however, he realized that there was danger that the British might be pushing too far. He reminded Lansdowne that the Russian government, by ordering the fleet to stop at Vigo and the responsible officers to be removed, had admitted the right of investigation. Only the form remained to be determined. Britain must not be too demanding lest she find herself held "responsible for an unjustified conflict if events got out of hand." He declared, "The Entente Cordiale will not survive a blow against our ally." The same day Benckendorff reported that St. Petersburg had agreed that the incident be investigated under the terms of the Hague Convention. This news, coupled with the friendly attitude of Lansdowne, left Cambon believing that the incident was closed.

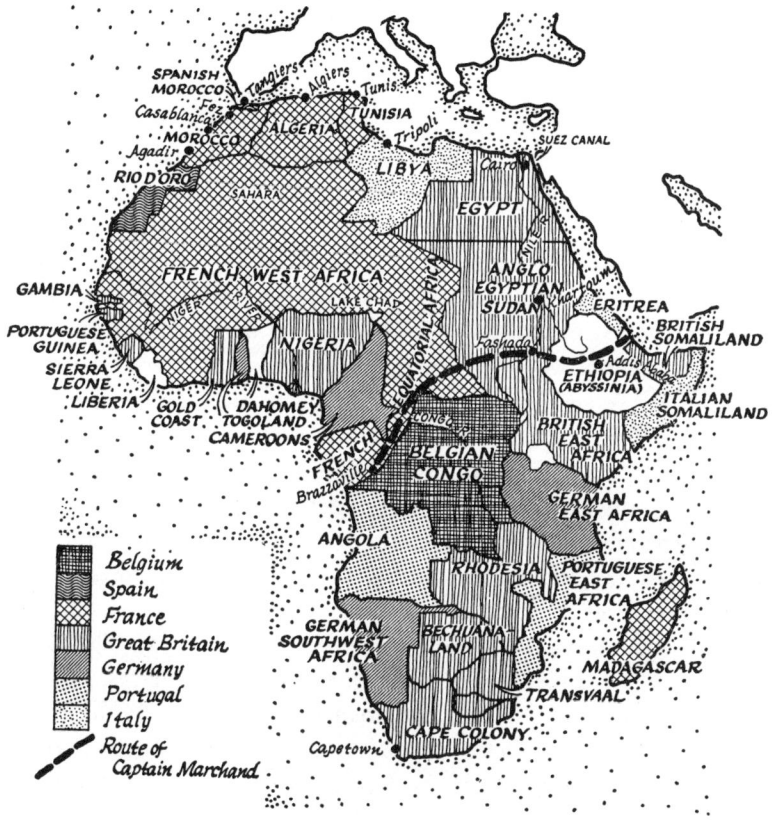

AFRICA, 1914

But the incident was not closed. News reached London on November 2 that the Russian fleet had left Vigo after only four officers had been removed, and they had been selected because of their knowledge of foreign languages! It was now a job for Cambon. That night he wrote: "I have spent the entire day between Benckendorff and Lansdowne attempting to explain, to clarify, and to suggest some solutions. These two men cannot talk; Benckendorff is too vague, Lansdowne is too reserved; when I am not between them, they live in two entirely different worlds. This is not finished."

Cambon intimated to Lansdowne that he now tended to base his judgments on information from conversations that might not have been too accurately reported. In proof of this, the French ambassador read a dispatch from his country's ambassador in St. Petersburg reporting that the officers who were "implicated" would be removed from the ships. Lansdowne admitted that he might have been hasty and decided to state officially that Britain would be satisfied if the officers "principally implicated" were detained. When Cambon showed this statement to Benckendorff, he would have none of it. "Implication" was derogatory to the admiral commanding the Russian fleet, whose report of the incident had been accepted as the truth in St. Petersburg. This was going too far, Cambon stormed; words were not that important. Lansdowne agreed to change his statement to read "especially implicated."

The argument over the wording of the convention, which was to convene the investigating commission, continued into mid-November. At last, on November 23, Cambon reported to Delcassé, with great relief, that the incident could be considered closed. The final arbitration was handed down on February 25, 1905. The Commission awarded the British government £65,000 damages, and decided that there had not been any Japanese torpedo boats in the North Sea on the night of October 21–22, 1904. The Russian fleet sailed on to defeat at the hands of the Japanese in the battle of Tsushima in May, 1905.[1]

In the midst of his worries over Anglo-Russian relations, Cambon was honored in June, 1904, with an honorary degree conferred by the

[1] Cambon to Delcassé, Feb. 18, April 20, May 7, Oct. 25, 26, 27, 28, 29, Nov. 1, 1904, *DDF,* 2 ser., IV, 377–79, V, 47–48, 464–65, 467–70, 472–73, 475–76, 481, 484–96; Cambon to Henri Cambon, April 16, Nov. 1, 1904, *Correspondance,* II, 134–36, 165–68.

University of Oxford. Lord Goschen, the new chancellor, had proposed the move as a sign of the new friendship between France and Great Britain. On June 22, Cambon journeyed to Oriel College, Oxford, where those to be honored assembled and were robed for the ceremonies. The distinguished company, which included John Singer Sargent, Guglielmo Marconi, Lord Curzon, General French, Cambon, and George Wyndham, moved off through the ancient streets of Oxford to the Sheldonian Theater. To Cambon it seemed that the theater was more of a church than a theater because it lacked scenery and contained two pulpits and an organ.

Before the learned assemblage Cambon was presented to the Chancellor by a sponsor who made the usual speech in Latin. In his reply granting the degree, the Chancellor commended Cambon as a "friendly interpreter." The new Dr. Cambon had been not a little apprehensive, before the convocation, that the students might embarrass Anglo-French relations, for they had been allowed great freedom in the past on similar occasions to say loudly what they thought of the candidates, sometimes to the point of rowdiness. But the university authorities had declared a holiday, and most of the students were enjoying themselves elsewhere rather than suffering in the hot theater.

After the degrees were granted to the perspiring candidates, the convocation continued. Cambon, in a letter to his brother, wrote:

> After the reception of the new doctors, a young preacher with glasses entered one of the pulpits and recited some Greek verses, then some Latin verses of his own composing. This was the laureate of the year. The Latin and Greek verses pronounced with an English accent were simply frightful. Scarcely had he finished than there appeared in the opposite pulpit another student who recited an historical composition; then another entered the pulpit.
>
> This alternation was dreadful. We had been there more than two hours; we were drenched with sweat; we were hungry; then in order to refresh us, a doctor of theology entered the pulpit and began an oration eulogizing the benefactors of the university. I did not make the least effort to pay attention; I was exhausted.

Luncheon finally saved Paul Cambon, L.L.D. As soon as possible, he divested himself of his robes, which by tradition he was supposed to wear all day while in Oxford. Dr. Cambon then set out on a sightseeing tour of the university. The evening ended with a formal dinner in cap and gown at Oriel College.

Cambon summed up his new honor: "This title of doctor of Oxford is much sought after and makes a considerable impression on the English public."[2]

The Entente Cordiale had withstood its first crisis without the destruction of the diplomatic arrangement, although the Entente had been hit at its weakest point. France was aligned with two nations whose political interests clashed, whose political systems were opposed, and who had been on the brink of war. Cambon, together with Delcassé and Lansdowne, had preserved the Entente through this crisis; a direct test of its strength had been avoided. But the next test, in the form of the first Moroccan crisis, could not be avoided. It was this test that brought down Delcassé.

The support and collaboration of Theophile Delcassé had been of major importance in Cambon's work in London. His accomplishments in the early years of his London mission would have been impossible without the aid of the patriotic Minister of Foreign Affairs.

Delcassé had also been burned by the fire of 1870. Well educated, he became a cub reporter on *La République Française,* where he eventually specialized in politics and international affairs. After a wealthy marriage, he deserted journalism for politics, and in 1889 was elected to the Chamber of Deputies. He became the undersecretary of state for colonies, and entered the Quai d'Orsay as foreign minister in 1898. His term of office was one of the great peaks of French diplomatic history; the agreements with Italy in 1900 and 1902 and the Entente Cordiale were to a great extent his work.

In creating a new diplomatic position for France, Delcassé worked closely with his ambassadors: Paul and Jules Cambon, Camille Barrère, and J. J. Jusserand. He failed to work closely enough with his colleagues in the cabinet. They were unaware of much that he

[2] Cambon to Henri Cambon, July 7, 1904, *ibid.,* 145–48.

was doing. Great was their shock when the Moroccan crisis burst on them in 1905.

Count Bernhard von Bülow, the German chancellor, and Friedrich von Holstein considered the Moroccan clauses in the agreement of April 8, 1904, detrimental to German prestige. German rights and interests in Morocco must be preserved. Germany would refuse to recognize the existence of the agreement; if France sent troops or warships to Morocco, Germany would do likewise until France asked Germany's price for good behavior.

At the insistence of Bülow, Emperor William II challenged the Entente Cordiale in a speech at Tangiers on March 31, 1905. The Emperor regarded the Sultan as a free and independent ruler. Under the Sultan's authority a free Morocco would be open to the peaceful commerce of all nations. Reforms should be instituted in accord with Moslem traditions and religion.

Paul Cambon did not foresee the importance of this speech. Although he warned Delcassé that Germany might make trouble, Cambon mistakenly believed that William II did not intend to seek an open quarrel over Morocco. Rather, William intended to inflict a humiliation on Delcassé and compel him to ask Germany for her conditions. Cambon prophesied: "For France events will in the end settle themselves, but it is possible that it will be the end of Delcassé."[3]

Germany called for an international conference on Morocco. To Cambon, this was an insult. On April 13, he consulted with Delcassé, urging him not to refuse a meeting with the Germans. At least he ought to talk with them and learn their intentions. Maurice Rouvier, the new premier, was frightened by the growing crisis and advocated a similar policy. Delcassé dined that same day at the home of Prince Hugo von Radolin, the German ambassador. Following the advice of Cambon and Rouvier, he informed Radolin that he was ready to discuss measures to dissipate the bad feeling between Germany and France over Morocco. As Cambon expected, Radolin claimed to be without instructions and so must refer this question to his government.

[3] Cambon to Henri Cambon, April 1, 1905, *ibid.*, 181–83.

Cambon was satisfied that France had called Germany's bluff by offering to talk. Throughout the entire crisis he maintained that the Germans were only bluffing. France had a good case; she needed only to stand fast and avoid appeasement.

In Berlin, Bülow chose to reject Franco-German negotiations and to press for an international conference over Morocco—all at Delcassé's expense. Foolishly he sought a diplomatic victory at the expense of France. If Delcassé were overthrown, so much the better.

During the six years that Delcassé had forged his foreign policy, French political interests had been centered on domestic affairs, particularly the Dreyfus Affair and the struggle over church-state relations. The sudden eruption of the Moroccan crisis alarmed many in influential positions. Many members of the cabinet were hostile to Delcassé. He appeared to be a most satisfactory scapegoat, for it was he who had failed to give the Germans official notification of the accord of April 8. Rouvier was disturbed by the threat of war: Britain could not be trusted because she would use France for her own perfidious ends; Russian aid was out of the question; Delcassé had blundered, and a businessman, such as Rouvier, must direct French foreign policy in seeking a satisfactory bargain with Germany.

In the Chamber of Deputies on April 19 the attack was loosed against Delcassé. Rouvier finally came to his rescue, but he assured the Chamber that he would be personally responsible for foreign policy in the future.[4]

The next day Delcassé appeared unnerved and spoke of resigning. Cambon counseled him to wait until the end of the Easter parliamentary vacation and then issue a review of the entire question in a yellow book (*livre jaune*). In this way he could explain the affair and recapture his influence over public opinion. Delcassé disagreed, and resigned on April 20, only to withdraw his resignation later in the day. On April 23, Cambon repeated his plea for a yellow book, but Delcassé had decided that it would only throw more oil on the fire.

[4] *Journal Officiel,* April 19, 1905.

Courtesy Historical Pictures Service

A contemporary drawing of the Marquis of Salisbury protesting the Armenian massacres, 1895.

Courtesy Culver Service

Cartoon of Jules Cambon drawn at the time of a visit to Washington in 1902.

Help now came to Delcassé from London. By April 22, Lansdowne had heard the story that Germany wanted a port on the Moroccan coast. This was out of the question in view of the growing German Navy and the strategic relation of Morocco to Gilbraltar. In a possible effort to bolster Delcassé's position, Sir Francis Bertie, the British ambassador in Paris, under instructions from Lansdowne, handed Delcassé a note on April 25 containing the statement that if Germany were to request a port in Morocco, the British government would give France all the support in her power. If this question were raised, the British government wanted Delcassé to give them "full opportunity . . . to concert with the French government as to the measures which might be taken to meet it."[5]

Cambon returned to London in early May and discussed the Moroccan crisis with Lansdowne. The French ambassador suggested that the conduct of the Emperor might be the result of some thoughtless act. Perhaps it was an attempt either to push Delcassé out of office or to gain a German port on the Moroccan coast. What, Cambon wondered, should they do if William obtained concessions or something worse? Quietly Lansdowne replied that there was nothing they could do except let William know of their agreement.

Cambon and Camille Barrère, the French ambassador in Rome, hurried to Paris and attempted to effect a reconciliation between Delcassé and Rouvier. The two ministers only railed at each other all the more. On May 15, Cambon, Barrère, and Rouvier met with the President of the Republic, Émile Loubet, in another attempt to bring about a meeting of minds. Cambon reminded them of the pledge which Lansdowne had made in writing on April 24. Cambon and Barrère agreed that Germany would not dare to provoke war; and both appealed for opposition to the German threats. Together with Delcassé they argued that Germany was not prepared to attack France, despite the weakness of Russia and the impotence of the French army. However, the German threats still terrified Rouvier,

[5] Lansdowne to Bertie, April 22, 1905, Bertie to Lansdowne, April 25, 1905, *BD*, II, 72–75.

who implored Cambon to discontinue his talks with Lansdowne lest the Germans learn of them and declare war.[6]

When he saw Lansdowne in London on May 17, Cambon asserted that attempts were being made to split the Entente. The accord must be maintained. They must counteract the allegations that Britain had embroiled France in the Moroccan question to obtain territory for herself. Lansdowne agreed, stating that the governments "must continue to treat one another with the most absolute confidence; they should keep one another fully informed of everything which came to their knowledge and should, so far as possible, discuss in advance any contingencies by which they might in the course of events find themselves confronted." Cambon informed Delcassé of this discussion, adding that such a statement would help to dispel the stories about the lack of solidarity in the Entente. However, he cautioned Delcassé to speak of it with reservations.[7]

A few days later, Cambon passed on to Delcassé a written statement from Lansdowne that he desired "full and confidential discussion between the two governments, not so much in consequence of some acts of unprovoked aggression on the part of another power, as in anticipation of any complication to be apprehended during the somewhat anxious period through which we are at present passing." In Cambon's eyes this letter covered a wider scope; it was not just a desire to concert if it became a question of unjustified aggression. "It is an immediate discussion and an examination of the general situation," he declared. If France remained silent and rejected this offer, she would discourage the British government. He concluded, "To accept would constitute, in reality, an alliance." Did the French Republic really want this? Cambon confessed that he did not know. He proposed to report to Lansdowne that Delcassé had read the letter with great interest and that this policy was now in practice

[6] Cambon to Henri Cambon, May 13, 1905, *Correspondance*, II, 193–95; Camille Barrère, *"La chute de Delcassé," Revue de deux mondes* (Aug. 1, 1932), 614–17. I have used the date given this meeting by Cambon because it seems to fit the chronology better.

[7] Cambon to Delcassé, May 18, 1905, *DDF*, 2 ser., VI, 520–23; Lansdowne to Bertie, May 17, 1905, *BD*, III, 76.

since they exchanged information where their interests were concerned. They would continue to do so in the future. But Delcassé exceeded Cambon's cautious acceptance, instructing him to inform Lansdowne that he had read the letter with great satisfaction and that the two governments should have confidence in each other more than ever. "I am ready," Delcassé declared, "to examine with him all the aspects of a situation which nevertheless is somewhat frightening."

Cambon purposely failed to inform Lansdowne of Delcassé's attitude, because it differed too much from Rouvier's. Instead, he berated Delcassé for responding to overtures that would lead France to an alliance. Had Delcassé forgotten the last words of Rouvier to Cambon on May 15 that they should not concert with the British because the Germans might hear of it? What would they do if Lansdowne pressed for talks between the chiefs of staff? This must be expected if Lansdowne's offer was accepted. Cambon warned: "You will surely not be followed by your colleagues in the cabinet nor by public opinion, and they would accuse you of preparing for war. I believe that it would be more prudent to respond cordially enough not to discourage the good-will of Lord Lansdowne and vague enough to put off the proposition for immediate concert." Much as he might desire a closer Entente with Britain, Cambon perceived that Rouvier would not support Delcassé if he created an alliance.[8]

By June 5 a new request for a conference over the Moroccan question had come from the Sultan of Morocco. In Paris the German pressure had become too much for Rouvier, who called a cabinet meeting on June 6. There Delcassé presented his view that Germany was only bluffing. He revealed the British offer of May 17 and demanded the conclusion of an immediate alliance with Britain. If France refused the offer, Britain might turn to Germany. Rouvier declared that Germany was serious. If France signed an agreement with Britain, it would mean a German declaration of war. France

[8] Cambon to Delcassé, May 29, June 1, 1905, Delcassé to Cambon, May 30, 1905, *DDF,* 2 ser. VI, 557–60, 563–64, 573; Lansdowne to Bertie, May 31, 1905, *BD,* III, 77–78. For further discussion of this event see Appendix A.

was poorly prepared; in the war she would bear the brunt of invasion, while Britain would be safe. Rouvier reminded the ministers that Britain had much to gain from the crisis, while France would expose herself to great dangers. The entire cabinet backed Rouvier. Delcassé resigned, ending his partnership with Paul Cambon in the making of French foreign policy.

A Havas dispatch brought the news of the resignation to Cambon. That night he wrote to his former chief:

> I am profoundly affected by your loss, because, in addition to the feelings of deep attachment which you have inspired in me, I have experienced a real satisfaction of spirit in marching with you. The friendship remains, the collaboration is no more than a dream, and I foresee all too well difficulties when you are no more there.
>
> I have not yet seen anyone. This evening there will be a dinner at Buckingham Palace for the King of Spain. I expect an attack because of your dismissal. What to say that will be intelligible to the English? How to explain a change in direction at the height of the battle? This is heartbreaking.

The next day an unhappy Cambon reported the change to Lansdowne. Rouvier had taken over the Ministry of Foreign Affairs, and it was his intention "to follow a loyal and firm policy by which the government of the Republic had always been motivated." In his report to Rouvier, Cambon underlined "loyal and firm policy." He added, "I can assure your excellency of my devoted and active cooperation."[9]

On June 7, Lansdowne received a note from the German ambassador demanding the conference that the Sultan of Morocco had requested. The Ambassador declared that Germany would oppose the retention of privileges by one power, and France was obviously that power. Because other members of the diplomatic corps would ask questions, Lansdowne turned to Cambon for advice. As there was a new foreign minister, Cambon did not yet know the wishes

[9] Cambon to Delcassé, June 6, 1905, *Correspondance,* II, 196–97; Cambon to Rouvier, June 7, 1905, *DDF,* 2 ser., VII, 2.

of his government. He suggested that Lansdowne submit the note to the British cabinet to give the French government time to readjust. Lansdowne agreed, and the next day the British cabinet rejected the proposal.

In Paris, Rouvier found a thorny path once he had given way to appeasement. Even though Delcassé was out of the Foreign Ministry, Radolin insisted on an international conference. If there were no conference, France would not be permitted any special privileges in Morocco. He cautioned, "It is necessary that you know that we are behind Morocco with all our forces."[10]

Cambon felt France should laugh at these statements. The policy of Germany was largely bluff. If France gave in, the Entente Cordiale would be destroyed. France must be calm and inflexible in her opposition to a conference, while asserting her proposal for direct settlement with Germany. The Emperor was not interested in Morocco. This was an attempt to expose the ineffectiveness of the Franco-Russian alliance and the Franco-English entente. If they accorded this satisfaction to William, he would demand more and more until they would have to recognize the hegemony of Germany in Europe.

His first meeting with Rouvier after Delcassé's resignation did not reassure Cambon:

> M. Rouvier is very intelligent and has some of the attributes of a statesman, . . . but he does not grasp the importance of the portfolio of foreign affairs. He imagines that diplomacy is limited to some conversations and to the drafting of dispatches which can be entrusted to the secretaries. In forty-eight hours he has seen that the work of the chief of foreign relations is infinitely harder than that of a minister of finances because it is more personal. It is necessary to read everything, to write a great deal yourself, to know everything yourself. In a word, it occupies a man day and night, and when one has not lived in this atmosphere, one is overwhelmed by so many questions that he is breathless.[11]

[10] Note of the Foreign Minister, June 10, 1905, *ibid.*, 28–29.
[11] Cambon to Henri Cambon, June 15, 1905, *Correspondance*, II, 197.

Every time Radolin talked with Rouvier the threats increased. If the Sultan asked for help from the German government, Germany would be unable to disregard the call. Cambon knew of the increasing threats; he learned that Radolin had offered concessions and a promise that the troubles would end if the conference were accepted in principle. To Cambon and Lansdowne this sounded ominous. Cambon had to return and consult with Rouvier. On June 14 he left London on the first Channel train.

In Paris he hurried to the Quai d'Orsay, where he found a distraught Rouvier frantically seeking some way out of the dilemma. "If I say 'no' to the proposal for a conference, it means war with Germany; if I say 'yes,' it means a rupture with England," moaned Rouvier. Cambon calmly suggested that he say neither "yes" nor "no" about the conference. Without definitely refusing the proposal, Rouvier ought to demand a preliminary agreement on the program. They would then possess a clearer idea of Germany's intentions. Above all, Cambon insisted, Rouvier should obtain the agreement of Britain to such a procedure. Before the conference broke up, Rouvier accepted Cambon's suggestions and authorized Cambon and Georges Louis, the political director of the Foreign Office, to draw up a note to Germany, which was presented on June 21.

In the note Cambon and Louis stressed the opposition of the French government to a conference. France intended neither to take over the internal affairs of Morocco nor to represent the Sultan abroad. France was willing to make any clarification of the accord of April 8, 1904, that any power might desire. If there should be a conference, the best way to insure its success would be for France to know precisely what Germany intended to discuss. The door was still open, but Cambon had helped to extract Rouvier from a tight position.

When the German reply arrived, Cambon sent a point by point refutation of the German charges to Rouvier to help him out of his difficulties. The Germans claimed that they had been deceived. France had been deceived because Delcassé had been discarded as the obstacle to all conversations. Bülow alleged that a prior agreement on the program of the conference could not be made because it would injure the Sultan's sovereignty and the rights of the other powers. Cambon repeated his claim that there had never been a conference without a prior agreement on the program.

Cambon warned Rouvier that if there were to be a conference without a previous accord, the smaller powers would soon desert France, followed by Italy and Spain. France would then be forced to accept internationalization of Morocco or risk an explosion. He cautioned: "Internationalization established through a European conference under German pressure is a more or less disguised form of a German protectorate over Morocco—that is the open door to all conflicts." Finally Cambon counseled the Premier to remember that if they adhered to the terms of their note and failed to obtain German acceptance, they would at least have public opinion behind them.[12]

Cambon's exhortations had been motivated by the fear that Rouvier might cede too much to the Germans. This had been observed by Radolin, who reported that he understood Cambon to be "the chief instigator" in pushing Delcassé's pro-British policy; Cambon sought to obstruct German plans and "to terrorize the weak Rouvier, who places himself on our side." His actions confirmed Rouvier's hint to Radolin that Cambon was the British candidate for the office of minister of foreign affairs.[13]

At last, however, Germany and France agreed to a conference over Morocco, to be held at Algeciras. The French decision had been hastened by the advice of the United States President Theodore Roosevelt to Rouvier that the conference be accepted in order to save face for William II. Roosevelt promised to oppose any German attitude that seemed unjust and unfair, but it was imperative, he insisted, that the conference take place so that peace might be preserved. Undoubtedly German knowledge of Lansdowne's offer of May 17 lessened the obstinacy of the Wilhelmstrasse, as well as the

[12] Cambon to Jules Cambon, June 22, 1905, *ibid.*, 198–99; note of Cambon, June 16, 1905, Rouvier to Radolin, June 21, 1905, Cambon to Rouvier, June 25, 1905, *DDF*, 2 ser., VII, 74–75, 97–100, 144–48.

[13] Radolin to the Foreign Office, June 29, 30, 1905, *GP*, XX, 492–94.

rumors that a British expeditionary force of 100,000 men was ready to land in Schleswig-Holstein.

A lengthy discussion followed about the program of the conference. Cambon insisted that France be awarded a mandate over all the Moroccan empire and that there be no internationalization of Morocco. He feared the creation of a situation similar to the one that arose when the Capitulations had troubled the French protectorate in Tunisia. In the program also must be mention of the Anglo-French entente over Morocco in order to keep the support of Britain and Spain. Lansdowne agreed with Cambon, and Rouvier followed his views in the final text of the letters exchanged between Paris and Berlin on the conference program.

Privately Cambon was eager that there be no break at this time in the Entente because "we have lost a great deal of credit in the last month." The panic among government officials, French newspapers, and French financiers had not raised France in the esteem of the world. France must be on guard, he wrote, because, "as Lord Lansdowne has made me understand clearly, those countries who depend on England will not speak for us if we do not remain faithful to the Entente." If France should lack a majority at the conference, "the Germans will strangle us."

Above all, France must stop being afraid. Cambon was disgusted with the conduct of some of the younger members on the staff of the Quai d'Orsay. Although they appeared to know everything, too many acted as if this were the funeral of France. He growled: "Fear is a pleasure like any other. It is a luxury of decadents, and we have too many of them in the Quai d'Orsay. All these young men have need of some virility."[14]

It is difficult to ascertain fully the part which Cambon played in the first Moroccan crisis up to the fall of Delcassé because many of the pertinent documents are missing. The editors of *British Documents on the Origins of the War* (Gooch and Temperley) reported that many of the papers dealing with this crisis were missing from British archives and, as a result, they were forced to resort to the

[14] Cambon to Georges Louis, July 3, 1905, *Correspondence,* II, 200–202.

archives of the Paris embassy to fill the gaps. Even then, they were certain that some of the documents had not been located. The French documents that have been published do not give a comprehensive account of the crisis, perhaps because Cambon and Delcassé met almost weekly and a complete record of their conversations either was not made or does not remain. On leaving the Ministry of Foreign Affairs, Delcassé destroyed many of his personal papers, which he kept in a mysterious box. It is probable, also, that he took many documents with him, possibly to use in defense of his policy or in an attack on Rouvier. Of course, he never did use them, perhaps because his revelations could have caused a crisis more dangerous to national security than the Dreyfus Affair. France could not stand such an ordeal again.[15]

Paul Cambon's conduct in this crisis was of mixed value to his country. In the early part of the negotiations he had been overly optimistic. He had not realized that Germany would be willing to push her action as far as she did. Not until the crisis had burst upon Europe did he discern the degree to which German vanity had been injured because she failed to receive compensation for the settlement of the Moroccan question. He had not comprehended how far Germany would dare to go in an effort to re-establish her prestige.

Cambon tended to regard the affair as a matter of the Kaiser's vanity, but that he should blame the Kaiser alone is surprising in view of the fact that Delcassé knew that Bülow and Holstein were behind the entire action. It would appear, therefore that Cambon lacked complete information about the situation in Berlin. After 1907, when his brother Jules became the French ambassador in Berlin, Paul Cambon's tirades against William's conduct of German foreign relations lessened. Probably Jules kept his brother better informed regarding the originators of German foreign policy.

From the evidence available it is apparent that Cambon, Barrère, and Delcassé all agreed that Germany was only bluffing. Even now

---

[15] Editors' note, *BD*, III, 72. Delcassé's revelations would have forced the disclosure of the cryptographic service of the Quai d'Orsay that deciphered the dispatches of Radolin.

it is difficult to discover the truth, but probably Bülow and Holstein believed that France would not fight and that it would then be easy to obtain an international conference in which victory would be theirs. Two factors disproved the theory that Germany was bluffing: As early as April 26, 1905, Rouvier had informed Radolin that he was prepared to sacrifice Delcassé; and the poor estate of the French Army meant that France had little with which to call Germany's bluff.

Delcassé's secretiveness towards the Chamber of Deputies and the cabinet finally helped to overthrow him. His overthrow was beyond the control of his friends, Cambon and Barrère. The politicians resented what they considered highhanded treatment by Delcassé. His attitude towards his fellow politicians probably resulted from the fact that in the past his policy had been too successful for his own good. The team of the brothers Cambon, Barrère, and J. J. Jusserand, the French ambassador to the United States, had worked too well. The impossible had been achieved in strengthening the diplomatic position of France since 1870, but in the spring of 1905, Delcassé and his advisers became overconfident, and as a consequence, the Entente was endangered.

The aspirations of Holstein and Bülow to rupture the Entente Cordiale and build a new empire for Germany in Morocco failed. The ambassadors of France, such as Paul Cambon and Barrère, remained on the job to carry out the policy of Delcassé. Although his partnership with Delcassé had ended, Cambon helped to maintain the Entente with Britain and to influence Rouvier in the adoption of a policy similar to that of the defeated Delcassé. The Entente would continue because the Germans failed to remove all of its creators.

VII. STRENGTHENING THE ENTENTE

In the fall of 1905, Conservative strength was fading as the party went down to defeat in the by-elections. Balfour resigned in December, hoping that the Liberals would be unable to govern successfully. If this should happen, the Conservatives, in the ensuing election, would return to power with a greater majority in Commons. On December 5 the Liberals formed a new government with Sir Henry Campbell-Bannerman as prime minister and Sir Edward Grey as foreign secretary. Immediately the Prime Minister asked for a dissolution and a general election in January.

The new Foreign Secretary lacked firsthand knowledge of Europe, although he had had some experience with foreign matters by virtue of his years as Parliamentary undersecretary for foreign affairs in previous Liberal cabinets. Handsome and quiet in manner, he had accepted his services in Parliament as a duty, while longing to wander among the glories of the English countryside. Grey brought deep sincerity to his work, and he served his country with all his strength.

The views of Grey and his party on foreign affairs were of great interest to Cambon. He was pleased when Grey announced in a speech to the electors of London that he desired no change in the Entente Cordiale. Grey had no objection if Germany wanted to improve relations with Britain, but nothing in the relations between Britain and Germany must injure those between Britain and France.

Cambon was more interested in the views of the Liberal party when he received disturbing news from Rouvier. On a recent visit to Berlin, Alfonso XIII, king of Spain, had been approached by William II with the suggestion that when war came with France, Alfonso should send forces to the French frontier to immobilize as many French troops as possible. Rouvier instructed Cambon to take this matter up with Edward VII because it involved another king.

At the first opportunity Cambon related the story to the King, who asked him to inform Grey at once. After Cambon had agreed to bring up the matter in a roundabout way because the information related to monarchs, Edward agreed to use his royal influence with Alfonso to stimulate resistance to the German demands.

Cambon then observed to the King that the Entente Cordiale regulated only colonial affairs. There were rumors, he said, that Britain could place 100,000 men on the Continent. "You could certainly do it," he added, "but we have not spoken of it."

"Yes, we could do it," Edward replied, "but—" The sentence trailed off with a gesture that Cambon did not know quite how to interpret. Did Edward mean that the Liberal government would not permit it? Or that any help would be limited to diplomatic action? Sensing his opportunity, Cambon asked if he might take up the promise that Lansdowne had made in the spring of 1905 to support France. The King agreed readily, and Cambon wrote for instructions.

Cambon saw Grey on December 20, when he casually brought the conversation around to Spain and the rumors of German influence in that country. He proposed that Sir Arthur Nicolson, now the British ambassador in Madrid, should alert the Spanish government. Grey approved the suggestion and instructed Nicolson to warn the Spaniards that if they went over to the German side during the Algeciras conference, Britain would not remain neutral but would throw her support to France.

On January 10, 1905, Cambon made his first official approach to Grey for both diplomatic support and armed help if Germany started a war. He suggested that a closer Entente might be necessary if the conference collapsed. He did not think that the German emperor actually wanted war, but he might arouse the military to such a

STRENGTHENING THE ENTENTE

degree that they would commit some foolish act. Previously Lansdowne had proposed a discussion of the danger that might occur during the Moroccan crisis; now it was time to talk. Specifically, Cambon wanted to know whether France could count on Great Britain in case of German aggression. "Will England," he asked, "range herself on the side of France and lend her armed aid?"

Grey replied that the Prime Minister was out of London, the cabinet members were busy fighting the election, and he would not know the opinion of the country until after the election, which would begin on January 12. Personally he believed that if France were attacked because of the Entente Cordiale, "public opinion in England would be strongly moved in favor of France." Cambon replied that he would repeat the question after the elections.

Grey, returning to the subject of the Algeciras conference, voiced the hope that a peaceful outcome favorable to France would result. Cambon observed that William II was using the conference only to weaken the Entente and that nothing would have a more quieting effect on him than the realization that if Germany attacked France, she would find England allied against her. Grey countered with the qualification that no minister could promise such aid since it would depend on the circumstances surrounding the rupture between France and Germany. But, argued Cambon, he was referring to some aggression growing out of French action to protect her Algerian border. Even then, replied Grey, he could promise only benevolent neutrality. To Cambon, this was unsatisfactory, and again he proposed to repeat the question after the elections. As the conversation ended, Cambon casually remarked that he hoped the unofficial talks between the military staffs might continue because the views exchanged would be of value in the event that the two countries were allied in a war. Grey agreed, as long as the action did not pledge either government.

This talk was so important that Cambon allowed Grey to read his dispatch of January 11 to Rouvier. Grey had only one correction—he did not approve of the unofficial military talks; rather, he merely reserved his opinion because he did not know the exact subject matter of the conferences. He would permit them to continue with the approval of the heads of the departments concerned.

Cambon had faced Grey with "the great question," as he described it. To Grey, any promise in advance would be contrary to the traditions of his country. Naturally, if France became involved in a war growing out of the Entente Cordiale, Britain must take part. Grey believed that a pledge given in advance went far beyond what Lansdowne had proposed in 1905. If France were to make any pledge, it must be conditional on Britain's rights to suggest concessions in the event of the failure of the Algeciras conference.[1]

By the time Cambon saw Grey on January 15, R. B. Haldane, secretary for war, and Campbell-Bannerman had approved direct talks between the French and British military staffs. Grey informed Cambon of this development, adding the restriction that "it must be understood that these communications did not commit either government,"[2] not realizing that the government had already committed itself by agreeing to official talks between the staffs. His failure to comprehend that he was talking one way and acting another was to cause Cambon untold agony during the crisis of July-August, 1914.

On January 31, after the Liberal victory at the polls, Grey and Cambon again took up "the great question." At once Cambon asked about the possibility of British support if France were attacked. Grey would not agree to any formal assurance; however, the military staffs were in conversation, and he had warned Count Paul von Metternich,

---

[1] Rouvier to Cambon, Dec. 18, 1905, Cambon to Rouvier, Dec. 21, 1905, Jan. 1906, *DDF,* 2 ser., VIII, 335–36, 359–66, 504–507; Grey to Bertie, Dec. 20, 1905, Jan. 10, 15, 1906, Grey to Nicolson, Dec. 21, 1905, Grey's minute to Cambon's dispatch of Jan. 11, 1906, *BD,* III, 172–74, 177–79.

[2] Grierson to Sanderson, Jan. 11, 1906, Grey to Bertie, Jan. 15, 1906, Sanderson to Grierson, Jan. 15, 1906, *ibid.,* 172–73, 177–79; Cambon to Rouvier, Jan. 15, 1906, *DDF,* 2 ser., VIII, 549–50. Early in January, 1906, Colonel Repington, the military correspondent of the London *Times,* had begun unofficial talks with Major Huguet, the French military attaché. Direct talks between the naval staffs, begun under Lansdowne, still continued.

the German ambassador, that an attack on France over a Moroccan disagreement would find public opinion too strongly pro-French for Britain to remain neutral. This, argued Grey, was as good as any formal agreement. In addition, any formal agreement would require that the French government consult the British government regarding her Moroccan policy. Did France want this? Was not the present situation satisfactory without formal assurances of British support?

Cambon assured Grey that although he saw no war resulting from the conference, they must consider every possibility. If the conference broke up without beneficial results, if Germany seized a few Moroccan ports along the Atlantic Ocean, pushed the Moroccans to violations of the Algerian frontier, and forbade France to retaliate—that, Cambon concluded, would mean war. He reminded Grey, "Hostilities break out today with a frightening rapidity; this is not a question of weeks, not even of days; it is a question of hours." Even though the Admiralty might intend to bar the Channel to German ships, if they had to await cabinet meetings and the reaction of public opinion, the action would come too late. He warned: "The German ships will have passed; this is an affair of twenty-four hours. It is necessary then to be in agreement before the commencement of hostilities."

Grey was unconvinced. Possibly future events might change the Entente into a defensive alliance, but the time had not yet come. Any change in the alliance would have to be in writing and would have to be submitted to the cabinet and to Parliament. Grey would agree only to take up this matter if circumstances warranted it.

Cambon sent his analysis to Rouvier: Britain would engage in hostilities only if she were certain that they were an absolute necessity, but if that necessity arose, France could depend on Britain. However, he omitted a vital aspect of the problem: Would France and Britain see the necessity at the same time?

Cambon had secured much more than Grey realized. In the staff talks, now official, lay the basis for future military co-operation. When co-operation led to commitments, the alliance would be a fact without signed documents. Although Grey might disclaim that the government would give formal assurances of support, the fact that the staff talks were permitted to continue cancelled any need for formal assurances. By attempting to keep his right hand from letting his left hand know what it was doing, Grey had given Cambon the substance of his desire. The rumored alliance of May, 1905, was now almost a fact.

Campbell-Bannerman, the prime minister, sensed something of what had happened. He wrote: "Cambon appears satisfied. But I do not like the stress laid upon joint preparations. It comes very close to an honorable undertaking; and it will be known on both sides of the Rhine."[3] The fact that it came so close to "an honorable undertaking" was to make the conduct of Grey incomprehensible to Cambon in the dark days of July-August, 1914. Unrealized by the actors, Britain had begun to take her stand for the future conflict.

In preparation for the Algeciras conference, Paul Cambon, his brother Jules (French ambassador in Madrid), and Sir Arthur Nicolson (British ambassador in Madrid) met to plan Anglo-French strategy. They agreed that the conference might collapse over the question of policing Morocco. Germany would probably suggest a smaller nation to police Morocco, France would object, and Britain would back her. The conference would break up, with Britain and France sharing the blame. Some other power must propose that France organize the police. Temporarily, France would share the policing of Morocco with Spain. Finances and a national bank must be discussed first, then the question of smuggling, and lastly the problem of the police.

Although Cambon watched the conference from London, he labored to keep France and Britain moving towards the same goal. The conference opened on January 16, 1906. When the question of the police came up, Germany proposed that the Sultan organize the police by using foreign officers of his own choice. An officer from a

[3] Grey to Bertie, Jan. 31, 1906, Memorandum of Sanderson, Feb. 2, 1906, *BD*, III, 180–85; Cambon to Rouvier, Jan. 31, 1906, *DDF*, 2 ser., IX, 149–53; J. A. Spender, *The Life of the Right Hon. Sir Henry Campbell-Bannerman, G.C.B.*, II, 257.

*Courtesy British Information Services
and Radio Times Hulton Picture Library*

The visit of Edward VII to France, 1903

The supreme moment of the Great Military Review at Vincennes on May 2, 1903: His Majesty King Edward VII, in field marshal's uniform, saluting the French regimental flags. The President of the French Republic, M. Loubet, is on the King's left.
On this state visit to France, King Edward laid the foundations of the Entente Cordiale.

Courtesy Culver Service

THE ALGECIRAS SEANCE

The Assembled Powers: *"Well, nothing seems to be happening."*

Cartoon from *Punch* depicting the Algeciras Conference of 1906.

STRENGTHENING THE ENTENTE

small power would inspect the police and report to the diplomatic corps at Tangiers. Grey and Cambon immediately agreed on a proposal, which was mainly Cambon's idea: Let a neutral power suggest that the Sultan organize the police with French and Spanish inspectors who would report to the diplomatic corps at Tangiers. A similar proposal was handed to the German representative at the conference on February 16, but it was turned down.

Spain next proposed that the Sultan organize the police under the control of the diplomatic corps, instructors to be Moroccan except for two, who would be Spanish and French. Rouvier asked Cambon's opinion. He was completely opposed, for such a plan would open the door to internationalization. Grey, still fearful of war, wanted to accept. No, argued Cambon, at the most they would merely allow the Sultan to tell the diplomatic corps what he had done, which was to invite the French and Spanish instructors to help. Brother Jules in Madrid voiced much the same opinion. Eventually the British and French governments brought Spain back into line.

From Austria came a plan for a division of the police in the Moroccan ports between Spain and France. Casablanca would be under a neutral power, which would inspect the other ports, and France would have Tangiers. Cambon rejected this plan as "inadmissible." Casablanca would only become a trouble spot, and any attempts at a uniform organization in Morocco would be destroyed. The proposal was directly contrary to the Entente Cordiale on the division of the ports. Jules Cambon and Barrère concurred, and instructions along the lines suggested by the three ambassadors were sent to Paul Révoil, the French representative at the conference.

An American proposal called for Spain and France to co-operate in equal numbers in the job of policing the ports. This had much appeal for the new French foreign minister, Émile Bourgeois (Rouvier's cabinet had fallen on March 7). Cambon claimed that the proposal was "the act of the Kaiser, who seeks any line of retreat whatsoever and who knows himself abandoned by the opinion of the powers." Jules Cambon objected because this plan would annul the accord of April 8, 1904. With British and Spanish support, the proposal was turned down by France.[4]

Germany finally gave in on March 27 and accepted a proposal of President Theodore Roosevelt that a joint mandate be given to France and Spain, who should divide the ports as they wished. Roosevelt originally intended to remain impartial, and the Kaiser thought that he would use his influence in behalf of Germany; however, Roosevelt came to mistrust Germany and to regard her as a bully intent on dividing Morocco into sectors. France appeared more likely to preserve the territorial integrity of Morocco, which Roosevelt wanted. Under the influence of Jusserand, Roosevelt became a supporter of France. His proposal for a joint mandate was actually a victory for France.

Cambon's ideas were not followed in the final settlement, signed on April 7. The ports of Morocco and the policing were divided between France and Spain. The banks were to be controlled jointly by Great Britain, Spain, France, and Germany.

In London, Grey and Cambon exchanged congratulations over the happy outcome. War had not broken out. Cambon had been right. As the result of teamwork among the French ambassadors, Germany had suffered a diplomatic defeat. The Entente Cordiale still existed, but an alliance was being created. Grey informed Cambon, unofficially, that it had been a pleasure to support France; he was happy that the conference had strengthened the Entente.[5] Only later did Grey realize how much.

The Conference of Algeciras ended the first Moroccan crisis with a German defeat; however, the political vacuum called Morocco was still an unsolved problem. Not all that Cambon desired had been achieved, but what he abhorred had not come to pass. To his way of thinking, the internationalization of Morocco would have been a defeat for France. Internationalization meant only mild anarchy,

[4] Cambon to Bourgeois, March 23, 1906, Jules Cambon to Bourgeois, March 23, 1906, *DDF,* 2 ser. IX, 688–89, 713–14.

[5] Grey to Bertie, April 3, 1906, *BD,* III, 329; Bourgeois to Cambon, April 3, 1906, *DDF,* 2 ser., IX, 783.

because the governing powers would be unable to rule the natives.

Cambon had little sympathy for the clumsy German tactics. The Germans had bungled the affair, but in so doing, they had aided Cambon in his task of strengthening the Entente Cordiale. German statesmen had helped France find a friend in Great Britain.

In the years after the Algeciras Conference, the Entente was strengthened through less spectacular negotiations, in which Cambon labored to reduce the possibility of friction. His task was difficult, for he had to protect French interests, avoid alienating the British government, and allow nothing to injure the alliance with Russia, whose interests often clashed with those of Great Britain.

The summer of 1906 saw the successful completion of negotiations over spheres of influence in Ethiopia, which could have been a source of conflict between France and Great Britain. The negotiations had begun shortly after the creation of the Entente Cordiale in 1904. The problem of Ethiopia was then fifteen years old.

In 1889, Italy established a virtual protectorate over Ethiopia. In spite of Italian protests, a Paris syndicate in 1894 negotiated a concession for an Ethiopian railroad line to terminate at Jibuti in French Somaliland. Little was done about the railroad until after Ethiopia defeated Italy at Adowa on March 1, 1896. In July, Menelik, the Ethiopian emperor, transferred the railroad concession to a French company, *Compagnie imperiale des chemins de fer ethiopens*. Only a small section of the line had been completed by 1902, because of the lack of funds, when the French government came to the aid of the company with a yearly subsidy of 500,000 francs. Angered by this development, since he had granted the concessions to private individuals and not to a government, Menelik concluded a treaty with Great Britain on May 15, 1902. The British government received the right to construct a railroad running north and south to connect the Anglo-Egyptian Sudan with Uganda. French interests in Ethiopia were now in jeopardy.

On May 9, 1904, Delcassé asked Cambon to bring up the problem of the French railroad line in Ethiopia. The question was important because Sir John Harrington, the British minister in Ethiopia, insisted that Menelik internationalize a section of the French railroad and grant Great Britain a share of control over the entire line.

Cambon did not view this problem as merely a question of ownership of a railroad. It was only one aspect of the larger problem that would be solved satisfactorily only when France, Italy, and Great Britain discussed Ethiopian affairs as a whole and agreed upon a plan of action. He believed that France lacked the means to exert exclusive influence in Ethiopia but that she must prevent domination by a single power in order to protect the interests of French investors. It seemed only a matter of time before Ethiopia "would . . . be surrounded and submerged by the British current which grew stronger daily in the Nile Valley."

With this in mind, Cambon took the matter up with Lansdowne. By May 18 he reported the results. Lansdowne tended towards internationalization, but Cambon reminded him that the French concessions had been obtained when the British control in the Nile Valley had been weak. France could not abandon her interests in Ethiopia without adequate compensation. A new situation had been created by the Entente Cordiale; therefore, they ought to seek an agreement that would prevent conflict over Ethiopia.

To all of this Lansdowne was sympathetic. He mentioned the possibility of including Italy. Cambon agreed and proposed an accord including Italy, France, and Britain. The spheres of influence would be delimited, and the maintenance of the status quo would be assured. They would prepare for any disorders following the death of Menelik. Such an arrangement would enable the three powers to pursue their economic aims unhindered within their respective spheres of influence. Lansdowne concurred and within a few days announced to Cambon the approval of the cabinet.

At Lansdowne's suggestion, Cambon discussed the latest developments concerning Ethiopia with Alberto Pansa, the Italian ambassador, who reported that Tomaso Tittoni, the Italian foreign minister, had already discussed the possibility of a tripartite agreement over Ethiopia. Thus the way seemed opened for serious negotiations.[6]

[6] Cambon to Delcassé, May 18, 1904, *ibid.*, V, 167–70.

STRENGTHENING THE ENTENTE

Tripartite negotiations were well underway by the fall of 1904. The Italian ambassador and Lansdowne had agreed on the independence of Ethiopia, the delimitation of the frontiers, and intervention without prior agreement in case of disorders. If the Empire were to break up, they would meet and discuss the zones of special interest. This last point produced a strong objection from Cambon when Lansdowne asked for his opinion. They must not wait until the collapse of Menelik's empire was imminent to decide on the zones of interest because they battled already over zones of interest in Ethiopia. They must immediately establish the zones of economic influence between themselves.

Throughout the fall and winter the negotiations continued. The first Moroccan crisis distracted the attention of the French government in the spring of 1905. Cambon had to remind his government that if this accord were to fail, relations with Italy would be harmed and destruction would threaten the Entente Cordiale.

When Delcassé fell from office, Cambon telegraphed Rouvier to push the Ethiopian accord. It would make a good impression in Britain, where recent events in France had begun to raise doubts in the minds of some. But no final decision was reached, and the discussions continued through the fall of 1905.

By January, 1906, Cambon was aware of hesitancy on the part of the Italian diplomats. He blamed it on their fear of German action similar to that in Morocco. Cambon proposed that France and Britain agree on their part of the accord and inform Italy before they signed, so that the danger of internationalization would not be increased. Italian lethargy ought then to end. Although Sir Edward Grey, now the foreign secretary, agreed with Cambon, his policy was not followed because Italian support for France and Britain was desired during the Algeciras Conference.

In March the news came that Tittoni, now Italian ambassador to the Court of St. James, would arrive in London with new instructions to settle the Ethiopian question. Cambon could not believe it. Tittoni would demand more changes; he would keep the railroad question open, and the Germans would be allowed to involve themselves more and more in the affairs of Ethiopia. As Cambon predicted, Tittoni called on Grey in April and announced that he was without instructions. His action so alarmed Grey that he agreed with Cambon that France and Britain should exchange declarations on the Ethiopian question.

Realizing the poor reaction to his announcement, Tittoni suddenly appeared in Whitehall on April 12 with instructions that forbade discussion of all matters relating to the future of Ethiopia. Cambon and Grey, disgusted with this procrastination, began to draw up the terms of letters that would be exchanged over Ethiopia. Grey enlightened Tittoni on the feelings of France over the Italian delay and advised him that there would be an arrangement by June 15. Italy was ready to sign by June 7. Last-minute haggling over details by the government in Paris delayed the completion of the accord for almost a month.

The agreement was initialed by Grey, Tittoni, and Cambon on July 6 and signed on December 31. The three parties agreed to maintain the status quo in Ethiopia, to preserve her territorial integrity, and to take action only to protect their nationals and their property. The accord included arrangements for the development and control of the railroads by British, French, and Italian companies.[7]

Like the accord of April 8, 1904, this was a practical arrangement resolving problems that could have caused strained relations among the three nations. Ethiopia, like Morocco, was a power vacuum. The threat of one nation's seizing control seemed imminent, thus in the interests of peace it was best to allot the zones of influence to the three nations. The agreement of July 6, 1906, was a selfish matter for France, Great Britain, and Italy: Ethiopia was not informed until after it was signed.

The treaty of 1906 disappeared in the smoke of war on October 3, 1935. Benito Mussolini would not abide by its terms, and neither

[7] Cambon to Rouvier, Jan. 24, Feb. 28, March 8, 1906, Cambon to Bourgeois, March 23, April 5, 7, 16, May 11, May 24, June 7, July 5, 6, 1906, Bourgeois to Cambon, June 12, 1906, *ibid.,* IX, 78–80, 435, 529–30, 696–97, 798–99, 810–11, X, 18–20, 73–75, 103–106, 137–42, 153–54, 206–13.

Britain nor France would force Italian compliance because the shadow of Nazi Germany loomed too large.

The following year another bond strengthened the Entente Cordiale. Early in January, 1907, Cambon took up the task of negotiating an accord among Great Britain, France, and Spain to guarantee the status quo in the Mediterranean area. The accord originated in a suggestion of Lansdowne's in 1905 that Spain promise not to alienate any of her possessions in the vicinity of the Straits of Gibraltar. Little was done until January 7, 1907, when Jules Cambon proposed officially to the Spanish government that Britain and France guarantee the Spanish possessions in the western Mediterranean and the Atlantic Ocean. The British Foreign Office was not a little piqued at the French tactics. Eyre Crowe, senior clerk in the Foreign Office, noted, "The French proceeding is not only maladroit in itself, but also very inconsiderate as regards this country." Grey would speak to Cambon about the matter.

Cambon found Grey friendly enough when he mentioned his brother's proposal on January 9, 1907. He excused his brother's conduct on the grounds that Jules was leaving Madrid soon and wished to come to an agreement with Spain over the Mediterranean, fearing German pressure on the Spanish government to force the granting of privileges in this important area. His explanation satisfied Grey, especially since Cambon emphasized the necessity of discussing the problem privately and doing nothing officially until they were agreed on the basic principles. Grey was sympathetic but would not commit himself further until he could consult with the cabinet at the next meeting in February.

On January 18, Grey remarked to Cambon that Prime Minister Campbell-Bannerman wondered if Spain should be brought into the discussions at this time in view of a ministerial crisis. Cambon insisted that the talks be started immediately so that whoever succeeded Pérez Caballero, the foreign minister, would find the negotiations under way.[8] Grey, acting on this suggestion, took up the proposal

[8] Minute of Hardinge, Dec. 8, 1906, Grey to Campbell-Bannerman, Dec. 12, 1906, Bertie to Grey, Dec. 25, 1906, Jan. 7, 1907, Grey to Bertie, Jan. 9, 1907, *BD*,

with Villa-Urrutia, the Spanish ambassador, on February 7. Within a week the three diplomats had agreed on an exchange of notes between the three powers. Grey preferred an Anglo-Spanish arrangement with France adhering later, but he acquiesced when Cambon insisted that France had as great an interest in this matter as Great Britain. Furthermore, the inclusion of France would make the arrangement more palatable to the Spaniards, who were still sensitive over the question of Gibraltar. Grey had insisted on an exchange of notes in order to avoid embarrassing questions in Parliament.

On May 16, Grey and Villa-Urrutia exchanged identical notes. Cambon gave Grey a copy of similar notes exchanged in Paris between Pichon and the Spanish ambassador. Each government agreed to maintain the status quo of its possessions in the Mediterranean and in adjacent areas in the Atlantic Ocean. Should conditions develop that threatened the status quo, the governments would communicate with each other in order to co-ordinate their actions. Cambon and Grey also exchanged written declarations acknowledging the exchange of notes and agreeing to communicate if the status quo was endangered. On June 6, Berlin, Rome, St. Petersburg, and Lisbon were notified simultaneously by identical notes.

Would Germany create another European crisis now that she knew of the exchange? Cambon wanted to be prepared for any eventuality; therefore, on June 8 he asked Grey whether France could depend on British support if Germany should take a threatening attitude, as she had in 1905, and bring pressure to bear on either France or Spain. Noting that the areas involved were near Morocco, Grey declared that the notes were a complement of the accord of April 8, 1904. The same spirit would apply and the same support would be forthcoming.

"In a word," Cambon asked, "if Germany seeks a quarrel with us, we can count on you?"

"Yes," Grey replied without hesitation.

VII, 4–11; Cambon to Pichon, Jan. 10, 18, 1907, *DDF,* 2 ser., X, 617–18, 624. Actually Jules Cambon had full authority in Madrid to negotiate on this matter.

STRENGTHENING THE ENTENTE

"You can count on us," Cambon concluded, "if Germany intervenes between you and Spain."⁹

On the surface these notes appeared harmless enough. Three concerned nations took steps to defend their interests in a crisis. Actually the notes were a logical extension of the accord of April 8, 1904, since they were protection for the weakest partner in the arrangement. The notes of May 16 tied Spain to France and Britain while denying a strategic area to German influence.

Apparently Grey did not sense that another cord had tightened the Entente Cordiale. Here was an additional step in the direction of a *de facto* alliance, particularly when Grey promised British aid if Germany intervened. The significance of the arrangement was not lost on Cambon.

With the Mediterranean accord France acquired protection for her Mediterranean frontier. In Eastern Europe, France had the assurance of support from the Russians in case of war with Germany. The Entente Cordiale settled French differences with Britain, and in time it was to be hammered into something more than a mere accord over colonies. There was, however, serious need of a *rapprochement* between France's partner in the Entente Cordiale and her eastern ally, and this matter became the next step in the strengthening of the Entente. Cambon played only a minor role in these negotiations.

When Benckendorff returned from St. Petersburg in March, 1906, he was enthusiastic for an Anglo-Russian agreement. Count Vladimir Lamsdorff, the Russian foreign minister, had spoken in favorable terms of an agreement similar to that of the Entente Cordiale. Would Cambon please help? Of course he would, and he asked Benckendorff if he had any idea of his government's point of view in regard to the problems, particularly Persia, the most important one. Benckendorff replied blandly that Russia would declare only that she was

---

⁹ Pichon to Cambon, May 4, 29, 1907, Cambon to Pichon, Feb. 15, May 14, 16, 17, June 5, 8, 1907, *ibid.*, X, 649–51, 792–93, 803–804, XI, 5–6, 9–10, 25–26, 28–31; Note from Paul Cambon, Feb. 14, 1907, Grey to Cambon, May 16, 1907, Grey to Bertie, Feb. 14, May 6, 9, 17, June 8, 1907, Grey to Bunsen, May 28, 1907, *BD,* VII, 12–13, 31, 38.

ready to talk; the initiative was up to Britain. Somewhat taken back at this method of diplomacy, Cambon replied, "I can only be of use to you in urging Sir Edward Grey to formulate his views."

Cambon informed Grey what had happened and proposed that Britain immediately produce ideas for discussion since they could not expect to obtain anything precise from Russia. Cambon thought that Sir Arthur Nicolson, now British ambassador in St. Petersburg, should handle the negotiations because this was too delicate a matter to be entrusted to the telegraph. Cambon remembered that the telegraph had snarled the Dogger Bank affair. Grey agreed and drew up a memorandum for the cabinet.[10]

On May 28, Nicolson arrived in St. Petersburg with definite instructions to begin talks that would lead to an entente with Russia over colonial questions. The British cabinet had not been eager for this accord because of the unstable political conditions in Russia, but pressure from Cambon helped to produce the instructions. The long negotiations started, with Cambon assisting wherever possible. Finally, on August 31, 1907, the agreement between Russia and Britain was signed.

Both parties recognized the neutrality of Tibet. Afghanistan would be a British sphere of influence; the northern sector of Persia would be a Russian sphere, the southern sector would come under British influence, and the central section of the country would be neutral.

Although it was not prominent in the negotiations, Cambon's work had been useful in achieving the desired result. He had helped create an accord thought to be impossible because Britain and Russia had quarreled too long ever to reach an agreement. Most important of all to him, the Entente Cordiale had been strengthened indirectly by the elimination of possible Anglo-Russian friction. Like the Entente, the Anglo-Russian agreement was nonmilitary. Only time and the bungling of German and Austrian diplomacy would make military allies out of the ententes.

But there was still the unanswered question—how much had the crisis over Morocco and the subsequent conference changed the

[10] Cambon to Bourgeois, March 23, 1906, *DDF,* 2 ser., IX, 693-96.

STRENGTHENING THE ENTENTE

relations between Britain and France? Cambon was deeply interested to learn of the conversation between Grey and Metternich, the German ambassador, on March 9. The latter asked if "the entente between France and England had anything which could worry the German government?"

Grey kept from smiling and replied: "The character of our *Entente* with France depends uniquely on the attitude of the German government. It is an arrangement of affairs, a guarantee of peace and of tranquility. Our *Entente* will be defensive and only in case the action of the German government would be threatening."

A month later, while in Paris, Campbell-Bannerman announced to Georges Clemenceau, the premier, that in case of German aggression Britain would intervene with all her naval forces. In view of public opinion, the sending of the army was another matter. Clemenceau was frightened. Had Britain changed her attitude? Cambon received instructions to inquire if there had been such a change. Grey explained calmly that it was a mistake, that Campbell-Bannerman meant to imply that Britain would be reluctant to go to war.

"Since the Moroccan incidents, if Germany attacked France, we were ready to help you on sea and on land," Grey declared. "In such circumstances it would be necessary, in order that action be effective, not to spare any effort."

"These circumstances could recur," Cambon replied, "and we think that your intentions would not change."

"Certainly not," said Grey.[11]

Thus was the Entente Cordiale strengthened by pledges of aid, co-operation in an international conference, and fresh agreements removing sources of discord. All of these developments were most heartening to Cambon, for they meant that there would not be another 1870. At least, so he hoped.

[11] Grey to Bertie, April 19, 1907, *BD,* IV, 27; Cambon to Pichon, March 9, April 20, 1907, *DDF,* 2 ser., X, 684–86, 767–68.

VIII. THE BALKANS AND MOROCCO

THE ENTENTES between Britain and France and between Britain and Russia were fundamentally loose arrangements that could be interpreted any way a member saw fit according to the circumstances. Co-ordinated action was possible only if the interests of the powers were similar or if all three were threatened by the same source. This problem became apparent in the Bosnian crisis of 1908–1909 and the Agadir crisis of 1911.

The Bosnian crisis originated on September 15, 1908, when Count Lexa von Aehrenthal, the Austro-Hungarian foreign minister, and Alexander Isvolsky, the Russian foreign minister, secretly agreed on the annexation of Bosnia-Herzegovina by Austria-Hungary, whose troops had occupied this area since 1878 under the terms of the Treaty of Berlin. In return, Austria-Hungary would not oppose Russian action to obtain an opening of the Dardanelles for Russian warships—a goal long sought by successive Russian governments. Isvolsky began a tour of the European capitals to obtain permission for this scheme, but before the completion of his tour, the newspapers broke the story on October 7 that Austria-Hungary had annexed Bosnia-Herzegovina without consulting Isvolsky. He found little support, however. The French government decided to await developments without giving him any pledge. Grey insisted that the Dardanelles should be open to all nations, not to Russia alone. Isvolsky's only hope lay in an international conference, but Aehrenthal, supported by Germany, refused to join such a conference. Europe was on the brink of war.

The Balkan area was of strategic importance to many powers. Austria saw it as a field for expansion, especially Bosnia, which she feared Serbia might acquire and so become strong enough to challenge Austria-Hungary. Germany decided to support her ally, Austria-Hungary, so that her reluctance would not weaken the Dual Alliance. Traditionally, Britain had been opposed to a Russian exit from the Black Sea. Although some members of the government wanted to accommodate Russia, the radicals in the Liberal party were unwilling. The outraged Serbian government thought seriously of war. The French position was awkward because her ally was involved in an area where France had few interests—she was not eager to risk her alliance in the Balkans but rather along the Rhine. Cambon was again faced with problems arising from an alliance for which he had little love.

At the news of the crisis Cambon talked with Grey, then hurried to consult with Count Albert Mensdorff, the Austrian ambassador, to whom he insisted that a conference would be the only way out of the present difficulty. Cambon tried to bluff Mensdorff with the hint that the conference might be held without Austria-Hungary.

By October 9, Isvolsky was in London. Grey and Cambon met with him to try to find some solution to the problem. Cambon was under a handicap in these talks because he knew little of what his superiors in Paris had said to Isvolsky, who assumed that Cambon had been informed. In order not to make his government appear too silly, Cambon did the best that he could to fake a knowledge of the Paris talks. Grey and Cambon worked out a program with Isvolsky, cutting out many of the irrelevant subjects that he wanted on the agenda of the conference. Their work was to no avail because the story leaked to the papers. Aehrenthal announced that any conference would only take notice of the annexation that had already occurred. This was obviously unacceptable to Isvolsky, who hoped to save something from the debacle through a conference.

Privately Cambon felt that both Isvolsky and Aehrenthal had

placed themselves in a poor position, for they had expected that a resolution upon which they had agreed secretly would be approved by all immediately. Cambon blamed Aehrenthal for attempting to be another Metternich or Bismarck. Cambon feared that if there was no conference, the Slav elements would break out in rebellion against Austria: "Europe will have a bomb at her feet which the slightest movement will explode."[1]

The Austro-Hungarian government found loyal support in Berlin, where there were hopes of a diplomatic victory at the expense of Russia. Serbia demanded that Russia obtain some compensation for her defunct scheme for expansion into Bosnia-Herzegovina. The Russian government was loath to fight over the issue, but the thought of submitting to Aehrenthal's coup was awful in its consequences for Russian foreign policy. Isvolsky could find little help from either Great Britain or France.

By February, 1909, Cambon was sufficiently worried over war that he wanted Pichon to advise St. Petersburg that France had only one aim, to prevent war. Whatever followed would be Russia's responsibility. If she contemplated war, France should at least be informed. Pichon quieted him with the news that the Russian government had been so advised.

Faced with an ultimatum from Germany and possessing an army still recovering from the Russo-Japanese War, Russia gave in on March 31 and accepted Aehrenthal's victory. Serbia received compensations neither in land nor in economic aid.

The French government had no desire to use the alliance with Russia for a war that did not involve the return of Alsace-Lorraine. Great Britain saw none of her interests threatened. Cambon thought that the trouble had begun when Isvolsky "lost his head," for diplomacy was a profession in which hysteria was out of place.[2] Isvolsky was forsaken because neither Britain nor France had a vital interest in supporting Russia.

[1] Cambon to Henri Cambon, Oct. 11, Nov. 27, 1908, *Correspondance,* II, 245-46, 260-61.
[2] Cambon to Xavier Charmes, March 30, 1909, *ibid.,* 282.

THE BALKANS AND MOROCCO

In spite of problems in international importance, Cambon was constantly annoyed by French citizens who called themselves artists. He complained:

> Don't speak to me any more of singers, pianists, or artists of any sort; I am sick of them. They come in packs with recommendations of every type. This morning I had a large woman of great talent call at my home; her husband is in the service of the Prince of Monaco. Léon Bourgeois recommends all the young pianists from Châlon-sur-Marne and every senator or deputy has some diva up his sleeve. As for painters, pastellists or aquarellists who forge false Monets, they swarm here and give exhibitions which they ask me to solemnly open at the homes of all the art dealers in London.[3]

If that was not enough, in the summer of 1909, Cambon was distracted by a visit from the author Pierre Loti, whom he had entertained in 1894 in Constantinople. He was a very agreeable young man, despite his habit of wearing high heels and painting his fingernails. Born Lucien Viau in Rocheford in 1850, he had spent his life as a naval officer, rising to the rank of commander. His avocation was writing novels based on the scenes of his travels. Plot was of secondary importance, for his great talent lay in description. Loti was an impressionist painter of landscapes, except that he painted with a pen. His work was unequaled, and, as Cambon found out, so was he.

Cambon and one of his assistants went to the railroad station to meet Loti on his arrival in London. A quick search failed to produce the literary naval officer. The frustrated diplomats were standing at the exit debating whether or not to return to the embassy when they heard a soft voice calling them. There was Loti dressed in a coat, cape, and cap of a particularly vile shade of blue. The diminutive author had lost his servant and his baggage; they could not be found. The Ambassador shepherded his charge back to the embassy. There Loti expressed his doubts about the trip.

He whined: "I think that I was wrong to come. They don't really

[3] Cambon to Jules Cambon, May 19, 1909, *ibid.*, 286.

need to see me. I'll lose my prestige. When they read my books, they think that I'm always young, and what will they say when they see that it is no longer so?" But Cambon assured his guest that there was no reason for his fears.

The lost servant arrived by another train with the baggage, and the Ambassador observed that "there were four bags of respectable dimensions which could have been those of a pretty girl who changed her clothes three or four times a day."

The following day Loti greeted Cambon with rouge on his cheeks and his mustaches curled and quite obviously dyed. The day's program included a tour of Oxford and Blenheim Castle, which he seemed to enjoy, although Cambon was never quite certain what his reaction would be. He might complain that there was nothing to see, nothing to visit, and that he hated museums—all in a voice that was "a lamentation, a whispering in a dolorous tone which makes you want to treat him brusquely as you would a whining child."

Then there was the audience with the Queen. "My God! If he doesn't get it?" Cambon cried. The alternative was unthinkable. The Ambassador wrote a letter to the Queen asking for an audience.

"When will she answer?" demanded Loti. Only an hour had passed.

"Why this silence? But can she already have answered? The letter should have arrived, she will answer this evening, or tomorrow—but then she can't have seen my letter. But if the answer does not come, if there is a refusal, what will I do? Maybe I should not go to that ball tonight at the United States embassy where I will surely meet her?"

"We will talk about that tomorrow evening if the answer does not come," Cambon sighed. "It's useless to get excited so soon."

Within two hours the answer came announcing that Her Majesty Queen Alexandra would receive Loti. For the moment he was calm. Then a flood of questions engulfed Cambon again. What frock coat should he wear? What color tie? What about the gloves? The coat?

The next day it started all over again when Loti appeared wearing a gray-gold waistcoat with black stripes. Should he wear it to the ball that night at the United States embassy? Cambon suggested a white one. What about the decorations? What about the hat?

By this time he was beginning to bother Cambon, but at least he was very friendly with everyone else and made a good impression. The Ambassador grumbled, "But that damn rouge on his cheeks is embarrassing!"

In the evening Cambon gave a dinner for Loti at the embassy with some attractive women among the guests, who found the author most enjoyable. "I must say that with his small, timid manner, his soft voice, his odd appearance, and his unknown age, he does produce quite an effect," Cambon admitted.

Later the same evening, Cambon took Loti to the United States embassy, where the King, the Queen, and the Prince and Princess of Wales were guests at the ball. Queen Alexandra hurried to tell Cambon that she would be happy to see Loti the next day. She was delighted when Cambon told her he was there that night. The Ambassador presented Loti to Alexandra, who seemed to like him immediately. They talked a long time, but at first Loti was more concerned with his trousers because the other men wore silk knee breeches, the accepted court dress. He did not try enough to make himself understood by Alexandra, who was quite deaf. Later Loti admitted to Cambon that he had not understood what she had said; and the Ambassador was certain that she probably had not understood him either. But Loti was enchanted with Alexandra, for she was just as he had imagined her to be. "He was in heaven," Cambon reported.

The Ambassador next presented Loti to the King, who asked: "They say that you are an Anglophobe?"

"Yes," Cambon said, "but I think that will pass away."

"Sire," replied Loti softly, "I am not one any more."

The next day, July 10, Loti prepared for the trip to Buckingham Palace by trying on various ties during the morning. On the way to the palace the usual flood of questions began.

Should he button or unbutton his frock coat? We decided that it should be left buttoned. Should he wear his gloves on his hands or carry them in one hand? We decided that he would carry his gloves in one hand. But wait! He slapped some splotches of rouge on his cheeks which gave him the appearance of a thirty-sous doll. What pained him the most was that he could not kiss the hand of the queen. I told him that she would not like it. But he returned to it again. "This is the first queen whose hand I cannot kiss!"

At Buckingham Palace, the little naval officer conquered the Queen. She complimented him, flirted with him, talked with him about their mutual friends. She took him on a tour of the palace, and to Cambon's surprise, showed Loti her bedroom. The Queen even asked for his photograph. Loti's happiness was complete.

In September, when *Figaro* ran a series of articles by Loti, Cambon hoped Anglo-French relations would not be harmed. To his astonishment, Loti reported: "There are some parks in the city. The policemen are numerous, hackney coachmen are silent, and the English taken individually are not so bad."[4]

On May 6, 1910, death came suddenly to King Edward VII. He was an old friend for whom Cambon had great regard. Because the French ambassador was dean of the diplomatic corps, he had to handle the large number of problems connected with the funeral. His thoughts went back to the chaos of Victoria's funeral. Let it not happen again! It did not, because the practice obtained through Victoria's funeral prevented similar disaster at Edward's.

Nevertheless, Cambon had his troubles. Many people who had shaken the King's hand in Paris or Biarritz wrote to the Ambassador that it was their duty to participate in the funeral. As the hours passed, more requests to take part in the ceremonies came to the French embassy. Angrily Cambon complained, "I don't know how to handle all of these people who pretend to have the right to figure in the cortege. All the Frenchmen are convinced that the late King was their personal friend and that it is their duty to march behind the funeral carriage in the company of the Emperor of Germany."

[4] Cambon to Mme Paul Cambon, May 14, 17, 21, 1894, Cambon to Comtesse d'Arnaux, July 9, 10, 1909, Cambon to Henri Cambon, Sept. 4, 1909, *ibid.*, I, 371–72, II, 287–89.

Special missions came to represent the heads of state. How, when, and where the missions would participate was one of Cambon's problems. Should they follow the cortege on foot? In a carriage? On horseback? Cambon wanted only French naval and military officers to follow the carriage on horseback, while the rest of the French representatives would meet the carriage at the railroad station at Windsor and follow the procession to the burial in St. George's Chapel. Some wanted all of the missions to follow the carriage on foot through the streets of London. With the thought of portly diplomats and generals limping along the streets in his mind, Cambon objected. Teddy Roosevelt aided the confusion by announcing that he would ride on horseback dressed in "khaki, in boots, with a Buffalo Bill hat, a saber, and pistols." Cambon shuddered—this was 1901 all over again. The Foreign Office and the Palace were of little help. At last a compromise was reached. The heads of the missions would ride in carriages in the cortege in London, while the rest of the delegations would join the procession at the railroad station in Windsor. Thus it was that Teddy Roosevelt and Stephan Pichon, the French representative, rode quietly, side by side, in a carriage through the silent London streets on May 20 as Britain paid her last respects to the dead sovereign.[5]

The year 1910 ended so calmly for Cambon that he left his work for a long vacation in the Adriatic, Greece, Athens, and Corfu. The climax came in a reunion with old friends in Constantinople. He needed the rest, because 1911 would see a new crisis over Morocco.

After the Algeciras Conference, France did not assume outright control of Morocco immediately. The Chamber of Deputies and the Senate did not ratify the Act of Algeciras until December, 1906; and not until January, 1907, did the French government announce the selection of the officers to handle the policing of Morocco. Consequently, the Moroccan empire was left open to internal disorders and foreign intervention. These conditions produced another Moroccan crisis, that further altered the Entente Cordiale in the direction of a

[5] Cambon to Henri Cambon, May 6, 7, 11, 14, 16, 1910, Cambon to Jules Cambon, May 10, 1910, *ibid.*, 298–303.

military alliance. Cambon played a prominent role in the story of this crisis.

In the months immediately after Algeciras, Cambon urged his government to adopt a resolute policy in Morocco in order to keep anyone else from superseding France. There was still no firm agreement between the Spaniards and the French over police arrangements in Morocco. Cambon could only hope that the Spaniards would not delay over the matter. However, the Spaniards did delay, and launched into interminable discussions over the creation of the police force. By October, Cambon and Sir Charles Hardinge, the permanent undersecretary in the British Foreign Office, agreed that something would have to be done about a temporary police force when the French troops were withdrawn from Casablanca. It was decided that one thousand troops might be sent in as police, and Pichon, the French foreign minister, proceeded to carry out this step.

Negotiations were under way for a Franco-German accord over trading rights in Morocco by December, 1908. The Germans agreed to recognize the special French rights in Morocco, France would not thwart German industrial and commercial interests, and the Germans would not compete for posts in Morocco that had a political character.

Grey feared that everyone would be squeezed out of Morocco except France and Germany. To quiet the Foreign Secretary, Cambon brought a copy of the completed accord to the Foreign Office on February 9, 1909. He pictured the accord as a means of preventing friction between French and German nationals working in Morocco.

Nonetheless, some members of the British government were convinced that France and Germany had hatched a deal that was detrimental to British rights. Even Grey was uneasy. At the next opportunity he emphasized to Cambon the necessity for the Entente Cordiale, now that the Bosnian crisis threatened Europe.

> We are engaged with you in Morocco, and it is to our interest that you are not involved in difficulties. We do not then consider your accord with Germany as injuring in the least the relations of

our two countries. But, on your side, do not think because there is nothing for the moment to fear from your German neighbors, that the Entente would no more be necessary for you. It has proven itself in the storm. It is not necessary to renounce it today because the sky is clear; it could be dark again. Now it is best to tighten anew our Entente.[6]

Thus once more Grey unconsciously altered the Entente Cordiale. Cambon was delighted to hear such sentiments, indicating the sympathies of Grey but not necessarily those of other members of the cabinet.

The Briand cabinet fell in February, 1911, and Pichon resigned as foreign minister. In the new cabinet Jean Cruppi was foreign minister. He knew little about the affairs of his ministry. Now Cambon would find little firm direction or help from Paris if a serious crisis developed. Within a month a new one arose over Morocco.

Cambon came to Whitehall on April 4 to inform Nicolson, now permanent undersecretary for foreign affairs, that unless the situation improved around Fez, the Moroccan capital, France would take some military measures. Action was necessary because rebels were besieging Sultan Moulay Hafid in Fez and Europeans were in danger. France could not stand by "with folded arms while the lives of Europeans were in danger."

By April 28 plans for the dispatch of troops had been drawn up by Cruppi in accordance with Cambon's advice. The military expedition would stay two or three weeks and withdraw after securing Fez. Fearing that the Spanish government, alarmed by the expedition, might demand a partition of Morocco and thus prompt German intervention, Cambon pushed Cruppi to make explicit statements regarding the French action to the Spanish.[7]

---

[6] Grey to Bertie, Feb. 6, 16, 19, 1909, *BD,* VII, 136–39, V, 602; Cambon to Henri Cambon, Feb. 7, 1909, *Correspondance,* II, 272–73; Cambon to Pichon, Feb. 25, 1909, *DDF,* 2 ser., XII, 70–72.

[7] Cambon to Henri Cambon, April 5, 1911, Cambon to Jules Cambon, April 27, 30, 1911, *Correspondance,* II, 312–13, 315–18.

May brought another visit by William II. This time it was for the dedication of a statue to his grandmother, the late Queen Victoria. He deliberately avoided political talk, and when Cambon asked if he would receive the diplomatic corps, the Emperor refused on the grounds that the visit was of a family character. They did meet at a garden party, and William seized the Ambassador's hand, saying merely, "Everything is fine." Later at a ball, Cambon reported that William avoided nearly all of the diplomats "like the plague." Not a few of them resented his impolite action.[8]

When the French forces reached Fez on May 21, the Europeans were safe. On June 12, Cambon learned that Spain had begun outright military occupation of certain posts in Morocco, claiming that such action was necessary because of injuries to a Spanish protégé. Once compensation had been received, she would withdraw.

The situation was doubly ominous because the Franco-German negotiations over economic problems in Morocco were not succeeding. It was difficult to keep harmony when dividing up mining interests, public works, and railroads. Alfred von Kiderlen-Wächter, the new German foreign minister, regarded the expedition to Fez as the first step on the road to a French protectorate over Morocco. In return for German acceptance of the protectorate, Kiderlen determined to extract compensations for Germany from France. He hinted to Jules Cambon, the French ambassador, that the expedition to Fez would end the Act of Algeciras. Germany would no longer be bound by this agreement and thus would regain freedom of action in Morocco.

In France, however, there had been another cabinet crisis, and Joseph Caillaux had become premier on June 27, with Justin de Selves as foreign minister. Once more France had an inexperienced hand trying to guide foreign affairs. Only a crisis was needed.

The German gunboat *Panther* dropped anchor at the port of Agadir in southern Morocco on July 1 to protect German business interests, although there were none in Agadir. Cambon advised Selves to voice astonishment at the German action and to view the

[8] Cambon to Jules Cambon, May 23, 1911, *ibid.*, 320–23.

presence of the *Panther* at Agadir as purely temporary. Most important of all, the government must not let itself be pushed into hasty action by the newspapers.

When Grey met with Cambon on July 3, he was ready for Britain to take part in a crisis that before this time had been considered a Franco-Spanish matter. Both men agreed that it was necessary to consider ordering British and French ships to Morocco, but not to Agadir. The next day Grey informed Cambon that although the cabinet would not sanction the dispatch of a British ship to Morocco, Britain would stand by her treaty obligations to France.[9]

In Berlin the other Cambon brother sought to learn Germany's price for this blackmail, but not until July 15 did Kiderlen make his demand explicit. Germany wanted practically all of the French Congo, and the *Panther* would remain at Agadir until the deal was completed.

Paul Cambon hurried to Paris and for three days conferred with Selves and the British ambassador, Sir Francis Bertie. Cambon pointed out the grand design in Kiderlen's blackmail: if Germany obtained the French Congo, she would next try for the Spanish colony, Río Muni, then for the Portuguese holdings at the mouth of the Congo River, and eventually for the right to take part in the partition of the Belgian Congo, if that should ever occur.

The three men met on July 18 to discuss the latest statement of Kiderlen. Since Germany had not been compensated when France made Morocco a sphere of influence, she required compensation now in the Congo, and in return would renounce her political interests in Morocco. Selves suggested an international conference to extract the country from this impasse. Cambon objected: "A conference is dangerous: first, because we are not sure of a majority; second, because the conference could question all the advantages which we have gained since Algeciras." Premier Caillaux, who joined the discussion, wanted to know Cambon's solution.

[9] Cambon to Grey, July 1, 1911, Grey to Bertie, July 3, 4, 1911, *BD,* VII, 323–24, 330–31, 333–34; Cambon to Caillaux, July 4, 1911, *DDF,* 2 ser., XIV, 17–18; Cambon to Henri Cambon, July 3, 1911, *Correspondance,* II, 327–28.

Cambon reminded Caillaux that first they must seek some way to begin the conversation in order to propose a solution. He continued: "We could say to Kiderlen: Your demand of the Congo is inadmissible. We can allot to you certain territories in the Congo but not everything, and above all, not our establishments on the coast. Then there are two possibilities: Kiderlen will restate his demand or he will say that he is staying at Agadir." If he chose the latter course, Cambon felt that they could reply: "If you please, you cannot remain at Agadir without the authority of the powers because it is not an open port. It is not dependent on you alone to open the ports on the Moroccan coast; you must have the consent of the Sultan and of the signatory powers of the Act of Algeciras. You force us then to a conference." If Kiderlen were to claim that he had no intention of seizing Agadir and that he sought only to protect German economic interests, they could not contest the statement. Then, Cambon added, they could request that the equipment from the *Berlin,* which had replaced the *Panther,* should be embarked from Agadir. French merchants should be sent to open their shops in Agadir and give France some economic interests. Caillaux seized a telephone and informed the others of the proposal.[10]

Back in London by July 22, Cambon informed Grey of the events in Paris and learned of the effects of the speech delivered by David Lloyd George at the Mansion House on July 21. Speaking with the approval of Asquith and Grey, the fiery Welshman proclaimed that Britain's world position would not permit her to be excluded from the Moroccan discussions. Soon Metternich appeared in the Foreign Office to announce that Germany had no intention of creating a naval base in Morocco, that she merely wanted compensation elsewhere for agreeing to the French position in Morocco.

Germany still would not modify her demands for compensation. The inexperienced Selves wanted to cry that the "last word" of France had been given. Cambon quieted him with a reminder that he

[10] Cambon to Fleuriau, July 18, 1911, *ibid.,* 329–31; Grey to Bertie, July 6, 10, 1911, Goschen to Grey, July 10, 1911, Bertie to Grey, July 17, 18, 1911, Nicolson to Goschen, July 18, 1911, *BD,* VII, 341–42, 345–47, 370–75.

could not really say the last word himself; guns would say it. They must work for a definite protectorate, avoiding any rupture. At the same time, Paul begged his brother: "Let us remain very calm, you and I, in the midst of this agitation which reigns about us. We are the only ones in a position to give Selves some reasonable direction."[11]

In early August, Cambon learned of the double-dealing of Caillaux behind the back of Selves. Jules Cambon had been receiving two sets of instructions: one from Selves and the other sent secretly by Caillaux, who was making proposals of an entirely different nature. This infuriated Paul because he depended on honest treatment from his superiors. "This is enough to drive one mad," he complained.

There were rumors of German troop movements, including the story that the German general staff was studying plans for debarkation of troops at Agadir. Cambon counseled Selves not to become alarmed; there was too much at stake for the Germans to risk a general war, but the German tactics might incite the French newspapers and the French people to push the government to some rash action. Now, more than ever, they must be prudent in the negotiations, for if they were not, it would become a question of national prestige.

In accordance with his ideas, Cambon returned a draft of a Franco-German agreement over the question of Agadir to Selves with criticisms aimed at making the agreement as easy as possible for the Germans to swallow. It was necessary, he insisted, "to place ourselves in such a situation that the German government could not reasonably refuse an understanding and that it would be impossible for the powers not to adhere to it."

In Paris on August 22, the brothers Cambon met with important cabinet members and fought to soften the draft agreement by making it more general. Too much detail would only give the Germans greater opportunities for raising their price and might even alienate

---

[11] Grey to Goschen, July 24, 25, 1911, Grey to Carnegie, July 25, 1911, *ibid.*, 394–95, 400–401; Cambon to Henri Cambon, July 25, 1911, Cambon to Jules Cambon, July 30, 31, 1911, *Correspondance,* II, 333, 334, 336, 339; Cambon to Selves, July 29, 1911, *DDF,* 2 ser., XIV, 143–44.

Great Britain. Not enough attention, however, was paid to the diplomats' advice.[12]

When the negotiations stalled in September, Grey insisted that France avoid, at any price, the responsibility for a rupture in the talks, for fear that British opinion would grow cool toward France. Cambon concurred and once more pressed Selves to eliminate from the draft agreement the details that had led to the haggling and had endangered the negotiations. "You are marching towards a rupture in the negotiations with Germany," he wrote Selves. It seemed to Cambon that the Quai d'Orsay was pleased to close the doors to compromise. On his last trip to Paris on August 21, he was frightened by those around Selves who treated the question too lightly, speaking blandly of "extreme limit, the last word." The brothers Cambon had been accused of not speaking loudly enough, of not sounding sufficiently patriotic. Such tactics, Cambon cautioned, would give Germany the opportunity to proclaim that France had forced the rupture. Britain would not support France. The Entente Cordiale would be doomed.

Selves needed clarification on the importance of advice from a veteran member of the French diplomatic service. Cambon did not hesitate. An ambassador was not a subaltern to carry out instructions but rather a collaborator. At the risk of giving offense, he must express himself frankly. Cambon, impelled by experience which some thought already too long, advised him to consider certain factors, to reject proposals bound to fail, to avoid haste or trifling that might jeopardize negotiations.

> I have been an ambassador for twenty-five years and for thirty years in the foreign service. Circumstances have led me to deal with questions similar to those now at issue with Germany. I may, therefore, allow myself to express an opinion: I am a little surprised when I

[12] Cambon to Fleuriau, Aug. 7, 1911, Cambon to Jules Cambon, Aug. 15, 1911, Cambon to Henri Cambon, Aug. 22, 1911, *Correspondance,* II, 339–42; Cambon to Selves, Aug. 14, 1911, notes of Jules Cambon, Feb. 1912, *DDF,* 2 ser., XIV, 208–11; Bertie to Grey, Aug. 22, 1911, Grey to Bertie, Aug. 23, 1911, *BD,* VII, 482–84.

see young fellows who have never left their desks lay down the law on everything and counsel you to take highly inexpedient steps.[13]

Despite the advice of Paul and Jules Cambon, the politicians in Paris and Berlin insisted on detailed clauses that prolonged the negotiations until November 5, when the signing at last came. Germany withdrew her opposition to the French protectorate in Morocco, and in return she received over 100,000 swampy square miles in the French Congo.

It was a double celebration for Paul Cambon, who was presented with a set of gold Louis XVI candlesticks from his friends on November 6, the twenty-fifth anniversary of his promotion to ambassador.

The Cambon brothers had helped avert war. Even the ordinary French citizen knew it. In December a railway porter in Lyon, catching the name of Jules Cambon, asked him, "Aren't you the ambassador at Berlin?"

"Yes."

"You and your brother in London have done us a great service. Without you, we would be in a fine mess."[14]

Paul Cambon's work in the Agadir crisis had not gone unnoticed in Berlin, where the Kaiser complained that Britain had continually made difficulties for Germany in the Agadir crisis because Grey was under Cambon's influence. The truth was that once more, as in 1905 and 1906, tactless German diplomacy had helped Cambon in his task of keeping Britain and France united. However, Grey's conduct was more than sympathetic for it implied British help if the negotiations with Germany were broken off through Germany's fault.

Cambon had divined the basic plan of Kiderlen to exploit the presence of the *Panther* at Agadir for what it was worth in the building of a German empire in central Africa. Had his suggestions about the details of the draft agreement and the attitude of the Quai

---

[13] Cambon to Selves, Sept. 6, 1911, *DDF*, 2 ser., XIV, 356–59, 361–62; Cambon to Selves, Sept. 9, 1911, *Correspondance*, II, 342–43.

[14] Cambon to Henri Cambon, Dec. 5, 1911, *ibid.*, 354.

d'Orsay been followed more closely, the negotiations would have ended earlier. Once again his work had helped strengthen the Entente Cordiale. Few realized the strength of this agreement. Little did any one imagine how profoundly its meaning would be altered in the near future by the exchange of two letters.

IX. ENTENTE OR ALLIANCE?

On September 30, 1911, Italy invaded Libya to obtain her share of the dying Ottoman Empire. This attack heralded a change in the balance of power in the Mediterranean area. Ultimately it produced a new feature of the Entente Cordiale embodied in the Grey-Cambon letters of 1912.

Cambon was surprised by the rapidity of the Italian attack, for he had not realized that Italy was so eager to create an empire in North Africa. Apparently he had forgotten his troubles with Italy during the years in Tunisia. He hoped that the conflict might benefit France because the Triple Alliance would be sorely strained if Italy sought territory in the vicinity of the Adriatic sea—an area dear to Austria-Hungary. Attempts to end the conflict failed, and it continued into the new year.

On New Year's Day, 1912, Cambon confessed his foreboding to his brother: "What does this year hold for us? I hope that the great conflict will be avoided." But the first rumblings of the great conflict had begun; the Italian invasion of Libya would lead finally to the first world war of the twentieth century.[1]

Early in the new year Cambon became aware of a fresh danger. If Italy conquered Libya and fortified Tobruk, making it available to the growing German navy, the British control of the Mediterranean would be seriously threatened. What then should be the new policy toward Italy? Barrère wanted to bring her into the Entente Cor-

[1] Cambon to Jules Cambon, Sept. 30, 1911, *Correspondance*, II, 348–49.

diale as a full-fledged member, but Cambon would not concur. To him, Italy would be "more embarrassing than useful as an ally." He predicted that in the event of a general war, Italian hostility for Austria would lead her to remain neutral and await the development of events before taking sides.

By summer, rumors of German intervention in the war led Cambon to embrace Barrère's suggestion for an arrangement with Italy. It should be discreet and confidential so that the Moslems in the British and French empires would not be angered, but it must prevent the entrance of Germany into the Mediterranean.

The war was terminated by fall when the Balkan countries attacked the Ottoman Empire, seeking to enlarge their frontiers at the Turks' expense. There was no entente with Italy over the Mediterranean. Apparently Cambon did not know that Italian neutrality had already been secretly pledged to France in 1902.

The Italo-Turkish war had underlined a new problem facing the Entente Cordiale: the security of the Mediterranean Sea and North Africa. The agreement of April 8, 1904 lacked provisions for such measures, but circumstances seemed to demand their creation. Such developments occurred in 1912, culminating in the famous Grey-Cambon letters.

Even though Russia had been linked indirectly to the Entente, France still desired closer military relations with Great Britain. This desire had been heightened by the two Moroccan crises, and it increased when Britain and Germany began to discuss ways and means of reducing their naval expenditures, thereby to end the race for naval supremacy.

Early in February, 1912, Grey informed Cambon that talks for this purpose would begin soon. Cambon replied that if the British government was entering these discussions because some of its members feared that increased British naval expenditures would bring war, they were wrong. Germany did not want war, and Austria would not go to war unless Germany gave her permission. There must be no undue haste in negotiating with Germany.

Privately Cambon noted a resurgence of pro-German activities.

ENTENTE OR ALLIANCE?

He thought that if Germany wanted Britain to be friendly, she must change her naval expansion program, although such a move appeared impossible. France was also involved, but in an unusual way: "We have need of England in order to consolidate our colonial empire.... Without need of renewing her ancient coalitions with Germany, Great Britain could shackle our actions; her friendship is precious to us, and whoever wishes her friendship ought to obtain her confidence."[2]

Here was a startling confession: the French Empire needed the help of the former enemy of Fashoda. Only with the succor of an old foe could France be secure. As a world power France would be dependent on the unity of the Entente Cordiale. This would then be the task of Cambon: to tighten the Entente for the preservation of the French Empire but not at the sacrifice of British confidence. It was the German failure to keep Britain's confidence that helped Cambon bind the Entente more closely.

He saw only failure and humiliation for Great Britain when he learned from Grey on February 7, 1911, that R. B. Haldane, secretary of state for war, would travel to Germany and examine the possibilities for a settlement of the naval question. Cambon observed, "Grey believes naïvely in the possibility of reaching an accord for the limitation of naval expenditures on the condition that England keep her supremacy on the seas. This is infantile...."[3] Haldane returned without a settlement—the only result of the meeting was a declaration that neither nation cherished aggressive intentions.

Meanwhile, negotiations over the Anglo-German naval question continued in London between Grey and Metternich, the German ambassador. On March 14, Metternich requested some assurance from Grey regarding British policy. "England will make no unprovoked attack upon Germany and pursue no aggressive policy towards her," was Grey's reply. Neither, he declared, was there any intention of aggression towards Germany in any treaty or agreement to which

[2] Cambon to Poincaré, Feb. 7, 1912, *DDF,* 3 ser., I, 631–35.
[3] Cambon to Xavier Charmes, Feb. 12, 1912, *Correspondance,* III, 10–11; Cambon to Poincaré, Feb. 10, 1912, *DDF,* 3 ser., II, 13–14.

Great Britain was a party. Metternich was not satisfied. On March 22, he demanded a statement of complete neutrality, which Grey would not give, although he would consent to a declaration of neutrality in the event of an unprovoked attack on Germany.

Learning of the proposed declaration, Cambon hastened to inform Grey that under such a formula Britain's hands would be tied. Germany would make it appear that she was a victim of aggression by moving troops to the border of Belgium, thus forcing France to attack her. Grey replied only that the formula would be put to the cabinet. And the cabinet, realizing the danger in such a formula, turned it down.

It was April in Paris, but Cambon found Raymond Poincaré, the premier, worried over the declaration. Both men agreed that it was only a means to entrap the British government into a written statement. Once it was written, the Germans would hasten to publish it with great fanfare. In France there were many persons still ready to twist the slightest fact that would imply that Britain was undependable and tied to Germany. The publication of this formula would give them additional ammunition. Cambon, however, saw no reason for excessive alarm since the Entente was still secure and would be as long as Britain wanted supremacy on the seas.

Poincaré asked Cambon to make new proposals to Grey on his return to London in mid-April. Because Grey was on a vacation, Cambon took the delicate problem to Sir Arthur Nicolson, now permanent undersecretary in the Foreign Office.

Poincaré's critics placed him in a weak position, Cambon declared. The Premier could say publicly only that France and Britain had sympathy for each other. The enemies of the Entente Cordiale in France were still unappeased. In a year or two an incident might lead to war with Germany. Poincaré longed to be certain that France could depend on Britain, because Germany might feel free to do as she pleased once she thought Britain was neutral.

Cambon asked Nicolson if they could seek a formula to reassure the worried and the dubious, at the same time admitting that the British government could not engage itself without Parliament's con-

Courtesy French Embassy, Information Division

Camille Barrère,
ambassador to Italy, 1897 ff.

Théophile Delcassé,
minister of foreign affairs, 1898–1905.

THE FRENCH DIPLOMATIC TEAM

Maurice Bompard,
ambassador to Russia, 1902–1907.

Jean Jules Jusserand,
ambassador to the United States,
1902–25.

Courtesy Culver Service

Pierre Loti, French naval officer and novelist.

sent. He saw no necessity for a signed accord. "We could be content with the exchange of verbal declarations which could be the subject of notes," he said. "That is what we would have done in 1905 with Lord Lansdowne if the resignation of M. Delcassé had not cut short our conversations."

Although Nicolson was sympathetic and would like to consolidate the Entente by a written agreement, he reminded Cambon that Grey and Herbert Asquith, now prime minister, could not enter into any written agreement without first consulting the cabinet. The present group of ministers would not dare ratify such an agreement. Many still thought that Germany had been denied her rightful place in the sun. Cambon argued in return that two of the most influential ministers, Lloyd George and Winston Churchill, first lord of the Admiralty, were now partial to the Entente Cordiale. This could not be denied by Nicolson, but they were not enough. It was best to leave things alone; the cabinet would not last, and when the Conservatives took office, a more definite arrangement could be made.

Later Grey told Nicolson that he agreed with his stand and would have made much the same statements to Cambon. In the future he would impress on the French ambassador that Britain would not be obligated to fight with France against Germany for any reason whatsoever, but he would not promise the Germans never to help France.

In the days that followed, both Nicolson and Bertie, the British ambassador in Paris, realized that Britain would have to make more definite arrangements with France and gave their superiors due warning. They advised Grey that Britain could not expect support from France without responsibility on Britain's part. Nicolson wanted agreements more with France and Russia than with Germany; these two allies could harm British interests more than Germany could.

By 1912 the threat of the German Navy had forced the Admiralty to reassess their war plans. No longer could Britain try to be strong both at home and around the world. A greater concentration of the fleet nearer the British Isles would be necessary. But who would insure the protection of the British trade routes elsewhere, particularly in the Mediterranean, where the Italo-Turkish War had seriously altered the balance of power? The only source of help seemed to be the French Navy, which was desirous of taking up naval staff talks, originated under Sir John Fisher, first sea lord, 1904–10.

In May, Cambon brought up the question of naval control in the Mediterranean by passing on to Grey the request made by the French naval authorities that discussions be held concerning future eventualities in this area. These discussions, begun under Sir John Fisher in 1905, had continued at irregular intervals. In 1911, a vague promise of renewal had been made. Nicolson admitted that he knew nothing about these talks. Cambon, nevertheless, had made his point. The naval talks no longer comprised discussions among technical experts; in the future, they would be a subject for diplomatic discussions.

On May 11, Grey announced to Cambon that Britain was redistributing her fleet and could not enter into serious naval talks with France until this redistribution was completed. Cambon insisted that in November, 1911, the First Lord of the Admiralty, Reginald McKenna, had asked the French naval attaché to join in discussions aimed at aiding Britain in the Channel in wartime. The British naval attaché in Paris had repeated the invitation in January, 1912; now France wanted to accept the invitation. Before committing himself, Grey had to talk with Winston Churchill, now first lord of the Admiralty.

Churchill would not discuss the matter with the French until after the meeting of the Committee of Imperial Defense. Early in June, at the meeting of the committee, support for Cambon came from the Sea Lords, who advanced an agreement with France over the defense of the northern French coasts and the Mediterranean sea.[4]

Late in June, Cambon learned that Britain planned to reduce the over-all number of her ships in the Mediterranean and to concentrate a swift striking force at Gibraltar, ready to speed wherever needed.

[4] Minute of Nicolson, April 15, 1912, Grey to Nicolson, April 21, 1912, Nicolson to Grey, May 4, 1912, Nicolson to Bertie, May 6, 1912, memorandum of Crowe, May 8, 1912, Bertie to Nicolson, May 9, 1912, Grey to Churchill, May 11, 1912, Grey to Bertie, May 24, 1912, Kitchener to Grey, June 2, 1912, *BD,* VI, 747–49, 751; X, pt. 2, 582–91, 594–95; Cambon to Poincaré, April 18, 1912, *DDF,* 3 ser., II, 369–71.

This was disquieting news to a diplomat who had spent many years worrying about the problems of the Mediterranean Sea. To Cambon, France had a great stake in the maintenance of British naval power in the Mediterranean, for reduction of Britain's fleet would affect her prestige and indirectly that of the Entente. "I would not then consider it advantageous for us that England withdraw her forces from the Mediterranean, unless this withdrawal had as a consequence the conclusion of a positive pact between her and us."

When Cambon saw Grey in July, he stressed the political importance of keeping a squadron at Malta. Grey answered that there was enough strength to insure that French and British naval forces would offset any Austro-Italian combination in the Mediterranean. As yet there was no decision on the dispositions of the fleets, but he hoped to have one by July 22.

On the appointed day, Grey announced to Cambon that the talks between the naval staffs could continue, whatever might be said, the freedom of action of both countries could not be impaired. The governments were not to be committed by the discussions of their naval staffs; of course, there was no formal agreement between the two governments. Cambon replied that "there was nothing but a moral entente which might, however, be transformed into a formal entente if the two governments desired when the occasion arose." This was going too far for Grey, who contended that the talks of the experts did not commit the governments but only enabled assistance when the need arose. To Grey, Cambon seemed quite satisfied. Well he might, because he knew that once military plans had been formed with another country, a military entente was in being although it might not be in writing.[5]

On July 24 a distraught Cambon hurried to see Nicolson after reading the draft of the naval convention under discussion by the naval experts. Nine-tenths of the French fleet would be concentrated in the Mediterranean, and France would abandon the defense of the Atlantic and the Channel to Britain—all without any guarantee from

[5] Cambon to Poincaré, June 27, 1912, *ibid.*, III, 176–81; Grey to Carnegie, July 11, 22, 1912, *BD*, X, pt. 2, 600–601.

Britain. France would be open to attack by sea if Britain did not wish to help her. This was entirely unilateral, Cambon argued; France was giving up the defense of the Channel coasts while moving all her fleet to the Mediterranean. Her Channel coasts were unprotected, but "England was free to aid France or not as she liked and under no obligation to do so." Cambon would take this up on his next trip to Paris.

Back in Whitehall on July 26, the Ambassador debated the draft agreement with Grey. Cambon was realistic enough to understand that France was definitely committing herself for the future, no matter how many pious declarations might be contained in the agreement. Churchill, in discussions with the French naval attaché, had claimed that the disposition of the two fleets had been made independently of each other. The convention was only using the existing dispositions and would not affect the liberty and the freedom of action of the governments. Such was not the case, Cambon argued, for in 1907, France had made moves towards concentrating her fleet in the Mediterranean as a consequence of discussions with Sir John Fisher.

Nor did Cambon like the preamble of the draft agreement containing clauses that seemed strange in any agreement of naval experts. According to these clauses, the agreement was based on the contingency that Britain and France were allies in war. The freedom of either government to enter such a war was unaffected. France had concentrated most of her fleet in the Mediterranean Sea; Britain had concentrated hers in her home waters. These were independent dispositions, made because they were the best for the interests of each nation. They did not originate in a naval agreement or a convention.

Cambon insisted that if these clauses were included, the governments must agree to communicate with each other if there was danger of war and plan joint action. The concentration of the French fleet in the Mediterranean could endanger the Atlantic and Channel coasts. France could not allow such a move without some knowledge of British intentions.

Grey was in an awkward position. He claimed that the government could not promise military action without consulting Parliament, but that did not deter Cambon. They did not have to engage themselves formally, the Ambassador argued. Private notes could be exchanged, such as Lansdowne's letter of May 28, 1905, in which he agreed that France and Britain should consult together for mutual protection if events seemed threatening. If such notes were exchanged, Britain and France could declare truthfully that no binding agreement to take action existed between them.

Grey found too many objections to the exchange of notes. If the story of the staff talks leaked out, it would be possible for a third nation to learn the state of affairs between France and Britain. Why could they not carry on in the future as they had in the past? Cambon was still unhappy.

The noncommittal clause should be omitted from the convention, he argued. If it were left in, France wanted assurances that the governments would co-operate when war threatened. If they could not agree on a military accord, it would be every man for himself. France would not police the Mediterranean alone. Perhaps it might be possible, Grey admitted, to find some formula for co-operation while avoiding accusations that the cabinet had contracted an alliance without Parliament's knowledge. He would think it over and take it up after his vacation.[6]

The situation made Poincaré unhappy also. A naval convention that stated that the governments were not concerned meant nothing. Because of the contradiction, why have the convention? He proposed to Sir Francis Bertie, the British ambassador, that if the interests of the two governments were threatened, talks should begin to implement the arrangements of the experts. The political reservations then could be removed from the naval convention, where they did not belong anyway, because political agreements should be made not by naval experts but by diplomats. He promised Bertie that Cambon would take up this problem when Grey returned from his vacation.

[6] Minute of Nicolson, July 24, 1912, Grey to Carnegie, July 26, 1912, *ibid.*, 603–605; Cambon to Poincaré, Sept. 21, 1912, *DDF*, 3 ser., III, 544–46.

In mid-September, chance almost ruined the negotiations for Cambon. A staff officer forwarded by mistake an order for the Third Squadron of the French Navy, stationed at Brest, to move to the Mediterranean. The order was premature since the movement would not occur until October 16; moveover, it was forwarded to the wrong officer. Somehow the newspapers picked up the item and speculated on the existence of a naval entente between France, Russia, and Britain. As the guesses of the newspapers increased, so did Cambon's alarm. He feared that the British government would achieve its aim without an accord protecting French interests. France might lose her best lever to pry an agreement out of Whitehall.

Although he lacked instructions, Cambon hurried to Whitehall on September 17 to cover the mistake. He described the movement to Nicolson as only a temporary shift occasioned by practice maneuvers. Any permanent shift would depend on the outcome of negotiations then in progress.

Two days later Cambon repeated to Grey much of what he had related to Nicolson, offering his personal suggestion for the form of the understanding. If either government feared aggression, they could discuss the problem and seek means for maintaining peace and preventing aggression. Undoubtedly Poincaré had already approved of this "personal" suggestion.

When Grey argued that such was already their practice, Cambon responded that France was dependent on Britain's good will without any assurance of the co-operation of the British cabinet. That was a matter for Grey to discuss with Asquith, the prime minister, and the cabinet. Asquith's reaction was favorable. He saw no harm in Cambon's formula, for he considered it almost a platitude. He found the exchange of notes impossible without communicating them to the House of Commons.

Cambon relentlessly pressed Grey and Asquith for an exchange of notes. At last they capitulated but on their own terms: instead of diplomatic notes, private letters that needed only the cabinet's approval would be exchanged. Cambon had no objection to cabinet approval because it would make the letters more official.

In the cabinet meeting of October 30, the letters were discussed, many of the ministers learning of the military and naval talks for the first time. To many, this was not a little frightening because politically they were interested in more peaceful pursuits. Of the changes that Cambon dreaded, one was made by adding a paragraph that the consultation and agreements of the naval experts did not commit the governments. Cambon regretted that they did not keep Poincaré's version of the proposal, saying, "Its precision and brevity perhaps forced it to be discarded because the English are insensible of the art of saying anything in a few words." The same day he received the notes for transmission to Paris for study.

By November 7 he returned with the approval of his government. After slight changes were made in the form of the letters, they were exchanged on November 23, 1912. Their content followed much the line desired by Grey: The consultations of the military and naval experts would not obligate either government to support the other with armed forces. The dispositions of the British and French fleets did not necessarily indicate co-operation in wartime. Both governments agreed that in the event of danger of an attack or a threat to the peace, they would discuss possible joint action and at the same time consider whether to put into operation the plans of the naval and military staffs.[7]

A great deal of print and paper have been employed in discussing the exchange and meaning of these letters. The argument centers around the question, To what exactly had Britain been committed? Grey thought that Britain had left her hands free while not committing herself to anything other than consultations. No automatic military action was involved. Not until after the discussions had occurred would any consideration be given to the plans of the military staff. Of the greatest significance to Grey was the statement, "It has always been understood that such consultation does not restrict the freedom of either government to decide at any time whether or

[7] Cambon to Poincaré, Sept. 19, 21, Oct. 13, Nov. 23, 1912, *ibid.*, 523–25, 544–46, IV, 318–22, 535–38; Bertie to Grey, July 30, 1912, Nicolson to Grey, Aug. 4, 1912, Grey to Bertie, Sept. 19, Oct. 30, Nov. 7, 1912, Asquith to Grey, Oct. 11, 1912, *BD,* X, pt. 2, 605–608, 611–14.

not to assist the other by armed forces." Thus Britain seemed to have her hands free. She would not become involved in a quarrel that was not of her choosing, such as a war to regain Alsace-Lorraine.

Grey forgot that whether or not Britain was committed, France was already committed by the withdrawal of her fleet from the North Sea. Churchill maintained that the disposition of each of the two fleets would have been necessary even if the other had not existed. He saw the danger in the letters and warned Grey that France would have a weapon to compel British intervention. France could say: " 'On the advice of and by arrangements with your naval authorities we have left our northern coasts defenseless. We cannot possibly come back in time.' " He argued that Britain had the obligations but not the advantages of a precise alliance. Churchill realized that Britain's honor would be involved, no matter what hypotheses might be placed on paper. The military dispositions committed both countries.[8]

In these letters Britain undertook a moral obligation. It was not a simple agreement merely to consult, as Grey imagined. Britain had taken on herself a moral obligation to defend the northern coasts of France. At the time, Cambon made no mention of this fact; in 1914 he remembered it.

On the French side, these letters were the result of collaboration by Delcassé, Poincaré, and Paul Cambon. Delcassé, now minister of marine, used the naval convention to achieve his frustrated wish for a closer relationship in the Entente Cordiale. Poincaré, alarmed by the criticism of the Entente, wanted a more concrete arrangement. Cambon's part is not clear because much that he said and did in London was the result of conferences in Paris of which no record is available. He sought the proper moment to suggest a closer entente; the negotiation of the naval convention gave him his opportunity. Because the naval convention was a British idea, he succeeded in having Grey agree to the letters. The French ambassador was aided by the influence of the Admiralty, the effect of the Italo-Turkish war on the balance of power in the Mediterranean area, and the Balkan

[8] W. S. Churchill, *The World Crisis 1911-1918*, I, 85-88.

ENTENTE OR ALLIANCE?

wars that broke out in October, 1912. The idea of these letters did not originate with Cambon alone, but he was certainly one of the fathers of the idea.

Cambon had Grey do what he did not want to do: commit the British government on paper to a future action. But Grey believed that he had protected himself against such an eventuality. Time would show that naval commitments spoke louder than vague phrases written on paper. These letters gave the talks of the military experts a value that they had lacked. Prior to November, 1912, there had been somewhat of a semi-official air about them. Such was no longer the case: the British and French governments had approved of them in writing, and the planning could continue at greater speed. The fact that the planning was so far advanced by 1914 helped save the Allied cause in the early days of the war.

Although there is little evidence available regarding his opinion of the letters, Cambon probably thought that because British opinion had changed, another 1870 would not occur. Britain would now realize that it would be detrimental to her interests to permit German domination of the coasts of northern France, where the growing German Navy would find good ports from which to harass British shipping. He knew that the British Admiralty was apprehensive of the strength of the German Navy. For strategic reasons it was to Britain's interest to prevent German domination of France. He erred in not realizing how long it would take for this danger to become apparent to the British government.

Cambon believed that the letters were the best he could obtain in view of the pacifist tendencies of the Liberal government. He was probably wrong in stating that if Grey had his way, the letters would be only a beginning. Grey was still very British and did not want to commit Britain to any future action.

For Cambon, this exchange represented the completion of a job started in 1905 with Lansdowne's offer to consult. He had helped to achieve what Rouvier had prevented when he overthrew Delcassé. The Entente Cordiale was no longer merely an agreement over colonies. But was it an alliance?

X. PRELUDE TO ARMAGEDDON

The growing crisis in the Balkans impelled the British cabinet to approve the Grey-Cambon letters. With the Ottoman Empire defeated by Italy, the small Balkan countries bestirred themselves to attack Turkey. By February, 1912, Serbia and Bulgaria, with the knowledge of the Russian government, signed a treaty pledging themselves to propose an attack on Turkey if internal conditions so warranted. If Russia then had no objection, hostilities would begin. By May, Greece and Bulgaria were allied. Bulgaria and Montenegro were allied in early September, and later that month Montenegro became an ally of Serbia. Each of these alliances had the same goal—concerted attack on Turkey.

Knowledge of the Serbo-Bulgarian treaty infuriated Cambon because he saw its inherent danger to the peace of Europe. To him, it was an instrument of Russian revenge for the annexation of Bosnia-Herzegovina. For Russia, it was a perpetual menace because Bulgaria might reveal the details at any time to Vienna to gain aid against Russia or blackmail Russia by threatening to reveal the treaty to Austria-Hungary. Only war could result from such an agreement.

As the tension continued, Poincaré proposed a meeting of the powers to discuss certain Turkish reforms that might calm the Balkan allies. Cambon agreed that a conference of the great powers who had interests in the Balkans was the best defense against war.

The time was past for a conference, however. Only force could prevent a conflict, and none of the powers were eager for that. Before Cambon could present Poincaré's proposal to the British Foreign Office, Montenegro had declared war on Turkey on October 8. The remaining allies presented their declarations of war on October 18, and before the end of the month all Turkish armies in the Balkans had been defeated.

Cambon did not desire a Turkish defeat, foreseeing dangers to the peace of Europe if the Ottoman Empire was dismembered. Should the Bulgarians reach Constantinople, they would never want to withdraw, and the complications would be frightening. It was imperative to prevent any hasty move by Austria that might push Serbia to rash action.

Involved discussions began among the powers over action to end the war and settle the Balkan problems. Poincaré wanted a full-fledged international conference in Paris. Grey advocated a conference of ambassadors in Paris to begin discussions of the pertinent questions. The latter proposal Cambon thought best because speed was essential and Poincaré's plan would waste time in preliminary negotiations. The diplomats must begin talking, for already rumors abounded that Austria was preparing for war.

Grey took the initiative and proposed a conference of ambassadors in Paris similar to the old consultation of ambassadors in Constantinople that Cambon knew so well. Poincaré inquired about his pro-proposal for a conference concerning Turkish reforms. Cambon insisted that such a discussion was too late; it was pointless to discuss reforms while there was war. A conference of ambassadors would unify the powers and immobilize Russia and Austria.

Poincaré was a burden to Cambon in this crisis. The Premier, after a legal education, by 1887 had been elected to the Chamber of Deputies, where he made a reputation as a financial authority. His career had flourished, bringing him to the premiership and the Quai d'Orsay in January, 1912. He was a solemn Lorrainer, who took himself too seriously, but he possessed great energy and self-confidence. Hatred of Germany on account of the Franco-Prussian war drove him on. His relations with Cambon were correct but never intimate and often irritating. Cambon felt a need to be on his guard against Poincaré, who blamed his agents if his efforts failed. Too often he lost himself in "telegrams, proposals, and red tape."[1]

Poincaré wanted the ambassadors to meet in Paris, where he hoped to preside over the final peace conference. It would be priceless publicity for a French politician with presidential ambitions. Cambon argued for London because the ambassadors there were on better terms. The German and Austrian governments favored London, also, because they wanted to avoid any meeting that included Isvolsky, now the Russian ambassador in Paris. When the Russians approved of London, Poincaré capitulated.

Cambon and Grey had been worried over the delay in meeting lest Austria-Hungary frighten Serbia into war. Fearful that France might find herself once more fighting her old Hapsburg rival of the sixteenth and seventeenth centuries, Cambon, on December 4, asked Grey what the British attitude would be in such a crisis. Grey replied that it would depend on how the war began and its effect on public opinion. Cambon reminded him that if a Continental war broke out and Austria attacked Russia with Germany coming to Austria's aid, France would enter the war. Should that occur, Cambon promised to repeat the question.[2]

At last, on December 17, the diplomats representing the powers assembled in the Foreign Office for the first meeting. They included Count Albert von Mensdorff for Austria-Hungary, Prince Karl Max Lichnowsky for Germany, the Marquis Guglielmo Imperiali for Italy, Benckendorff for Russia, Grey, and Cambon. The meetings were secret, verbose, and too long even for ambassadors. Cambon lamented that the conference "would continue till there were six skeletons sitting around the table."[3]

The problems facing the conference included Albania's boundaries (all agreed on the necessity to create an independent Albania), Ser-

[1] Cambon to Jules Cambon, Nov. 28, 1912, *Correspondance,* III, 29–30.
[2] Grey to Bertie, Dec. 4, 1912, *BD,* IX, pt. 2, 244; Cambon to Poincaré, Dec. 4, 1912, *DDF,* 3 ser., IV, 642–43.
[3] Viscount Grey of Fallodon, *Twenty-five Years, 1892–1916,* I, 256.

Balkan Peninsula, 1914

bian access to the sea, and the disposition of the Aegean Islands. Solutions were not easy because the balance of power in Eastern Europe was at stake.

Early in the conference, the ambassadors agreed that Albania should be autonomous and under the protection of the powers. More difficult to settle was the question of its size. Austria wanted a large satellite to control the eastern shores of the Adriatic. Serbia, the enemy of Austria-Hungary, wanted a small Albania. The other allies, bordering on Albania, Montenegro and Greece, both wanted parts of Albania.

The disposition of Scutari, in northern Albania, involved the ambassadors in a long argument. Austria wanted it for Albania, and Russia wanted it for Montenegro. Meanwhile, a Montenegrin army besieged the city. Throughout January, February, and most of March, the Triple Entente demanded a Montenegrin Scutari, and the Triple Alliance argued for an Albanian Scutari. By March 21 a compromise gave Scutari to Albania and two other towns to Montenegro and Serbia. The conference agreed on a naval demonstration to force the withdrawal of the Montenegrin army. On April 22, Scutari fell to Montenegro. The meeting of April 25 was devoted to a heated argument over the use of coercion. Benckendorff wanted immediate debarkation of an international contingent to force the surrender of the city. As in the days at Constantinople, Cambon sought to restrain his Russian colleague by advocating a demonstration after they had heard from King Nicholas of Montenegro. The meeting ended without agreement.

Mensdorff demanded either a bombardment, coercion, or an occupation in the meeting of April 28. Cambon countered with the argument that a bombardment would have no better effect than a debarkation. They must bring Nicholas to comply with their request through a promise of compensation for Montenegro. King Nicholas solved the problem by evacuating the city, and international detachments landed by May 14.[4]

[4] Cambon to Pichon, April 28, 30, May 1, 2, 4, 5, 1913, *DDF,* 3 ser., VI, 477–

The ambassadors next turned to the organization of the government of Albania. Austria and Italy proposed a plan that Cambon found quite insufficient. They wanted a prince, probably from some minor German family, Cambon thought; he would be incompetent, an expensive luxury, and would meet a violent death, offering an opportunity for Austrian intervention. Cambon wanted a high commissioner, with a term of three to five years, to govern Albania and set up the police system under instructors from the six powers. The country would be divided into sectors with an officer in charge of each sector. He very definitely opposed the selection of a prince by Italy and Austria. To please Russia, Albania must remain under Turkish sovereignty.

Cambon fought the Austro-Italian proposal so vigorously that Mensdorff thought that this time the French ambassador had gone too far. Even officials in the British Foreign Office agreed. They thought that Cambon had allowed his honor to become involved and now could not retreat, and that Grey ought to quiet him. When the question of the Albanian government came up for discussion in June, the seventy-year-old French ambassador returned to the fray with vigor. He stoutly maintained that they should not send a prince to this region, which lacked law and order; a provisional regime should be set up first. The ambassadors finally created a commission to study the problem. The police system would be erected under the leadership of an officer from a neutral country. By July 29 a compromise was reached; the sovereign prince would be designated by all of the powers, the police would be under the control of Swedish officers, and a commission would supervise the civil and financial administration.[5] Cambon's struggle had not been in vain.

80, 495, 519–22, 528–30, 548–49, 559–61; Lichnowsky to the Foreign Office, April 30, May 1, 1913, *GP,* XXIV, pt. 2, 769, 779–82.

[5] Cambon to Pichon, May 20, June 6, July 29, 1913, *DDF,* 3 ser., VI, 654–57, VII, 37–40, 535–39; Mensdorff to Berchtold, May 27, 1913, *Österreich Ungarns Aussenpolitik von der Bosnischen Krise bis zum Kreigsausbruch* (hereafter cited as *OUA*), VI, 538.

When the ambassadors turned to the delimitation of the southern border of Albania, Cambon took a strong pro-Greek stand in line with his thinking that the advance of the Austro-Hungarian empire in the Balkans must be stopped before it reached the Aegean Sea. The proposed frontier lines gave Albania too much Greek territory. His opposition was so fierce that Grey had to remind him that he was making the meetings drag on forever. They must have a vacation.

Mensdorff admitted that Cambon was "a learned and a very distinguished colleague who today is the dean of all the active ambassadors in Europe," but he had allowed the interests of Greece to become a matter of his own self-conceit. Eventually Cambon gave up the struggle, which Mensdorff thought made him "more Greek than the Greeks." An international commission would settle the question of the border.[6]

In the final days of the conference there was much skirmishing over the eventual disposition of the Aegean Islands. Italy sought to obtain as many of them as possible, particularly the Dodecanese Islands. Cambon fought to keep all of the Aegean Islands for Greece. He was even willing to let the Turks return to the islands, but not the Italians. All of the Aegean Islands in the hands of one of the Triple Alliance would seriously upset the balance of power in the eastern Mediterranean. The conference accepted Grey's proposal: as the Turks evacuated territory in North Africa that now belonged to Italy, the Italians would evacuate those Aegean Islands that they held, and the powers would then take up the disposition of the islands.

The final meeting of the conference came on August 11. Peace had been maintained among the powers who were at odds over the disintegration of the Ottoman Empire. The meetings had been long and tiring, but rather these than a world war. Mensdorff attributed the length of the conference to the fact that Cambon had been too "stiff-necked" over the question of Albania.[7] In view of Cambon's

[6] Cambon to Pichon, March 31, April 8, 9, June 9, 1913, *DDF,* 3 ser., VI, 176-77, 298-300, 307-309, VII, 70-73, 117-20; Mensdorff to Berchtold, May 9, 31, June 6, 21, 1913, *OUA,* VI, 398-400, 572, 607-608, 693-94; Grey to Bertie, May 28, 1913, Grey to Carnegie, June 26, 1913, *BD,* IX, pt. 2, 820-21, 869-70.

Courtesy United Press International, Inc.

Viscount Grey of Fallodon, British secretary of state for foreign affairs, 1905–16.

Courtesy Wide World Photos

At the height of his glory

Wearing a Hussar uniform replete with decorations, Germany's Kaiser Wilhelm is shown at left during a review of his troops in Braunsweig, Germany, in 1913, a year before the outbreak of World War I.

ideas about Austrian aspirations in the Balkans, it was inevitable that he would oppose the Austrian attempt to make Albania a satellite.

Throughout the conference Cambon worked closely with Benckendorff and Grey. So closely did he co-operate with the Russian ambassador that Benckendorff believed that his ideas guided Cambon. Grey appreciated Cambon's help in drafting documents of the conference, "and he sat through all our proceedings and took part in the drudgery of drafting without a sigh of impatience." But Grey felt that Cambon was not satisfied with his impartiality as chairman of the conference because "he feared that Russia might again suffer in prestige and this might react unfavorably upon the Franco-Russian alliance and the Entente with us." To prevent this, "he would have liked a little less neutrality, even a little more partisanship" from Grey. Probably Cambon thought Grey "somewhat wooden and wanting in resource to make the conference move when it stuck on some trivial difficulty."[8]

The three representatives of the Entente powers met almost daily before the meeting of the conference. If anything, these three diplomats co-operated too well. Small wonder that the German government did not want an ambassadors' conference in the July–August crisis of 1914.

Cambon had glimpsed the danger to peace in Austria's desire to push down the Balkan peninsula, but he overlooked the equally strong thrust in the same area from Russia. Once he had been only too much aware of it. Possibly the threat from Germany made him forgive the sins of France's ally. Throughout the conference Cambon was aware of the factor that might keep Europe from an overwhelming conflict: the concert of Europe. If the diplomats would sit around a table and negotiate, the chances of a conflict were lessened because the nation which broke off the talks to commence hostilities would

---

[7] Cambon to Pichon, Aug. 11, 1913, *DDF,* 3 ser., VIII, 12–16; Mensdorff to Berchtold, Aug. 15, 1913, *OUA,* VII, 146–47.

[8] Benckendorff to Sazonov, Feb. 12, 25, 1913, Alexander Graf von Benckendorff, *Diplomatscher Schriftwechsel,* III, 114–119; Grey, *Twenty-five Years,* I, 264.

be branded the aggressor. The conference had been a useful safety valve. But would the powers be willing to sit around a table and negotiate when the next Balkan crisis came?

The year 1914 saw a strengthening of the Entente through military agreements involving not only France and Britain but also Russia. In February, 1914, Sergei Sazonov, the Russian foreign minister, proposed that the Entente be tightened by a formal conference between Grey, Benckendorff, and Cambon. Such a meeting would speed up agreement on policies. Gaston Doumergue, now French foreign minister, suggested that Cambon discuss the matter with Grey because the conference would end the wavering of the Entente in the face of the disciplined union of the Triple Alliance.

All of this appeared quite useless to Cambon. He conferred daily with Benckendorff, and the two saw Grey when it was necessary. What value would there be in a solemn conference presided over by a chairman? Doumergue was insistent, however, claiming that such a conference would improve the Entente and produce the dispatch of concerted instructions simultaneously to the Entente embassies in the capitals.

Cambon presented this suggestion to Grey, but his attitude spoke louder than his words. Nothing came of the proposal. In time Doumergue came to agree with Cambon that Sazonov's idea was much too vague and imprecise. It happened also that the Triple Alliance was not as disciplined as Doumergue imagined—a closer study of the archives in the Quai d'Orsay would have dispelled his fears.

The validity of Cambon's stand appeared questionable in March, 1914, when he learned that Russo-British relations in Persia were far from friendly. There had been disorders in the central sector, which was neither a British nor a Russian sphere of influence. Actually, Russian agents had long been at work in this pseudo-neutral area. Relations had also been injured by the discovery of oil, which the Admiralty coveted.

Cambon blamed imprecision in defining the rights of both parties in the central sector of Persia. Revision, however, would only cause more trouble. He counseled Doumergue to avoid intervention but to help with advice whenever possible.

In April, 1914, the King and Queen of England journeyed to France for a state visit, which offered the diplomats an opportunity to examine the problems of the Entente powers. Cambon warned his government to prevent the discussion of the revision of the Anglo-Russian accord since it would involve the Persian question. In the midst of the festivities, Cambon, Doumergue, Grey, and Poincaré, now president of the Republic, met to discuss mutual affairs. From the available records it appears that Cambon's contribution was slight since this was a matter for the politicians.

As a result of this conference, however, Grey consented to discussions among the military staffs of Britain, Russia, and France. Later, Cambon was instructed to seek some agreement on consultations among the naval staffs of the Triple Entente. For the moment, the battle over Home Rule for Ireland held the attention of the British cabinet. Not until May 14 did Britain agree to naval arrangements with Russia similar to those between Britain and France.

Cambon and Benckendorff met in the Foreign Office on May 19, 1914. There Benckendorff saw the letters that Cambon and Grey had exchanged in 1912. Grey explained the form of the Anglo-French arrangement, whereupon Benckendorff demanded to see the written agreements between the parties. Cambon dissuaded him with the explanation that these were of little political importance and only of a technical nature. A well-grounded fear of security leaks in the Russian diplomatic service prompted Cambon to this step. His action was wise, because the naval agreement between Britain and Russia was soon known in Berlin and accounts of it appeared in the newspapers. A German agent had been working in the Russian embassy in London since 1909, so that often Berlin learned about the work of the Russian ambassador before St. Petersburg.

Cambon had urged Asquith to accept the invitation of the Russians. If it were to be turned down by the British cabinet, he feared that the pro-German elements in St. Petersburg would be aided. He viewed the arrangement as important for its political rather than its military scope. The Anglo-Russian Entente could only be reinforced by it. Russia would be more secure against German seductions.[9]

The Triple Entente, which Paul Cambon had helped to create, was on the brink of its greatest trial. The past had been a preparation for a bloody future. The strength of the Entente was deceptive, for the Anglo-Russian dispute over Persia threatened to tear it apart and force France to make an agonizing choice. Only a war would make the Triple Entente a complete alliance. The summer of 1914 brought that war.

[9] Cambon to Jules Cambon, April 29, 1914, *Correspondance*, III, 63–66; Cambon to Doumergue, April 30, May 14, 16, 19, 1914, *DDF*, 3 ser., X, 297–98, 361–62, 371–74, 389–90; Grey to Bertie, May 21, 1914, Goeschen to Grey, May 23, 1914, *BD*, X, pt. 2, 789–92.

XI. WAR!

THE SPRING OF 1914 was pleasant in England. Only the suffragettes made life unhappy for the police and members of Parliament as they cut up pictures in the Royal Academy, exploded bombs in Westminster Abbey, tried to force an entrance into Buckingham Palace, and insulted political speakers whenever possible. From Paris the latest report on women's fashions proclaimed the end of the tight skirt—in the future, skirts would flow. The London County Council was engaged in a solemn debate over the teaching of sex hygiene in the elementary schools. Throughout June the correspondence columns of the *Times* were filled with arguments over the merits of the "aeroplane" and submarine against the battleship. A Russian opera company, led by Chaliapin, filled Covent Garden with successful performances of *Boris Godunov* and *Prince Igor*. The Royal Geographical Society heard a stirring account of the Brazilian adventures of the former Rough Rider, Teddy Roosevelt.

Sunday, June 28, 1914, was quiet. There was some news the next day about the assassination of a foreign archduke. A unique figure passed from British politics when Joseph Chamberlain died quite suddenly on July 2. On July 14 the London *Times,* reviewing the first licensed performance of Ibsen's *Ghosts*, reported, "Its modernism is no longer its most salient feature; it can still appal, but no longer shocks." The politicians were too preoccupied with a bitter struggle over Home Rule for Ireland to pay much attention to a shooting in Sarajevo. There, about 11:30 A.M. on a sunny June 28, the Archduke Ferdinand, heir to the Austro-Hungarian throne, and his consort, Sophia, died of bullet wounds inflicted by Gavrilo Princip.

The assassination impressed Cambon so little that he intended to take a fortnight's vacation in the latter part of July. On July 8, Grey voiced his fears to Cambon that an Austrian *démarche* resulting from the assassination might arouse the Serbs and eventually Russia. Cambon did not think the Austro-Hungarian government seemed inclined to blame Belgrade for the assassination. He hoped that the matter would not cause trouble. The attitude of the French ambassador was conditioned by intelligence from his government that the military fanatics in Austria-Hungary had been curbed.

As early as December 4, 1912, Cambon had foreseen the possibility of trouble between Austria-Hungary and Serbia. He had presented a brilliant analysis of the possibilities in a dispatch to Poincaré. He regarded Austria-Hungary as the "principal creator" of the problem of eastern Europe. The future peace of Europe was dependent on Austria's attitude towards Serbia. For over two hundred years Austria had been expanding eastward at the expense of the Ottoman Empire. This policy had continued with the blessings and help of Berlin. But the Balkan wars had ruined Austrian plans because the Balkan allies seized territory that Austria coveted. Cambon believed that Austrian ambitions still moved in the direction of the Aegean Sea and would result only in war, "immediate or future, in any case inevitable." He was certain that Germany would support Austria in this policy until the two nations' territories would extend from the North Sea to the Aegean.[1]

In spite of this astute appraisal, Cambon treated the assassination lightly. He may have thought that German permission for Austria-Hungary to start a small-scale war would not be given merely because of the assassination of the heir apparent to the Austro-Hungarian throne. From London, the Serbian government did not appear to Cambon to have any connection with the assassination. Surely Germany would not give Austria-Hungary a "blank check" because of the action of a fanatical assassin. Cambon was certain that Berlin

[1] Cambon to Poincaré, Dec. 4, 1912, *DDF,* 3 ser., IV, 647–50.

would restrain Vienna because the assassination did not seem to involve German interests. Since he relied on Germany to curb Austrian foreign policy and did not imagine that the German General Staff could be so irresponsible, Cambon failed to see the imminent danger in the events of June 28, 1914.

Not until July 22 did Cambon again report to Paris on the crisis. In this report he admitted that the feelings of the diplomatic corps in London were not reassuring. Too many people were apprehensive; possibly the Austro-Serbian quarrel would not quiet down. To Cambon the danger lay in the fact that "you cannot reason with those people in Vienna; they have closed minds as if they wore blinders."

The bloody future became plain when Cambon learned of the Austrian ultimatum to Serbia. It meant war. He knew what would happen. "If the British government puts its foot down on the thing today, peace might be saved. But Grey is going to wobble and hesitate. Meanwhile, the Germans will go ahead in the belief that England does not dare intervene. England is sure to join us in the end, but too late."[2] How much Grey would hesitate Cambon did not realize at that moment. Now he prophesied that if the Russians took the part of Serbia, Europe would be exposed to a world war.

When Cambon met Grey on July 24, the latter proposed a four-power mediation by Britain, France, Italy, and Germany at Vienna and St. Petersburg. Cambon countered with the suggestion that they "ask the German government to take the initiative of a *démarche* at Vienna in order to offer a mediation of the four disinterested powers between Austria and Serbia." If Germany would favor such a proposition, time would be gained. Grey claimed that if Serbia took action, he would be powerless to do anything; he did not want to take any action against Austria unless she attacked Serbia. Cambon pointed out the fallacy in Grey's thinking. If they waited until Austria had attacked Serbia, Russia would have to take some action, and it would be too late for any mediation. The important factor was

[2] Cambon to Bienvenu-Martin, July 22, 1914, *ibid.*, X, 791–93; Cambon to Henri Cambon, July 22, 24, 1914, *Correspondence,* III, 68; André Giraud, "Diplomacy, Old and New," *Foreign Affairs,* XXIII (1945), 259–60.

for Germany to propose mediation at Vienna, thus gaining time. Grey came around to Cambon's point of view and agreed to speak to Lichnowsky about it. Cambon believed that Germany was the only power able to restrain Austria-Hungary, who would not make war without the permission of the Wilhelmstrasse.[3]

In Paris, J. B. Bienvenu-Martin, minister of justice, was acting minister of foreign affairs in the absence of René Viviani, the premier and minister of foreign affairs. Viviani had gone to St. Petersburg on a state visit with President Poincaré. In need of advice, the inexperienced Bienvenu-Martin asked Cambon to come to Paris. Leaving London on the afternoon of July 25, Cambon was in Paris that evening. Here a second crisis divided his time and attention: his daughter-in-law was about to make him a grandfather.

The published documents are silent about what Cambon said and did in Paris; he alleged that his work was of little importance. Bienvenu-Martin was unaware of the crisis that involved the ally of France; he saw little danger to the world if Serbia and Austria settled their quarrel by themselves. Cambon probably opened Bienvenu-Martin's eyes to the danger of world conflict, for this was no longer a mere Balkan squabble.

By July 26, Cambon had convinced Bienvenu-Martin to call for the return of Viviani and Poincaré. The same day Aimé de Fleuriau, embassy secretary, telegraphed from London, "Sir E. Grey, Sir A. Nicolson, and Count Benckendorff are most embarrassed at your absence, and they eagerly desire your prompt return. Your presence here Tuesday will probably be useful."

Bienvenu-Martin, probably at the prompting of Cambon, began to take a stronger stand against the rush to war when he warned Baron Wilhelm von Schoen, the German ambassador, that if Austria entered Serbia, "the situation would force Russia to declare herself and would precipitate the war which Germany wished to avoid." When the Austrian ambassador announced that Austria would use force to punish Serbia for her failure to yield on all points of the

---

[3] Cambon to Bienvenu-Martin, July 24, 1914, *DDF,* 3 ser., XI, 22–23; Grey to Bertie, July 24, 1914, *BD,* XI, 77–78.

WAR!

ultimatum, Bienvenu-Martin warned the Hapsburg representative that in demanding complete adherence, Austria "would assume a heavy responsibility in unleashing a war of which no one could measure the extent."

But it was time for Cambon to return to London, from which Grey had gone to the country for the week end at 6:00 P.M. on July 25. This was indicative of Grey's attitude—he had informed Lichnowsky that the only chance for peace was for Austria and Russia to avoid crossing their frontiers after they had mobilized. He still saw no need for intervention between Austria and Serbia. Someone was needed to alert Grey to the dangers of his gropings. Cambon arrived back in London late on July 27.[4]

The wisdom of Cambon's leaving London in the midst of a crisis has been questioned. Certainly a strong, experienced hand was needed in Paris at this time, with the President of the Republic and the Foreign Minister hundreds of miles away. Once Viviani was back in Paris, France again had a foreign policy. Cambon was needed to open Bienvenu-Martin's eyes to the realities of the situation. But Grey was as unaware of the impending calamity as Bienvenu-Martin. Cambon's presence was needed in both capitals.

Probably it would have been better for Cambon to advise Bienvenu-Martin by telegraph. Bienvenu-Martin had already done his worst by leading the Austrian and German foreign offices to feel that Austria could devour Serbia without involving either Russia, Germany, or France. The moral is apparent: if foreign ministers (or foreign secretaries) must be absent, return quickly, but leave competent men in charge; the fate of millions may depend upon them.

When Cambon saw Grey early on July 28, he voiced approval of Churchill's order for the fleet to remain together after the close of the current maneuvers. For, Cambon declared, "if once it were assumed that Britain would certainly stand aside from a European war, the chance of preserving peace would be very much imperiled."

[4] H. Cambon, *Paul Cambon,* 265–66; Ferry to Fleuriau, July 26, 1914, Fleuriau to Bienvenu-Martin, July 26, 1914, Bienvenu-Martin to Bapst, July 26, 1914, circular of Bienvenu-Martin, July 27, 1914, *DDF,* 3 ser., XI, 77, 81, 122–23.

Hourly, the situation grew more confused and desperate. Serbia had accepted the Austrian ultimatum with certain reservations that were unsatisfactory to Vienna. Grey proposed a mediation between Austria and Russia of four "disinterested" powers—Britain, Germany, France, and Italy. But Sazonov, the Russian foreign minster, began direct talks with the Austrians without waiting for mediation. Such tactics annoyed Cambon because the erratic Russian would only aggravate the crisis that the four nations might have pacified. The German Foreign Office, which had no intention of moderating Austrian action, used Sazanov's suggestion to sidetrack the four-power mediation until Austria and Russia could complete their talks. Before anything could be concluded, however, the Austrian declaration of war on Serbia on July 28 brought the world to the brink of war.

When Grey saw Lichnowsky on the twenty-ninth, the British foreign secretary would not make any statement of British intentions in view of the Austrian declaration of war. Later the same day, Cambon requested a statement on British intentions and Grey's response was indicative of future trouble for Anglo-French relations. To Grey, the crisis was not analogous to the Moroccan crises in 1905 and 1911 when Anglo-French arrangements were involved. It was a matter of Austrian or Russian supremacy in the Balkans. "That one or the other of these two powers obtains pre-eminence matters little to us, and if the conflict remains limited to Austria and Serbia or Russia, we are not going to involve ourselves in it." Grey admitted that the situation would be radically altered if Germany aided Austria against Russia and France were involved. "Then it would be a question concerning the European equilibrium, and England would have to consider whether she ought to intervene." He alleged that Britain was secretly making dispositions of her armed forces, and that Lichnowsky had so been informed.

Cambon replied, "We await from one hour to the next for Germany to demand that we remain neutral while she attacks Russia. Such assurance we cannot give her. We are obliged to aid Russia in case she is attacked."[5]

[5] Grey to Bertie, July 29, 1914, *BD*, XI, 180; Cambon to Viviani, July 29,

WAR!

Here was the misunderstanding that caused Cambon untold anguish in the next few days. Grey sought to maintain British neutrality, which the staff discussion and naval convention had destroyed. To Cambon, there was the danger of another 1870—Germany would overrun France and become the arbiter of Europe while Grey pondered legal technicalities. Cambon regarded the problem from a strategic standpoint, Grey from a legal one. The British foreign secretary was undoubtedly sympathetic to Cambon's plight, but he had to contend with a cabinet whose members inclined toward pacifism and a Parliament whose support in war was doubtful.

Under instructions from Viviani, who had returned to Paris, Cambon called on Grey on July 30 and informed him of German troop movements. No longer was this a conflict of influence between Austria-Hungary and Russia; France was menaced by aggression. Cambon showed Grey reports that Germany was more advanced in military preparation than France. Because Germany would probably demand that France remain neutral in a Russo-German war, Cambon wanted a discussion of every hypothesis. In particular, what would Britain do if France were attacked by Germany? Grey would give no answer; he promised a reply on July 31 after the cabinet meeting.

On the afternoon of the next day, Cambon gave Grey a telegram from Jules Cambon in Berlin reporting that Britain's indecision aided the German militarists. Grey retorted that this was not true. Germany had been warned that the question of British neutrality was still undecided; if the war became general, involving France, Britain could be drawn in. Cambon changed the subject and asked for a reply to his request of the previous day. Grey answered that the cabinet could not make a pledge. Because of the present attitude of public opinion and Parliament, the cabinet could not make any formal declaration. Parliament could not be committed in advance. Up to the moment no pledges seemed to be involved, but the violation of Belgian neutrality could change this situation. Cambon, deeply disappointed, grasped at the one remaining chance. Would Britain support

1914, *DDF*, 3 ser., XI, 228–29; Raymond Recouly, *Les heures tragiques d'avant-guerre*, 48–49.

France only if she were invaded by German forces? Again Grey could not give a pledge in advance. He cautioned Cambon that Russia's mobilization on July 31 might make it appear that she had forced mobilization on Germany. Cambon would not be put off by this reflection on the ally of France. He insisted that Germany had rejected proposals for peace at the very start of the crisis. The measures that Germany had taken on the French frontier showed her intentions. If the British were indifferent, they would repeat the error of 1870, Cambon declared. It would be more perilous because Britain would be isolated and dependent on a victorious Germany.

Again he begged Grey to insist on some guarantee from the cabinet. Grey would say only that if the situation changed, he would ask the cabinet to take up the matter again. The painful interview ended. As he left the Foreign Office, Cambon's old friend Nicolson gave him what consolation he could, assuring him that the cabinet would meet the next day and Grey would take up the discussion again.

Telegrams began to come to the French embassy from Paris reporting German troop movements. Warlike acts had occurred near the French frontier. Around midnight, Cambon sent a copy of a telegram relating German troop movements to Nicolson for Grey's use at the cabinet meeting. It might shock the cabinet into action.[6]

August 1 began with the news of a German ultimatum to St. Petersburg, demanding that Russian mobilization cease. At the same time Germany began preparations for mobilization and inquired about the French attitude.

After the cabinet meeting on August 1, Grey announced to Cambon that the cabinet was opposed to any intervention. He reminded the Ambassador that this was not the Moroccan crisis; therefore, Britain had no obligations that would justify the use of British arms. It would be unfortunate if France could not take advantage of the German offer to remain neutral in a Russo-German war. This did not mean that under no circumstances would Britain assist France,

[6] Cambon to Viviani, July 31, 1914, Viviani to Cambon, July 31, 1914, *DDF*, 3 ser., XI, 329–30, 365–66, 375–76; Grey to Bertie, July 31, 1914, Cambon to Nicolson, July 31, 1914, *BD*, XI, 225–27; Recouly, *Les heures*, 50–51.

WAR!

but France must make her own decision without reckoning on assistance that the British government could not promise.

Cambon refused to transmit this statement to his government; he would say that the cabinet had not reached any decision. But, Grey countered, they had reached a decision; they could not ask Parliament to send an expeditionary force to the Continent unless British interests were more deeply involved. Cambon was shocked, for it seemed to him that British interests were very much involved. He implored Grey to have the matter reconsidered. As a last resort, he reminded Grey that France had left her coasts undefended in accordance with the naval convention of 1912. French troops had been drawn back ten kilometers from the frontier to prevent any incidents and to pacify British public opinion. By land and by sea France lay open to invasion; indeed, only a few old ships guarded the Channel. Had the naval convention been concluded just for the sake of Britain, Cambon bluntly asked? "Although there is not a formal alliance," he pleaded, "does not Britain have a moral obligation to help us, to at least give us the help of your fleet since it is on your advice that we have sent ours away?" If there was no aid for France, would not the Entente end? What would be Britain's position after Germany had conquered France? Grey conceded the force of Cambon's arguments. Possibly a German attack on the undefended French coast and a violation of Belgian neutrality might change public opinion. Cambon could inform his government that the question of Belgium was being discussed. Grey would bring up the question of the French coasts in the cabinet meeting on August 2.

Although Cambon knew that Grey was meeting resistance in the cabinet, this interview unnerved him. He faced ruin, for he had assured his government that British support could be depended upon when the time of great danger came. Would all this be thrown back in his face by his enemies at the Quai d'Orsay?

Close to hysteria, his face white, he staggered from Grey's office into the adjoining room, where Nicolson guided him to a chair. "They are going to drop us; they are going to drop us," he muttered as Nicolson tried to comfort him. Nicolson rushed to ask Grey if the government had refused aid to France. Grey answered only with a despairing shrug. Angrily Nicolson snapped, "You will render us a byword among nations." Nicolson returned to Cambon, who had recovered his composure. He murmured, as he left, that perhaps it was time to produce publicly *"mon petit papier,"* referring to the Grey-Cambon letters of 1912.[7]

In Paris, Viviani had informed the German ambassador that "France will act in accordance with her interests." By 3:45 P.M. the same afternoon, the French government ordered mobilization of the armed forces. The Imperial German government ordered mobilization at 5:00 P.M. and declared war on Russia by 6:00 P.M.

The uncertainty of the opposition's position contributed to Grey's indecision. If they allied with the pacifists in the Liberal party, the government would be outvoted and a Parliamentary crisis would result. Agreement on war policy seemed impossible under these circumstances, although such was not the case.

Lord George Lloyd and Leopold Amery, Conservative leaders, unhappy about the information they had received that the government would desert France, on the thirty-first began to rally members of their party to stronger support of France. Lloyd and Leo Maxse, editor of the *National Review,* seeking more information from Cambon, called on him on August 1 after his painful interview with Grey. They found him bitter over the British attitude and quite blunt.

He conceded that Britain was under no written obligation, for not even a scrap of paper existed. But there was more—the general staffs had consulted, Britain had seen French plans and preparations, the French fleet was in the Mediterranean because of their arrangements, and the coasts of France were open to Germany. During the last few years, every British action seemed to assure British support. Now neutral Britain would deliver the French coast to the Germans. "If you stay out and we survive, we shall not move a finger to save you

---

[7] Viviani to Cambon, Aug. 1, 1914, Cambon to Viviani, Aug. 1, 1914, *DDF,* 3 ser., XI, 393–94, 424–25; Grey to Bertie, Aug. 1, 1914, *BD,* XI, 253–60; Recouly, *Les heures,* 51–54; Nicolson, *Sir Arthur Nicolson,* 419–20; interview with Harold Nicolson.

from being crushed by the Germans later," Cambon cried. "If we lose, you will share our fate anyhow, and your condition will be even worse."

The aged ambassador's voice crackled with fury as he cried, "Honor! Does England know what honor is?"

Lloyd was shaken by the outburst from the normally calm Frenchman. He asked the government's opinion, and Cambon replied that the Foreign Office insisted that the opposition could not be counted on to support the government in any line of action that might lead to war. Lloyd denied this. But, Cambon demanded, "Where are your leaders?" Lloyd had no answer, because most of the Conservative leaders were in the country enjoying the Bank Holiday.

Worried over Cambon's report, Lloyd and Amery hurried to round up the Conservative leaders. A midnight meeting followed at Austen Chamberlain's home. Those present agreed to force some action from the most prominent absentees: Bonar Law and Lansdowne, the Conservative leaders in the Commons and in the House of Lords. By 10:00 A.M. the next morning Chamberlain had won Landsdowne and Bonar Law over to positive action. A letter was sent to Asquith announcing that the opposition offered its support and adding a warning about the danger to the honor and security of Britain if she did not aid France in the crisis.[8] Asquith and Grey now knew that no matter how many defections there might be in the Liberal party, with the help of the Conservatives they would be able to muster enough votes to aid France.

The orders for full mobilization of the French Army were posted outside Albert Gate House. They were little noticed by the average Londoner, who was more interested in enjoying the pleasant Bank Holiday.

In a last effort to influence the government, Cambon sent a note to Nicolson on the afternoon of the first reminding him that France had moved her fleets to the Mediterranean with the understanding

---

[8] C. F. Adams, *Life of Lord Lloyd,* 59–60; Sir Austen Chamberlain, *Down the Years,* 94–101; Ian Colvin, *The Life of Lord Carson,* III, 14–20; L. S. Amery, *My Political Life,* II, 15–19.

that Britain would protect the northern and western coasts. Now there was a record in the files of the Foreign Office on the official attitude of the French ambassador toward Britain's policy. Nicolson forwarded Cambon's reminder to Grey, who agreed to take up the matter with the cabinet on August 2.

One of the early risers among the secretaries at Albert Gate House on August 2 found a telegram announcing the invasion of Luxembourg and numerous violations of the French border. Cambon read it as he finished dressing. He thought that perhaps this might influence the British, and had a call put through to the Foreign Office requesting an interview. Grey balked at seeing Cambon until 3:00 P.M., after the cabinet meeting, but the Ambassador's insistence led Grey to see him in the morning. While Cambon finished dressing, a secretary looked hastily through the embassy files for a copy of the treaty guaranteeing the neutrality of Luxembourg to which Germany and Britain had agreed.

At their meeting, Cambon showed Grey the copy of the treaty of 1867 guaranteeing the neutrality of Luxembourg. Surely this would produce British aid. Grey adopted the point of view of a previous administration and claimed that the treaty was a collective instrument. If Germany violated the treaty, Britain was released from her obligation. Cambon argued that the invasion of Luxembourg indicated that a violation of Belgian territory would be next. Grey would say only that he had warned Lichnowsky to expect opposition by British public opinion to any violation of Belgian neutrality, but he did promise that the cabinet would discuss the use of British naval forces to protect the coasts of France.

Cambon returned to the embassy to await the outcome of the cabinet meeting at 11:00 A.M. Meantime, Wickham Steed, a foreign correspondent of the London *Times,* called at the embassy. In an interview with Cambon, he mentioned the violation of the neutrality of Luxembourg. Cambon pointed to a copy of the treaty and, trying to control his emotions, said: "There is the signature of England. I have asked Grey whether England means to respect it."

"What did he say?" asked Steed.

WAR!

"Nothing, nothing," Cambon replied. His voice was heavy with sarcasm as he snarled, "I do not even know whether this evening the word 'honor' will not have to be struck out of the British vocabulary!"[9]

That afternoon Cambon returned to the Foreign Office to hear the result of the cabinet meeting. Grey announced that conditions in Egypt and India prevented the use of British troops, but he handed Cambon a note stating that the British fleet would protect the coasts of France if German warships attempted to come through the North Sea and into the English Channel. He still maintained his earlier interpretation of the treaty guaranteeing the neutrality of Luxembourg. Belgium was a different case, however, because Britain had guaranteed her neutrality as an individual nation. If Belgian neutrality were violated, he was willing to ask that it be considered a *casus belli*. Further, he took great pains to remind Cambon that the pledge to protect the coasts of France did not mean that Britain would go to war with Germany. Cambon asked only if two British divisions could be sent to France for their moral effect. Grey refused the request, saying that Britain could not safely send her troops out of the country at the moment.

Possibly Grey and the cabinet did not realize that once they had committed the fleet to action against Germany in the North Sea, it would be only a matter of time until all the armed forces of Britain would be engaged. With great relief, Cambon realized that he had won his greatest battle. He observed, "A great country does not really make war in halves. From the moment that it decides to make war on the sea, it is fatally led to make war also on land."[10]

Long into the night of August 2–3 crowds demonstrated for France in front of the embassy. Although the seventy-one-year-old ambassador appreciated their sentiments, he wanted to sleep after a trying

---

[9] Cambon to Nicolson, Aug. 1, 1914, *BD*, XI, 252; Viviani to Cambon, Aug. 2, 1914, Cambon to Viviani, Aug. 2, 1914, *DDF,* 3 ser., XI, 579; François Charles-Roux, *Trois ambassades français à la veille de la guerre,* 58–59; H. W. Steed, *Through Thirty Years,* II, 13–16; interview with H. W. Steed.

[10] Cambon to Viviani, Aug. 2, 1914, *DDF,* 3 ser., XI, 468–70; Grey to Bertie, Aug. 2, 1914, *BD,* XI, 274–75; Recouly, *Les heures,* 55–56.

day. Not until after 1:00 A.M. were peace and quiet restored to Albert Gate House.

Before Grey went to the House of Commons on August 3, Cambon tried unsuccessfully to obtain something further than the statement of August 2 regarding the fleet. Grey would not be definite because he was not sure of the reaction of the House of Commons to his remarks. He assured Cambon that the British fleet would give full protection to the French coasts. A German attack there would mean war with Great Britain.

Cambon telegraphed early that evening to Paris that Grey's speech in the House had been enthusiastically received. He had been supported in his wish to enforce the treaty guaranteeing the neutrality of Belgium—the House would vote money to the government for war. Paul Cambon's career would not be ruined.

That same evening, the Quai d'Orsay received the German declaration of war. Grey's pledge to Cambon had not come too soon.

Late on August 3, Grey informed Cambon that his government could announce officially the pledge of British naval aid. They could even announce the completion of the mobilization of the British fleet and the issuance of orders for the mobilization of the British Army. An ultimatum would be sent to the German government on the subject of Belgian neutrality.

On August 4, Grey told Cambon of the dispatch of the ultimatum to Germany. The German government had been asked to cease her violation of the Belgian neutrality; failing a satisfactory reply, the British government would take the steps necessary to uphold the treaty to which she was a party with Germany. Cambon asked what would happen if the German answer was in the negative.

"War!" Grey replied.

"How will you make war?" Cambon asked. "Will you embark your expeditionary force immediately?"

"No," Grey replied, "we will blockade all the German ports. I have already explained to you that we have need of our forces to prepare our defenses at certain points and that public opinion is not favorable to an expeditionary force."

WAR!

"Your explanations do not satisfy me," Cambon answered. "I do not think that you should hamper yourself by such fragile considerations. As for public opinion, it is not what it was three days ago. It wants war with all its might. The moment is decisive; a statesman would seize it. You will be forced by pressure of public opinion to intervene on the Continent, but your intervention must be immediate in order to be effective."

Taking a pencil and map, Cambon indicated to Grey the necessity for British military support on the left flank of the French line. He reminded Grey that in the staff talks between France and Britain, it had been agreed that "the embarkation of material and provisions ought to commence the second day of the mobilization." This would last five days, and "each instant lost would lead to complications in the execution of the French program." Cambon appealed for a discussion of this matter with the cabinet, and Grey agreed. At the cabinet meeting of August 5, the military leaders convinced the cabinet of the necessity of an immediate dispatch of an expeditionary force to the Continent.

Cambon returned to the embassy around 10:30 P.M., August 4, after seeing Grey and obtaining the latest information on the ultimatum to Germany. Before he went to bed after another tiring day, he stopped to talk with some of the secretaries. As the clock struck eleven, all fell silent. "Gentlemen, England has declared war," Cambon quietly remarked.[11] The Entente Cordiale had become a fighting force.

Certainly Paul Cambon did not bring Britain into the war alone. Forces and events beyond his control saved him from disaster, for he was almost helpless. He called August 2, 1914, "the day through which I passed the darkest moments of my life." Because he could see little military value for France in the Russian alliance, he dreaded a repetition of 1870, when France had been forced to face Germany alone. By 1914, he believed that there had been such a change in

---

[11] Cambon to Doumergue, Aug. 4, 1914, *DDF,* 3 ser., XI, 531–32, 552; H. Cambon, *Paul Cambon,* 271; Charles-Roux, *Trois ambassades,* 71–72. The ultimatum expired midnight Berlin time, or 11:00 P.M. London time.

British opinion that it would be obvious where British interests lay. He tried to impress on Grey that British interests could not endure a German victory. As late as August 2, the British government's policy was not to intervene to save France. The German ultimatum and invasion of Belgium changed British policy and saved Cambon. France was saved also by the military agreements involving joint planning, which had been drawn up and completed at Cambon's insistence.

Cambon may not have realized the extent of the opposition in the cabinet to British intervention on the Continent. Here he was saved by the offer of the Conservatives to support the government and by the invasion of Belgium. Years later, he admitted that the delay had been helpful because it had enabled public opinion to rally behind the government.

More than Grey and Asquith, Cambon recognized that it was only a fiction to maintain that neither government was committed to the other and, consequently, a free agent. At the same time, Grey's failure to commit Britain so frightened Cambon that he wondered if he had been wrong to depend on Britain.[12]

In this crisis Cambon was not the Machiavelli some have claimed he was. He was a frightened diplomat who feared that his country would be destroyed and his career ruined. He was constantly working against time during this crisis, thus he could not write any personal letters. He had thought that Great Britain would understand her commitment and that she would move quickly because speed was so essential. Britain would not wait for prolonged Parliamentary discussions to influence public opinion. The invasion of Belgium accomplished what Cambon could not, for it forced a speedier British decision to intervene on the Continent.

The road had been long and rough from the dark days of Fashoda, and darker days lay ahead, but the erstwhile opponents had become allies in a terrible world struggle.

The issue was now in the hands of the generals who had super-

[12] Cambon to Xavier Charmes, Aug. 20, 1914, Cambon to Henri Cambon, Aug. 2, 1914, *Correspondance,* III, 119–20; interviews with Henri Cambon and H. W. Steed.

seded the diplomats. Armies raced to grapple with each other. General staffs planned and plotted to find the death blow for their enemies. Crowds thronged the streets of the belligerents' capitals crying for swift victory and cheering the departing warriors. They believed that victory would be sweet and swift, but it was neither. Massed troops struggled with each other; strategy was forgotten and neglected. It was a war of power against power, producing a bath of blood undreamed of by civilized men. In the West, the British, French, and Belgian armies slowed down the German avalanche and broke it at the First Battle of the Marne. Thereafter it became a dreary, bloody struggle in the mud of the trenches. The swift Russian advance on the East disrupted the German plans and saved France. The holocaust had become a stalemate not to be ended until more than four years later.

Until the British and French governments open their archives to the historian, the diplomatic history of the first world war of the twentieth century will be necessarily incomplete. Thus there can be no full story of Paul Cambon's work.

The war produced a change in Cambon's tasks. In addition to negotiating diplomatic agreements, he had to foster the military co-operation of the allies. Co-ordinated action between Britain and France was difficult to achieve, for their recent history gave them little experience in co-operative military effort, with the exception of the Crimean War, where mistakes were the rule and not the exception.

Cambon on his own initiative helped to negotiate an economic accord between France and Britain on August 21, 1914, whereby Britain would handle the supply problems for both allies. A mixed commission, meeting in London, would allot the supplies. Before the end of August, the plan saved Paris, cut off from supplies because of the German advance. Despite the accord, differences in economy and mistakes in planning produced varying shortages and led to quarrels between the allies.

The Entente powers became a formal, wartime alliance when Benckendorff, Cambon, and Grey signed an agreement on September 5, 1914, pledging their nations to make no separate peace and to agree on terms prior to any negotiations with the enemy. Only the Russian Revolution would invalidate this promise.

Early in the war, the Entente powers sought to make Italy an ally. Sazonov sent instructions early in August, 1914, for Benckendorff to unite with Cambon in pressing Italy to enter the conflict. Delcassé, once again foreign minister, sent similar instructions to Cambon. Both ambassadors objected, claiming that if pressure were placed on San Giuliano, the Italian foreign minister, Italy would feel her prestige had been injured. More subtle tactics should be used. The Entente should wait until they had won more substantial victories. Sazonov could speak to the Italian ambassador in the name of the Entente. The Italians would have the illusion of acting independently and according to their own wishes and interests.

By December, 1914, Italy had begun to bargain with both sides, although formal negotiations did not begin until March, 1915. On April 26, 1915, the Treaty of London was signed by Cambon, Benckendorff, Grey, and Imperiali. Under it, Italy would receive territory in which Italians lived within the Austro-Hungarian frontiers, in addition to Turkish territory in Asia Minor, some of the Dalmatian Islands, and additional territory in Africa.

At the time of the present writing, it is impossible to discover exactly the part played by Paul Cambon in these negotiations because of the paucity of documents. Benckendorff reported that Cambon appeared to be the happiest person at the signing of the treaty. He had been restless and dissatisfied at the delays during the negotiations, and now a great burden seemed to be lifted. Probably Cambon saw this treaty as a device to give France another ally and avoid the debacle of 1870. The price agreed on was outrageous; it would be difficult to render payment; but it was a war, and in such times nations must often make promises that later prove impossible to keep. In the words of Delcassé: "We may have done wrong, but we were placed in a terrible position. Italy put a pistol at our heads."[13]

Relations between the wartime allies were not always smooth. In

[13] Steed, *Through Thirty Years,* II, 66.

WAR!

May, 1915, a Major Richardson returned from France and published a letter in the London *Times* criticizing the British government for its failure to institute conscription for the armed forces when France had begun to call up her last reserves. The British government decided to prosecute the *Times* for breach of security regulations and, at the same time, silence the *Times's* criticisms of the war effort. The government claimed that the case had been instituted at the insistence of the French military attaché. When questioned about this matter, Cambon replied that he had not known about it and had not authorized it. Without success, he tried to have the case dropped. He could obtain only the government's promise that after the conviction the announcement would be made that the French government had had nothing to do with the institution of the case.

Cambon was satisfied to let the matter drop there, but Steed, of the *Times,* pointed out that if this statement were made at the trial and the *Times* acquitted, it would appear that the French government sought to escape the discredit of the prosecution's failure. If the *Times* were convicted, the statement would imply that the French government wanted to avoid the odium of instigating the condemnation. Cambon immediately authorized Steed to publish a statement regarding the French government's attitude, declaring, "I authorize you to state that the French government neither desired, knew, nor approved of this prosecution; and you may add that had I known of it or been consulted about it, I should have protested against it. I know that the only object of the *Times* was to help in winning the war." He was prepared to be a defense witness for the *Times*. Eventually the case was quashed because French and German papers were full of similar stories about the British war effort.[14]

Cambon was present at the first meeting of the heads of the French and British governments held at Dunkerque on October 27, 1914, and at many of the subsequent meetings. Since air travel across the English Channel had not yet been developed, the tiring journeys had to be made by boat-train. As the meetings became larger, the embassy often served as a hotel.

[14] *Ibid.,* 72–74; interview with H. W. Steed.

In the summer of 1915, Cambon helped to facilitate a meeting of Allied military and civilian leaders at Calais. Here he failed to secure the withdrawal from Gallipoli of the Allied forces, which were bogged down in an effort to outflank the Central Powers. In December, Cambon obtained a meeting to discuss the evacuation of Salonica, where an Allied force was halted in an effort to aid Serbia. Against the British, he supported the argument that the evacuation would have disastrous political consequences, but no decision was taken then. Through a later decision, the Allied force stayed, and in 1918 the collapse of the Central Powers began on this front.

Cambon took part in subsequent meetings, but his role in them will not be clear until the historian can examine the documents. By 1916, he was convinced the meetings of the leaders of the Allied powers occurred too frequently and with little gain for the Allied cause. Too often, he found, the ministers only exchanged useless proposals about trivial matters. After the trip, they could give the cabinet a lengthy report of their adventures and the receptions held in their honor. They were allowed to issue a statement extolling the concessions they obtained, yet nothing had been accomplished.

In 1917, Cambon was furious when another meeting was called in London. The members of the French cabinet trooped over to Britain for a vacation from Paris and the Chamber of Deputies.

As Marshal Ferdinand Foch descended from the train, he asked Cambon, "Do you know what we came here to do?"

"No," the ambassador replied.

"Neither do I." Foch muttered.[15]

The war dragged on through 1916. Cambon was amazed when the British finally instituted conscription in this year. It was a revolution and "the most extraordinary thing that we have seen during the war."

In December, 1916, Cambon observed the eighteenth anniversary of the beginning of his mission to London. With not a little pride he wrote that his mission "will be longer than the reign of Louis-

[15] H. Cambon, *Paul Cambon*, 275–78, 280–82; Cambon to Henri Cambon, Jan. 20, 1916, Oct. 11, 1917, *Correspondance*, III, 98–99, 198.

Phillipe, which itself was longer than any of the regimes which succeeded each other in France since the Revolution."[16]

In 1917, Cambon brought his prestige and influence to bear on Alexandre Ribot, the new prime minister, to stop the French military staff from maintaining a liaison officer in the War Office in London. Cambon claimed that the French staff was carrying on secret relations with their opposite numbers on the British staff. An agent of the French staff had become an amateur ambassador and had begun to intrigue in behalf of David Lloyd George, now British prime minister. The latter wanted the French staff to help in the removal of Douglas Haig from his post as commander-in-chief of the British Armies. Cambon warned Ribot, "There cannot exist in France a military government independent of the government over which you preside and which, as you have proclaimed, is the supreme director of the war." Cambon's objection was on the grounds that this arrangement placed the military outside the control not only of the embassy but also of the ministry of war and the government itself. Although Cambon helped to end this first attempt, a later one succeeded.[17] Probably this was an attempt by the military chiefs of France to make up for the lack of a combined general-staff organization. Constitutionally Cambon was correct, but militarily the arrangement left much to be desired.

Austria-Hungary began to put out peace feelers in April of 1917. Prince Sixte of Bourbon-Parma, brother-in-law of the Austrian emperor and a Belgian army officer, came to Paris in April with an offer of a separate peace between France and Austria. The peace proposals did not contain any compensations for Italy and denied France Alsace-Lorraine. These omissions doomed them.

Sixte, in search of advice, talked with Cambon in the latter's apartment on the Boulevard Haussmann in Paris on April 14. Cambon advised him to discuss the proposals with the Italians, but warned him that they would make huge demands that would need trimming.

---

[16] Cambon to Henri Cambon, May 6, Dec. 8, 1916, *ibid.,* 104–106, 133–34.
[17] Cambon to Henri Cambon, May 3, 1917, *ibid.,* 165–66; Cambon to Ribot, March 27, 1917, *Journal d'Alexandre Ribot,* 48–49.

He observed, ironically, that the Entente was supposed to be fighting for nationalities, but already the Italians had installed themselves on the island of Corfu, which was Greek. Because Sixte contemplated a trip to Britain to talk with Lloyd George, he asked Cambon for his opinion of the fiery prime minister. Cambon answered that Lloyd George was more Gallic than English and what he said was not to be depended upon. However, Cambon admitted, Lloyd George was valuable because he kept the cabinet well informed and was willing to resort to slightly unconstitutional means to get on with the war.

Back in London in May, Cambon arranged for a meeting between Sixte and Lloyd George, which was unsuccessful. Little could be achieved because of the Italian demands and the Allied insistence that either Austria-Hungary impose terms on Germany or assist the Allies against her. Contrary to the statements of Lloyd George, Cambon did not destroy this peace offer. Rather, it was doomed from the start.[18]

When Cambon traveled to Windsor Castle on September 1, George V sent for him immediately on his arrival. The King asked him to accept the Order of the Bath for his nineteen years of service to the two nations. Deeply impressed, Cambon accepted it in the same room in which he had presented his letters of accreditation to Victoria in 1898. He could think only of the differences that time and diplomacy had made in the relations of the two nations—once enemies over Fashoda and now allied in a world struggle.

The winter of 1917-18 was grim for Cambon. The Kerensky government collapsed before the Bolsheviks. Yet he realized that bad though the present might be, the future looked worse.

In February, 1918, Great Britain introduced meat rationing, a step Cambon thought unnecessary if there were properly organized distribution. When the ladies of the diplomatic colony learned of the size of their ration, they annoyed Cambon until he asked the Foreign Office for a larger one.

"But what if they do nothing about it?" the ladies moaned.

[18] Prince Sixte of Bourbon-Parma, *L'offre de paix séparée de L'Autriche,* 122-27, 204, 211-15; Ribot, *Journal,* 60-66, 71-73.

"We will assemble the entire diplomatic corps, both men and women," Cambon retorted, "and will draw lots to see who will eat!"[19]

By April, 1918, the old ambassador's spirits were low.

> Poor Europe, who destroys herself, and who will be tortured worse than ever as soon as she recovers, in spite of all the efforts of the ingenious spirits who imagine they can count on a perpetual peace after this war. . . . I ponder with sadness what will become of her.
>
> In setting things aright, she will turn to the American school where she will modernize herself; this will no longer be the Europe which we belong to and which we love. I am too old to assist in this catastrophe.
>
> This will be the result brought on by what they call scientific progress: the worst enemy of beauty, politeness, elegance, and good manners. After the war, the women who are aviators, factory workers mechanics, surgeons, and, at least in England, pretend to carry rifles, will no longer be women. Already they wear pants. They will keep them. They will ride astride a horse; there will not be any more riding skirts. They will march; they will smoke; they will swear like men: that will be the end of all that remains of good society.[20]

Cambon's sadness turned to joy when he heard the news in September, 1918, of the mounting defeats of the Central Powers. "What success!" he cried. "It is like a dream." As the German defeats continued through October and the end of the war seemed at hand, the diplomat could not avoid worry over the peace problems: "What messes, what difficulties in order to reach an agreement between the Allies for peace! All the little ones, the oppressed ones, all the Balkans will have open mouths. Italy is insatiable; she demands everything. What quarrels for the future!"

[19] Cambon to Xavier Charmes, Nov. 15, 21, 1917, Cambon to Henri Cambon, Feb. 12, 1918, *Correspondance,* III, 198–99, 224.

[20] Cambon to Boppe, April 18, 1918, *ibid.,* 249–50.

Cambon wanted immediate discussions over the peace conditions before hostilities ceased. Pichon, now foreign minister, shied away because he thought such discussions might cause unpleasantness with the Italians. "We have reserved for ourselves some future embarrassments," prophesied Cambon, "from which the Germans will not fail to profit."

At last on November 11, came the end of a terrible war. At the moment of triumph, Paul Cambon was uneasy over the future of Germany. "I fear greatly," he wrote, "the future constitution of a great socialist federation which will create a Germany that will be more unified and stronger than that of the Empire." The Germany he described would one day vanquish the Third Republic, in whose behalf he had labored so long. But for the moment, it was sweet peace: "I dare not think about the great difficulties we have reserved for ourselves, but, whatever they may be, I will have seen the revenge for 1870, and I can leave this earth without regrets."[21]

[21] Cambon to Henri Cambon, Sept. 30, Oct. 18, Nov. 11, Cambon to Xavier Charmes, Oct. 9, 1918, *ibid.,* 273–77, 281–82.

XII. PEACE AND RETIREMENT

THE CLOSE OF WORLD WAR I brought with it the inevitable burden of seeking a peace settlement. Paul Cambon's role in the Paris Peace Conference was largely that of a tormented observer. He followed the accounts of the conference closely and was ever ready to offer advice and comment. As the outcome of the conference became clearer, his frustration and his comments grew more bitter.

Probably in accordance with his instructions, Cambon left some preliminary notes on the peace conference at the Foreign Office in December, 1918. He proposed that guarantees be given for the demilitarization of the left bank of the Rhine, that Poland be restored, that Germany pay reparations for all damages that she had caused the Allies and neutral states, and that goods and material requisitioned by Germany in Alsace-Lorraine and occupied France be restored. He also proposed that German payments for the entire cost of the war be continued until 1975, that the indemnity extracted from France in 1871 be repaid with compound interest, that all of the enemy investments in France should be taken as indemnity, and all French investments in Germany, liquidated during the war, be repaid.[1]

This was the extreme position taken by those Frenchmen who had not forgotten the days of 1870. Since Cambon did not qualify any of these points, he must take some of the responsibility for such vindictiveness. However, he saw the necessity for speed in feeding the German people, whose government must sign the peace treaty.

[1] Philip M. Burnett, *Reparations at the Paris Peace Conference,* I, 438–44.

As the opening of the Paris Peace Conference drew near, hordes of delegates descended on Paris. The more Cambon saw of them, the unhappier he became. The American, British, Italian, Chinese, and Japanese delegates, as well as delegates from the newly born nations, filled Paris hotels under the pretext of working at the peace conference. "They have turned Paris into a bawdy house!" Cambon exclaimed. "What a mess they will make and what future wars they will prepare!"

On his next trip to Paris, Cambon urged Georges Clemenceau, the premier, to speed up the peace conference in order to accelerate demobilization. Already Britain was troubled with a mutiny at Folkstone, and there were dangers of strikes by unions filled with Bolshevik ideas. Clemenceau was not worried, claiming to be in close contact with the French unions. As he left, Cambon cautioned Clemenceau to beware of his enemies in the Chamber of Deputies.

The flood of foreign politicians into Paris, promising more than they could obtain, sickened Cambon; he must leave Paris quickly. "I can find nothing good here; I cannot approve of what is being done. . . . I leave weary and disgusted."[2]

The Paris Peace Conference opened on January 18, 1919. In its early meetings progress was too slow to satisfy Cambon, who was an advocate of a speedy preliminary peace—a consummation never achieved. The inclusion of the League of Nations and the colonial mandates in the conference violated all of his ideas regarding the conduct of diplomacy. Nor could he take comfort in Wilson's belief that the League would rectify all of the mistakes in the peace treaty. To Cambon, Wilson was a "vague dreamer" who possessed "an imagination sailing before every wind." Clemenceau disappointed him by permitting the discussions to stray to subjects that were out of place in a peace conference. Both Clemenceau and Lloyd George, the British prime minister, seemed to Cambon to have conceded too much to Wilson. There was no conference, Cambon declared, but a meeting of prime ministers and foreign ministers to whom Pro-

[2] Cambon to Henri Cambon, Dec. 11, 27, 1918, Cambon to Fleuriau, Jan. 19, 1919, *Correspondance,* III, 292–93, 297–98.

fessor Wilson delivered lectures. Clemenceau did not understand the importance of the questions he was discussing, Cambon alleged, and Lloyd George knew nothing. They had abandoned themselves to the caprices of Wilson.

Cambon insisted that poor preparation in the French Foreign Office had given Wilson his opportunity to take control of the conference. If French diplomats had known what they wanted, as a result of pre-conference work, Cambon believed that Wilson would have followed their desires.

Only Clemenceau could talk privately with Wilson and Lloyd George because he knew English, but his duties as premier limited such methods of diplomacy. Little could be accomplished privately, Cambon believed, if an interpreter had to be constantly present.[3]

As the time for the signing of the Treaty of Versailles drew near, the conservative Cambon was shocked at the elaborate preparations.

> The papers are full of the future signing of the peace with the plan of the Hall of Mirrors at Versailles. Nothing else than this plan could indicate such a profound revolution in the customs of diplomacy. There are found a hundred seats and tables for the assistants and the plenipotentiaries, as well as that table on which the treaty will be placed, in a type of theater. They lack only music and ballet girls, dancing in step, to offer the pen to the plenipotentiaries for signing. Louis XIV liked ballets, but only as a diversion; he signed treaties in his study. Democracy is more theatrical than the great king.[4]

When Lord Curzon, acting British foreign secretary, met Cambon in London and asked him if the Germans would sign, Cambon grimly remarked: "No doubt about it, they will sign—with a firm resolve not to execute it." However, when the treaty had been signed, Cambon was uneasy and dissatisfied. It reminded him of explosives that would one day burst all over the world. He preferred to see the

---

[3] Cambon to Xavier Charmes, Jan. 23, 1918, Cambon to Jules Cambon, Feb. 4, 1919, *ibid.*, 298, 303–304. See Appendix B.

[4] Cambon to Jules Cambon, June 28, 1919, *ibid.*, 340.

treaty signed in Berlin after an invasion of Germany. His wish was unfilled.[5]

His criticisms were colored by his memories of 1870 and his fears of the future. He was a methodical and systematic diplomat, and to him the politicians at the conference had been anything but systematic and methodical. There was much truth in his verdict, but the problems that crowded in on the men of the Paris Peace Conference were immense and required immediate action. System sometimes had to be forgotten because newly liberated peoples were changing frontiers, overthrowing governments, and clamoring for immediate solutions of their national problems.

Cambon's views would have been different had he been in Paris as a negotiator. But he would have been frustrated by the tendency of the politicians to negotiate and let the professional diplomats stand and wait. Certainly too much was attempted by men who were unsuited to the diplomatic profession and to the vast problems. Cambon realized this, but he could do little save dread the future.

He was of the generation whose ideas and methods were now considered out of fashion. In the future, the heads of governments in summit meetings would solve the problems of the world without professional advice, and with faulty procedure and disorganization. The great conflict was over, but its effects would linger on to poison the relations between nations, both allies and former enemies.

The fall of 1919 brought no cessation to the world's torment. Strikes in England, and riots in Italy, Rumania, Poland, and Czechoslovakia led Cambon to see anarchy everywhere. When President Woodrow Wilson suffered a stroke on October 2, 1919, the future of the treaty was indeed black. Cambon sadly noted: "If Wilson dies or if the American Senate rejects the League of Nations, what will become of the treaty? We must wish for Wilson's recovery."[6]

With the threat of Germany gone, the Entente Cordiale under-

[5] Cambon to Henri Cambon, June 29, 1919, *ibid.,* 341–42; H. Cambon, *Paul Cambon,* 303.

[6] Cambon to Henri Cambon, Sept. 27, Oct. 11, 19, 1919, *Correspondance,* III, 342, 358–62.

went a strain over dividing the remnants of the Ottoman Empire. During the Paris Peace Conference in May, 1919, Lloyd George proposed a British mandate over Constantinople, Anatolia, Armenia, and Syria. Later he offered Syria to the United States, but the Sykes-Picot Agreement of 1916, which Cambon helped to negotiate, placed Syria in the French sphere. Clemenceau was bitter, but Cambon assured him that Britain would not try to exclude France from Syria. In London he obtained assurances from Curzon that there were no changes and that Lloyd George probably did not know where Syria was located.

A month later the tension over Syria increased when Georges Picot assured the Syrians, in a public speech in Beirut, that France would free them from British control. Curzon was incensed. Cambon hastened to apologize and seek an end to such inflamatory outbursts.

The problem of Persia next disturbed the Entente, in July, 1919, when the Persian government, under French pressure, appointed French professors of law in Teheran. Curzon testily inquired of Cambon why these were necessary in a land of Moslem law. To him they sounded like amateur politicians. What if Britain were to do the same in areas reserved for French influence? Would not Cambon be quick to complain? With a sigh Cambon asked if the professors were confined to medicine, surgery, and similar fields of knowledge, would Curzon and his government be satisfied? With Curzon's assent, Cambon would attempt a change in his government's policy.

But Curzon was not finished. French propaganda beamed at Constantinople implied that France was the only friend of the Turks and should handle their interests. Britain could follow a similar policy, but it would only help the Turks play one nation off against the other. Cambon promised to make further inquiries in Paris because France did not want preponderance in Turkey.

Cambon encountered another list of complaints on September 22 when he saw Hardinge, again permanent undersecretary for foreign affairs, who complained that French papers were filled with criticisms of British policy in Syria, where Britain's actions were completely legal. Cambon argued that his government could not silence these influential papers, and, furthermore, some of the criticisms were justified. Hardinge dismissed this as past history that British agents on the spot had rectified. Returning to the attack, Hardinge asserted that in Teheran there was an active Franco-American policy that was anti-British and directed at the recent Anglo-Persian agreement to supply British advisers, army officers, and money to the Persian government. Had not Cambon twice before proclaimed his government's lack of interest in this area? Cambon had to confess that he had done so, but he assured Hardinge that Paris would hear of this complaint. He excused his government, since no warning had been given that such an agreement was in progress.

The next meeting of Cambon and Curzon in October was even more heated. Curzon berated Cambon for a recent note from the French embassy alleging that the British were giving arms to the Arabs in Syria and preparing to use them against the French, once British troops had evacuated the area. This Curzon denounced as "an insulting message." Cambon admitted "that its tone was of an unusual character and he expressed no surprise at its rejection; but he informed me [Curzon] incidentally that it had the distinction of having been composed by M. Clemenceau himself." Curzon reminded Cambon that similar notes had been received in the Foreign Office in recent months. Cambon could only deplore the fact that such messages were not handled through the foreign offices exclusively and that such language had been used. France was taking full advantage of the flexibility of her language to insult Britain, Curzon retorted; if he had done this for the past six months, what would Cambon have done? "I could imagine the speed with which you would have come to the Foreign Office and the vigor of the protest you would have made." Britain was prepared to publish papers showing how loyal she had been to France in Syria.

Cambon regretted that the settlement of the Turkish problem must await the outcome of Wilson's illness. Possibly this observation made Curzon realize at last that Cambon had not been fully informed by his government and did not know the full text of many of the documents that had passed between London and Paris.[7]

PEACE AND RETIREMENT

Cambon took a very minor part in the negotiations over the revision of the 1839 Belgian neutrality treaties. The Belgian government desired mutual guarantees of the frontiers without a pledge of neutrality, as required in the 1839 treaties, which prevented Belgium from making defensive arrangements with Great Britain and France. The negotiations did not reach the conclusion of a new treaty because of failure to agree on subsidiary issues.

According to the available records, Cambon was a silent ambassador when the Allied prime ministers and foreign ministers met again in London for three days in December, 1919, to consider secondary peace problems. Clemenceau, as befitting the "new diplomacy," led the negotiations. Cambon lent only his official presence.

In February and March, 1920, Cambon was a delegate to the Allied conference preparing the preliminaries for the Turkish peace treaty. Alexandre Millerand, the French premier, had not kept Cambon informed of the decisions made in Paris on this problem. Leaving the ill-prepared ambassador in charge of the negotiations, he returned to Paris and the Parliamentary battles.

The work of the conference was complicated by Mustafa Kemal Atatürk, the Turkish general who had placed himself at the head of a powerful nationalist movement in Turkey, determined to create a modern Turkish nation and defy the powers seeking the division of Turkey. To the embarrassment of the conference, there was no Allied force available to stop him.

Cambon realized that it was too late for the Allies to impose their will on Turkey. Fifteen months earlier they might have been successful, but now it was too late. They could do little, and the Turks knew it. To him the trouble with Turkey stemmed from the Allied promises of Turkish territory to Greece—which the Turks would not permit. Under the circumstances, Cambon could only make proposals of a general nature about improvements in the Turkish financial system; they meant little, and he knew it. Millerand hampered

---

[7] Curzon to Derby, May 30, June 11, July 4, Oct. 22, 1919, Curzon to Crowe, Sept. 24, 1919, *Documents on British Foreign Policy 1919–1939* (hereafter cited as *DBFP*), 1 ser., IV, 254–55, 274–75, 419–20.

his freedom of action by refusing assent to the propositions that the French delegates referred to him. Cambon felt that he was assisting in the sabotage of French interests in the Middle East. The treaty seemed unsuitable to him. He regretted his association with it.

As Cambon predicted, the Allied treaty of Sèvres, dealing with Turkey, which was completed in August, 1919, was not enforced. The powers could not agree on their aims. No nation was prepared to enforce the treaty alone. Once more he met the trouble that hampered his diplomacy in Constantinople during the 1890's. Many were willing to propose and talk about Turkey; no one was ready to act.[8]

More embarrassment followed for Cambon. On April 1, 1920, French troops occupied Frankfort and Darmstadt because German troops had entered the Rhineland to suppress revolts connected with Dr. Wolfgang Kapp's attempt to overthrow the republican government in Berlin. The French government claimed that the German action violated the demilitarization clauses of the Versailles Treaty.

In the presence of Lord Curzon on March 31, Cambon had dismissed reports in the newspapers of such impending action as mere gossip. The next day Curzon learned of the occupation through his morning newspaper. Cambon was speedily summoned to the Foreign Office to face Curzon's denunciation of the move as incompatible with the alliance and mutual understanding of the two nations. If France did not alter her policy, Curzon threatened to have the British troops withdrawn from the occupation areas.

It was the most painful moment of Cambon's career in London, for his government had not informed him and so made him appear a liar. By the end of May, the French government had apologized and withdrawn the offending troops.[9]

The Frankfort-Darmstadt affair revealed the deterioration of

[8] Cambon to Henri Cambon, Feb. 18, March 7, 17, 1920, Cambon to Jules Cambon, Feb. 27, 29, March 4, 9, 14, 1920, *Correspondance*, III, 375–83; David Lloyd George, *Memoirs of the Peace Conference*, II, 822–27; *DBFP*, 1 ser., VII, contains the records of the meetings.

[9] Earl of Ronaldshay, *The Life of Lord Curzon, being the Biography of George Nathaniel Marquess Curzon of Keddleston*, III, 231–33; Harold Nicolson, *Curzon: the Last Phase 1919–1925*, 199–200.

PEACE AND RETIREMENT

Anglo-French relations. The aged ambassador could not watch his work of twenty-two years collapse before his eyes. On every side disagreement and dissension surrounded him. "The unfortunate thing," he lamented, "is that neither in Paris nor in London is there enough intelligence to reduce the disagreements to the essential points and to disregard the trifles."

While he was in Paris on October 3 for the birth of his fourth grandchild, a digestive disturbance confirmed for him the idea of retirement. Shortly after his return to London, he informed the Quai d'Orsay of his decision to retire by the new year.

He knew that he must retire because he was completely at odds with his chief, Georges Leygues, minister for foreign affairs. Leygues advocated a policy antagonistic to Great Britain. This was the policy of Fashoda, and Cambon wanted none of it.

At the news of his retirement, letters of regret with invitations to banquets and dinners in his honor poured into Albert Gate House. Overwhelmed by the affection of the English, he hastened his departure to escape the invitations.

On December 10 the foreign press association gave him a banquet. In his toast, Andrew Bonar Law, leader of the Conservative party declared: "M. Cambon will take away with him not only the good wishes and respect and affection of all who had come in contact with him, but something more valuable still—the consciousness that through a career of unique length, he has deserved well of his country and ours."[10] Curzon gave Cambon and Imperiali, who was also leaving, a farewell banquet with the Prince of Wales as a guest. On December 15, after a dinner with his old friend Sir Thomas Sanderson, the aging ambassador became ill, and his doctor put him in bed for two days. Banquets and dinners already arranged, including one by King George V, had to be cancelled. On December 20, Cambon presented his letters of recall to the King and left London on December 22. A mission and a career unique in diplomatic history had come to an end.

Cambon returned to a quiet life in his apartment on the Boulevard

[10] London *Times,* Dec. 10, 1920.

Haussmann in Paris, seeing old friends and once more enjoying the way of life peculiar to Paris. As his health permitted, he made trips to the Pyrenees, to Rome, and to London for the last time in May, 1922. His brother Jules, still in an active diplomatic career, kept Paul informed on foreign affairs. In Paris he visited regularly the weekly meetings of the Academy of Moral and Political Sciences, of which he was a member. He was regular in attendance at the board of directors meeting of the Suez Canal Company, of which he was a member, as well as the meetings of the board of directors of the Paris-Lyons Railroad.

In 1923 his health began to deteriorate, and after breaking a bone in his right leg in March, 1924, he was bedridden. Cardiac asthma increased his suffering and hastened the end. Henri Cambon hurried from his post in Rome. At the last, Paul Cambon's mind wandered back to the Franco-Prussian War—so important in his life. At 5:00 P.M. on May 28, 1924, he died in the arms of his son and was buried beside his wife in the Montparnasse Cemetery.

On November 27, 1926, Monseigneur E. L. Jullien, bishop of Arras, who took Cambon's seat in the Academy of Moral and Political Sciences, delivered the eulogy on Paul Cambon's career: "He has done honor to his country through the truly magnificent way in which he served her. In London, as well as at Constantinople, he was, and he remains 'the grand ambassador.' "[11]

[11] H. Cambon, *Paul Cambon*, 317–23; E. L. Julien, *Notice sur la vie et les travaux de M. Paul Cambon*, 47.

XIII. AN EVALUATION

THE STORY OF A CAREER is ended. The final estimation of Cambon was mixed. To some of his contemporaries he was the supreme diplomat and to others only shrewd and cunning.

The London *Times* declared that Great Britain owed Paul Cambon a great debt, "for he will live in history as one of the chief architects of the Entente which laid the foundations of the alliance that was to save the liberties of the world ten years later on the stricken fields of France."

A different opinion came from Viscount Esher: "Shrewd and pliant, he gives an impression of possessing powers of mind that are in truth lacking. . . . He is courteous and cunning."

The journalist, J. A. Spender, wrote: "Cambon was a classic figure. With his courtly manners and air of taking everything seriously, he seemed to come straight out of the eighteenth century."

And Sir Edward Grey declared, "His great knowledge and experience had made his judgment mature; he felt the ground carefully before he ventured on it or advised others. He was above all petty maneuvers. . . . I felt safe with him: he wanted British policy to support France, but he would never use it for a passing advantage in a way that would result in his losing touch with it and forfeiting our confidence."

An interesting view came from the writer Octave Homberg. He found Cambon to be a great ambassador, a statesman, the superior of his brother, but somewhat pompous. "You had the feeling that even at night, alone with himself, in the intimacy of his bedroom, at bedtime, he would say to himself: 'His Excellency, the Ambassador of France, will now put on his night shirt.' "[1]

The Franco-Prussian War had a profound effect upon Paul Cambon. The spectacle of his country's defeat impelled him to prevent the repetition of such a catastrophe. There must never again be another 1870, never another time when France would face Germany alone. Cambon, like many of his generation, sought to rebuild France in national prestige. He did not want a war, but he fought to insure that France would have as many allies as possible if war should come. When the dread day dawned, Cambon and his colleagues had given France a strong international position.

As a diplomat, Cambon displayed independence in dealing with the Quai d'Orsay. He was no robot who wrote what his superiors wanted, nor did he try to satisfy a committee of the Chamber of Deputies. Much of his independence had developed through the trials and tribulations of the years in Tunisia when he struggled alone and unaided. In his later years, he sometimes filed his instructions in the wastebasket when he disagreed with them. This practice did not hurt his standing, but rather aided him. "I have a certain authority in the ministry only because, without worrying myself about the opinion of Paris or the pretended inclinations of the government, I have always expressed my ideas in complete freedom, and I have never deviated from this."[2]

The constant turnover in the office of minister of foreign affairs increased his independence. Cambon alone could provide the necessary continuity in the conduct of relations between France and the nation to which he was accredited. Not until the last years of his career in London was he hampered by sudden visits of foreign ministers and premiers who disrupted his negotiations with unpleasant

[1] London *Times,* May 30, 1924; Reginald Viscount Esher, *Journals and Letters,* III, 213–14; J. A. Spender, *Life, Journalism, and Politics,* I, 171–72; Grey, *Twenty-five Years,* II, 240–42; Octave Homberg, *Les coulisses de l'histoire,* 132–34.

[2] Cambon to Mme Cambon, Jan. 27, 1896, *Correspondance,* I, 400–401.

results. For much of his career, he was blessed by superiors who stayed in Paris.

Cambon practiced diplomacy as a good doctor would practice medicine, basing his diagnosis on sound principles. Tact and patience, coupled with quiet dignity and self-confidence, helped him in his work for France. Seeking only the possible, he shunned high-sounding generalities so beloved of "summit meetings."

He never spared those who he thought had acted foolishly—William II, French politicians, Russian diplomats, French diplomats, and even his personal friends. His criticism created the dislike that appeared for him in certain quarters of official Paris. Because he would not flatter the Quai d'Orsay, he was not well loved there in his later years.

During much of his work in London, Cambon was part of a team developed by Delcassé. With Barrère in Rome, Jules Cambon in Madrid and later in Berlin, Jusserand in Washington, Maurice Bompard in St. Petersburg, and Paul Cambon in London, France possessed an ambassadorial team unparalleled in recent French history. The collaboration of these men gave French foreign policy the cohesion and emphasis that it otherwise would have lacked. Paul Cambon's work would not have been as impressive or as efficient if the rest of the team had not existed.

Cambon favored "secret diplomacy," not to hatch nefarious deeds, but to accomplish the job at hand in the most efficient way. He advocated a method of diplomacy in which diplomats would talk privately with those whom they trusted and respected. The bargaining might be hard and sharp, but they sought an honorable and fair arrangement. By this method, the diplomats could achieve their goal without interference from public opinion or government propaganda. A point conceded in discussion could not be magnified by a hysterical public reading exaggerated accounts in a circulation-mad newspaper.

Before he left London, Cambon's style of diplomacy was considered out of date. The "new diplomacy" was fashionable—confused meetings between government leaders and foreign ministers with the professional ambassadors as spectators. Career diplomats were suspect, and politicians would be more effective negotiators. As diplomats, the politicians were often bad amateurs. Although well briefed, their knowledge of the subject was spotty. They gave lip service to "open covenants openly arrived at"; their half-secrecy only bred rumors harmful to sincere diplomacy.

Improvements in communications and transportation robbed the diplomat of more authority and influence. Too often he was a highly paid messenger boy, whose warnings and observations were disregarded by the politicians. In some quarters of the "new diplomacy," ambassadors were considered incompatible with democracy because they were loath to practice "front page diplomacy": negotiations carried on in an auditorium with reporters present to send every word around the world. The necessity to maintain a rigid ideological position in public negotiations prevented effective diplomacy. Public condemnation of a country's actions injured national prestige, creating more rigidity.

The diplomats of Cambon's generation had much in common and negotiated within a generally recognized frame of reference that disappeared after 1918. The subsequent growth of conflicting political ideologies, each with its promise of earthly paradise, made sincere negotiating almost impossible. The invasion of Poland in September, 1939, revealed the bankruptcy of the "new diplomacy." Despite the differences in conditions surrounding the "old and new" diplomacy, the principles practiced by Cambon had much value. Tragedy came when the principles were forgotten.

In Tunisia, Paul Cambon's work was illustrative of the French dilemma over how to equate control of empire with revolutionary ideals. The protectorate, in theory, tried to bridge that gap, but the noble ideal was forgotten, and Tunisia became a field for French exploitation of the natives. Cambon had seen the same tragedy in Algeria and hoped to avoid it in Tunisia. His work will always influence Tunisia, although his original intentions were forgotten.

Cambon contributed significantly to the creation of the French empire in North Africa. Most of his gains were lost because of the

AN EVALUATION

basic reasons that created the quarrel with Boulanger: the exploitation of Africa for the selfish interests of Frenchmen at the expense of the natives. The device of the protectorate in Tunisia could have been utilized to enhance French prestige if the needs of the natives had been kept foremost.

Cambon's years in Turkey were the least successful of his career. In the dying Ottoman Empire were the seeds of a great world conflict. If this conflict were to be avoided, the clash of spheres of power must somehow be adjusted peacefully. Cambon struggled helplessly with the problem of this empire; he sensed that it could destroy many unless agreement were reached and the power vacuum filled. Experience made him more aware of the relation of Russia to the Balkans and the Middle East. Circumstances forced him to draw closer to Great Britain and develop more sympathy for her policy. Thus Turkey prepared him for London and a twenty-two-year mission.

The years of Cambon's stay in London were the climax of his career. They were crowned by the negotiating of the Entente Cordiale, which at one time seemed impossible to the Wilhelmstrasse. His achievement was remarkable because he arrived in London when many despaired of Anglo-French amity. He was successful because he sought only what was possible. He tried to be a quiet, reliable old friend whose advice was in the best interests of Great Britain.

His mission was aided by what appeared to be a German menace. When Britain felt that she was threatened by a foe whose naval power might surpass hers, she turned to the nation who would be willing to give help. As a result of the groundwork laid by Cambon, France seemed to be the power to whom Britain naturally should turn.

The mission in London was successful because Britain, at the last moment, did not fail Cambon. If Britain had betrayed his trust in the great crisis of July-August, 1914, his career would have been ruined. But "perfidious Albion" went along with France, and one reason for her loyalty was the trust of Grey and Lansdowne in Cambon's word.

Cambon became a realist about his own nation. He knew that France could not stand alone against Germany, and, much as he hatred to admit it, she must have the aid of Russia—this became all too apparent in 1940. At the end of his career he even had to fall back on Britain to help France maintain her empire.

Paul Cambon's work was one of the fruits from the seed which Bismarck sowed when he united Germany by blood and iron. The defeat and the revolution of 1870–71 produced a generation of men who desired to create a stronger France. Of this generation, Paul Cambon was an outstanding member. Friends of France can only hope that the trials of 1940–44 will produce men with similar talent and vision.

APPENDIX A

CAMBON'S DISCUSSION WITH LANSDOWNE ON MAY 17, 1905

CAMBON'S INTERPRETATION of his talk on May 17, 1905, with Lansdowne has and will continue to puzzle historians until more documents are available—if they still or ever did exist.

G. P. Gooch wrote, "It is a curious instance of an experienced statesman taking the wish for the deed."[1]

Luigi Albertini implied that Cambon had misunderstood Lansdowne, who intended that they meet only to discuss the means of controlling events, not measures in case of German aggression. He wrote, "That Cambon was mistaken in repeating to Paris that it would be easily possible to have an alliance with England if it were desired is proved by documents of those dates."[2]

In April, 1906, Grey denied the existence of such an offer. In 1912 and 1927, Lansdowne denied the story also, agreeing with statements made already by Sanderson to Harold Temperley in a letter of August 17, 1922. Sanderson wrote:

> There is no record of this offer of an alliance by Lansdowne in our archives, nor has Lord Lansdowne any recollection of it. All that is to be found is that he and Lord Bertie laid stress in conversation on the need for frank and intimate communication and

[1] *Studies in Diplomacy and Statecraft*, 90.
[2] *The Origins of the War of 1914*, I, 155–57.

consultation with a view to harmonious action in opposition to any designs of Germany to acquire a port on the west coast of Morocco. It is possible that M. Cambon may have taken down in writing the phrases used by Lord Lansdowne in this respect . . . .[3]

A. J. P. Taylor asserted, "This was not an offer of an alliance, nor even of military support; it was a warning that France could not make any concession to Germany without British approval."[4]

It is difficult to believe that a diplomat of Paul Cambon's experience could have so misinterpreted Lansdowne's statements. The truth may be that to a certain degree both men were right in their interpretations. When this crisis burst on Europe, Lansdowne took the practical course and proposed conversations to unite policy. He did not propose a formal alliance; rather, he offered a practical solution for the immediate problem. But Cambon realized that the practical solution, when followed to its logical conclusion, would ultimately amount to an alliance. He foresaw that joint talks on policy would mean joint action, should Germany resort to aggression, and that would constitute an alliance in fact if not in theory. This actually proved to be the case.

[3] Grey to O'Connor, April 9, 1906, *BD*, II, 87; Sanderson to Temperley, Aug. 17, 1922, *ibid.*, III, 87; Newton, *Lord Lansdowne*, 343.
[4] *The Struggle for Mastery in Europe 1848–1918*, 431.

APPENDIX B

CAMBON'S INABILITY TO SPEAK ENGLISH

IT IS AMUSING that Cambon was critical of the inability of French diplomats to speak English—a language that he could not speak except to ask for his carriage and footman. His mission to London might have been aided by the use of English in his diplomacy. As far as is known, he never spoke English, even after living for twenty-two years in London. He read and understood English, but as a diplomat he felt that accuracy demanded that he use a language in which he was proficient. He did not want to place France in an embarrassing position because of the improper use of a foreign tongue.

Lansdowne and Salisbury spoke French, but Grey spoke the language very poorly. When Cambon and Grey talked, Cambon spoke slowly in French, and Grey spoke very slowly in English. Cambon usually repeated Grey's important statements in French to insure that he had correctly understood. Richard von Kühlmann, the counsellor of the German embassy, claimed that Cambon's social life was hampered by his lack of English. On one occasion Kühlmann was invited to a week end at Belvoir Castle to interpret for Cambon.[1]

[1] Richard von Kühlmann, *Erinnerungen*, 325-26; Charles-Roux, *Souvenirs*, 248; interview with H. W. Steed.

SELECTED BIBLIOGRAPHY

MANUSCRIPT SOURCES

Foreign Office Library, London, Nicolson Manuscripts.
Public Record Office, London, Manuscripts, Foreign Office, Tunisia, France, Morocco, Turkey.
"Rapport de la commission pour l'examen de la situation administrative en Tunisie," December 24, 1885. (Typescript.)

PRIMARY PRINTED SOURCES

Amery, L. S. *My Political Life.* 3 vols. London, 1953.
Barrère, Camille. "La chute de Delcassé," *Revue des deux mondes*, August 1, 1932, 602–18.
Benckendorff, Alexander Graf von. *Diplomatischer Schriftwechsel.* Edited by B. von Siebert. 3 vols. Berlin, 1928.
Bourbon-Parma, Prince Sixte. *L'offre de paix séparée de l'Autriche.* Paris, 1920.
British Documents on the Origins of the War. Edited by G. P. Gooch and Harold Temperley. 11 vols. London, 1926–38.
Cambon, Paul. *Les conditions du travail en Espagne.* Paris, 1890.
———. *Correspondance, 1870–1924.* Edited by Henri Cambon. 3 vols. Paris, 1940–46.
———. "Lettres de Paul Cambon au Président de la République Félix Faure," *Revue d'histoire diplomatique,* LXVIII (1954), 189–201.

SELECTED BIBLIOGRAPHY

———. "Lettres de Tunisie," *Revue des deux mondes*. 15 May 1931, 373-98.

Chamberlain, Austen. *Down the Years*. London, 1935.

Charles-Roux, François. *Souvenirs diplomatiques d'un âge révolu*. Paris, 1956.

Churchill, Winston Spencer. *The World Crisis, 1911-1918*. 2 vols. London, 1938.

Documents on British Foreign Policy, 1919-1939. Edited by E. L. Woodward and Rohan Butler. 1st series. 8 vols. London, 1947-.

Eckardstein, Baron von. *Ten Years at the Court of St. James 1895-1905*. London, 1921.

Esher, Reginald, Viscount. *Journals and Letters*. Edited by Oliver, Viscount Esher. 3 vols. London, 1938.

France, Ministère des Affaires Étrangères. *Documents diplomatiques. Affaires Arméniennes, projets de reforms dans l'Empire Ottoman 1893-1897*. Paris, 1897.

———. *Documents diplomatiques, français, 1871-1914*. 3 series. 39 vols. Paris, 1929-.

———. *Documents diplomatiques français, correspondance concernant la déclaration additionnelle du mars 1899 à la convention franco-anglaise du 14 juin 1898*. Paris, 1899.

Grey, Viscount, of Fallodon, K. G. *Twenty-five Years, 1892-1916*. 2 vols. New York, 1925.

Die grosse Politik der europäischen Kabinette 1871-1914. Edited by Johannes Lepsius, A. Mendelssohn-Bartholdy, and Friedrich Thimme. 40 vols. Berlin, 1922-27.

Homberg, Octave. *Les coulisses de l'histoire*. Paris, 1938.

Journal de Alexandre Ribot et correspondances inédites. Edited by A. Ribot. Paris, 1936.

Journal Officiel.

Kühlmann, Richard von. *Erinnerungen*. Heidelberg, 1948.

London *Times*.

Lloyd George, David. *Memoirs of the Peace Conference*. 2 vols. New Haven, 1939.

Österreich-Ungarns Aussenpolitik von der Bosnischen Krise 1908 bis zum Kreigsausbruch 1914. Edited by Ludwig Bittner, A. F. Pribram, Herbert Srbik, and Hans Uberaberger. 8 vols. Vienna, 1930.
Spender, J. A. *Life, Journalism, and Politics.* 2 vols. New York, 1927.
Steed, Henry Wickham. *Through Thirty Years 1892-1922.* 2 vols. New York, 1924.

SECONDARY SOURCES

Adam, Colin Forbes. *Life of Lord Lloyd.* London, 1948.
Albertini, Luigi. *The Origins of the War of 1914.* 3 vols. London, 1952-57.
Amery, Julian. *The Life of Joseph Chamberlain.* Vol. 4. London, 1951.
Burnett, Philip M. *Reparations at the Paris Peace Conference.* 2 vols. New York, 1940.
Cambon, Henri. *Histoire de la régence de Tunis.* Paris, 1948.
———. *Paul Cambon, ambassadeur de France.* Paris, 1937.
———. "Paul Cambon et les préliminaires de l'Entente cordiale," *La revue de Paris,* XLIV (1937), 545-64.
Charles-Roux, François. *Trois ambassades françaises à la veille de la guerre.* Paris, 1928.
Colvin, Ian. *The Life of Lord Carson.* 3 vols. New York, 1937.
Eubank, Keith, "The Fashoda Crisis Re-examined," *The Historian,* XII (Feb. 1960), 145-62.
Giraud, André. "Diplomacy, Old and New," *Foreign Affairs,* XXIII (1945), 256-70.
Gooch, G. P. *Studies in Diplomacy and Statecraft.* London, New York, 1942.
Jullien, E. L. *Notice sur la vie et les travaux de M. Paul Cambon.* Paris, 1926.
Newton, Lord. *Lord Lansdowne.* London, 1929.
Nicolson, Harold. *Sir Arthur Nicolson, Bart. First Lord Carnock.* London, 1930.
———. *Curzon: the Last Phase, 1919-1925.* New York, 1939.

SELECTED BIBLIOGRAPHY

P. H. X. (de Constant d'Estournelles). *La politique française en Tunisie, le protectorat et ses origines 1854-1891.* Paris, 1891.

Recouly, Raymond. *Les heures tragiques d'avant-guerre.* Paris, n.d.

Ronaldshay, Earl of. *The Life of Lord Curzon. Being the Authorized Biography of George Nathaniel Curzon of Keddleston.* London, n.d.

Serres, Victor. "Le protectorat Tunisie," *L'Afrique Française,* XL (1932), 329-46.

Spender, J. A. *The Life of the Right Hon. Sir Henry Campbell-Bannerman, G. C. B.* 2 vols. London, 1923.

Tabouis, Geneviève. *Jules Cambon par l'un des siens.* Paris, 1938.

Taylor, A. J. P. *The Struggle for Mastery in Europe, 1848-1918.* Oxford, 1954.

INDEX

Abdul Hamid II, Sultan of Turkey: 32, 38, 40–41, 43, 44, 46 ff., 60
Academy of Moral and Political Sciences: 200
Admiralty: 147–48, 154–55, 164
Adowa, battle of: 117
Aegean Islands: 160, 162
Aehrenthal, Count Lexa von: 126 ff.
Afghanistan: 124
Agadir Crisis: 126, 136–42
Albania: 158, 160–63
Albert Gate House: 64, 117 ff., 199
Albertini, Luigi: 207
Alexandra, Queen: 130–32
Alfonso XIII: 32, 34, 102, 110
Algeciras Conference: 105, 111, 114–17, 133; program, 106; P. Cambon, J. Cambon, and Nicolson discuss strategy, 114
Algeria: 13, 20, 21, 26, 30, 33, 59, 83
Alsace-Lorraine: 60, 128, 154, 191
Ambassadors' Conference over Balkan Wars: 157–64
American Indians: 32
Amery, Julian: 70 n.
Amery, Leopold: 176–77
Anatolia: 195
Anglo-French Naval Agreement: 147–52, 175
Anglo-Japanese Alliance: 69–70
Anglo-Russian Entente: 123–24, 126, 166

Armenia: 45, 47 ff., 195; Armenian question, 46–47, 52–53
Asia Minor: 46, 48, 50, 51, 53
Asquith, Herbert: 138, 147, 165, 177, 182; approved Grey-Cambon letters, 152
Atatürk, Mustafa Kemal: 197
Aumale, duke d': 24
Austria-Hungary: 35, 36, 39, 50, 64 n., 115, 126 ff., 158, 161, 168 ff., 187, 188

Bahr el Ghazal: 66
Balfour, Arthur J.: 71, 76, 87, 109
Balkan Wars: 154–57; ambassadors' conference, 157–64
Barcelona Exposition: 35–36
Barrère, Camille: 99, 107, 108, 115, 143–44, 203
Belgium: 178 ff., 182, 197
Benckendorff, Alexander: 123, 158, 160, 163 ff., 170, 183; quarrels with Lansdowne, 90–91; Dogger Bank incident, 91–94; opinion of P. Cambon, 184
Berlin: 138
Berthelot, Marcellin: 50
Bertie, Sir Francis: 99, 137, 147, 151, 207
Bienvenu-Martin, J. B.: 170–71
Billot, General Jean: 14
Bismarck, Otto von: 3, 35, 206

INDEX

Bittis, Armenia: 48
Blowitz, Henri: 23
Boer War: 67–68, 70, 76, 81, 88
Bompard, Maurice: 203
Bonar Law, Andrew: 177, 199
Bonhoure, editor of *La Lanterne*: 30
Bosnia-Herzegovina: 126, 128, 156
Bosnian Crisis: 126–28, 134
Boulanger, Georges: 24, 32, 33, 36; struggle with Cambon, 25–31
Bourgeois, Émile: 115
Bourgeois, Léon: 129
Brest, France: 61, 152
Brisson, Eugene: 28 f.
British Documents on the Origins of the War: 106
Broglie, Duke de: 12
Buette, engineer: 7 ff.
Bulgaria: 156
Bülow, Count Bernhard von: 97, 98, 107–108
Bureaus, intelligence: 25

Caballero, Pérez: 121
Caillaux, Joseph: 136 ff.
Cambon, Anna: 11, 32, 59
Cambon, Henri: 11, 31 n., 66
Cambon, Hippolyte: 3
Cambon, Jules: 3 f., 7, 59, 107, 114, 115, 121, 136 ff., 173, 200, 203
Cambon, Paul: birth, education, 3–4; secretary to mayor of Paris, 5–6; and Paris Commune, 6–10; escaped attack on Hôtel de Ville, 7; aided escape of Jules Ferry, 8–10; effects of Franco-Prussian War, 10, 200, 202; appointed prefect, 11; marriage and birth of son, 11; resignation after crisis of May 15, 1877, 12; dispersed religious orders, 12–13
――――, Tunisia: appointed minister, 13; preliminary report, 14; departure from France, 14–15; arrival in Tunisia, 17; report to Freycinet, 17–18; Paris trip, May 20, 1882, 18; presented treaty to Bey, 19; negotiated return of refugees, 19; obtained decree of March 27, 1883, 20–21; signed La Marsa Convention, 21; speaker in Chamber of Deputies (April 1, 1884), 22–23; struggle with Boulanger, 24–31; opinion of Boulanger, 24–25; dissatisfaction with Cambon's administration, 25–26; Tisi affair, 27; letter to Freycinet (June 15, 1884), 27–28; decree of June 23, 1885, 28; sought help in Paris, 28–29; administration investigated, 30–31; awarded Legion of Honor, 31; record in Tunisia, 32–33, 204–205
――――, Madrid: appointed Spanish ambassador, 32; presented credentials, 34; Spain in Triple Alliance, 35; Barcelona Exposition, 35–36; letter to Spuller (March 11, 1889), 36–38
――――, Constantinople: appointed, 39; arrival, 41; Egyptian question, 41–45; alarmed by Armenian question, 47; massacres and investigations, 48–49, 52; work with ambassadors for reforms, 50–51; advocated more forceful policy, 52–53; Cretan question, 53–55; doubts concerning Russian alliance, 56–58; attracted toward Great Britain, 58; meeting with William II, 59; departure, 60; results of mission, 60, 205
――――, London: accepted post, 59; proposed as ambassador, 62; arrival, 62; appearance and daily routine, 62–63; first meeting with Salisbury, 64; reception by Queen Victoria, 64–65; speech before French colony, 65; speeches before chamber of commerce, 65, 80; discussed Newfoundland question, 66, 71–72; alarmed by Boer War, 67; Leandre cartoon, 67–68; attended Queen Victoria's funeral, 68; meetings with

215

William II, 68–69, 136; reaction to Anglo-Japanese alliance, 70; discussion with Joseph Chamberlain, 70; discussed New Hebrides question, 72; discussions over Morocco, 73–78; disturbed by Maclean trip, 73; cessation of negotiations over Morocco, 78–79; negotiated loan for Sultan of Morocco, 79–80; state visit of Edward VII, 80–81; state visit of Loubet, 81–82; negotiated Entente Cordiale, 83–87; opinion of Entente Cordiale, 88; role in negotiation of Entente Cordiale, 89; Lansdowne-Beckendorff quarrels, 90–91; negotiated Dogger Bank incident, 91–94; received degree at Oxford, 94–96; first Moroccan crisis, 97–108; Lansdowne statement (May 17, 1905), 100–101, appendix A; interested in Grey's views, 109; problem of German influence in Spain, 109–10; requested British aid against German aggression, 110–14; discussed strategy for Algeciras Conference, 114; Algeciras Conference, 114–17; negotiated Ethiopian Agreement, 117–21; negotiated Mediterranean Agreement of 1907, 121–23; interested in Anglo-Russian Entente, 123–24; Grey's pledge in 1907, 125; Bosnian Crisis, 127–28; problems with artists, 129; entertained Loti, 129–32; funeral of Edward VII, 132–33; Moroccan problem, 134–36; Franco-German accord over Morocco, 134–35; Agadir crisis, 136–42; advised Selves, 140–41; affected by Italo-Turkish War, 143–44; disturbed by Anglo-German negotiations, 144–46; requested Anglo-French declaration, 146–47; Anglo-French naval agreement, 147–52; negotiated Grey-Cambon letters, 152–55; Balkan wars, 156–57; ambassadors conference, 157–64; Grey's opinions of Cambon, 163, 201; tightened Triple Entente, 164–66; unimpressed by assassination, 168; analysis of Austro-Serbian relations, 168; July-August crisis, 169–82; learned of Austrian ultimatum, 169; talks with Grey, 169–76, 178, 180–81; trip to Paris, 170–71; meeting with Conservative leaders, 177–78; reminded Nicolson of movements of French fleet, 177–78; interviewed by Steed, 178–79; announced Britain at war, 181; evaluation of work in July-August crisis, 181–82; and World War, 183–90; negotiated economic accord, 183; signed alliance (Sept. 5, 1914), 183–84; signed treaty of London, 184; opposed prosecution of *Times,* 184–85; participated in meetings with Allied leaders, 185–86; opinion on British conscription, 186; observed eighteenth anniversary, 186–87; opposed liaison officer in War Office, 187; discussions with Prince Sixte, 187–88; awarded Order of Bath, 188; opinion on meat rationing, 188–89; despair over future, 189; prophecy of Nazi Germany, 190; opinion of Paris Peace Conference, 191–94; preliminary notes on peace conference, 191; warning to Clemenceau, 192; opinion of League of Nations, 192, 194; opinions of Wilson, 192–93, 194; dissatisfied with Versailles Treaty, 194–95; saddened by strains of Entente Cordiale, 195–99; troubled by Syrian question, 195–96; participated in Belgian negotiations, 197; worried by Treaty of Sèvres, 197–98; embarrassed by occupation of Frankfort and Darmstadt, 198–99; decision to retire, 199; retirement, 199–200; death, 200; *Times* opinion, 201; Esher's opinion, 201; Spender's

INDEX

opinion, 201; Homberg opinion, 201–202; independence, 202–203; practice of diplomacy, 203; secret diplomacy, 203–204; "new diplomacy," 203–204; work in London, 205–206; discussion with Lansdowne, 207–208; inability to speak English, appendix B
Cambon, Virginie: 3, 7, 9
Campbell-Bannerman, Sir Henry: 109 ff., 121, 125
Campenon, General Jean: 25, 28
Capitulations: 14 n., 17 ff.
Casablanca: 115, 134
Chamber of commerce: 65, 73, 80
Chamber of Deputies: 21–24, 42, 48, 108, 133, 157, 186, 192, 202
Chamberlain, Austen: 177
Chamberlain, Joseph: 64, 67, 69, 70, 82
Churchill, Winston: 147 ff., 171; opinion of Grey-Cambon letters, 154
Clemenceau, Georges: 11, 125, 192, 195
Compagnie imperiale des chemins de fer ethiopens: 117
Congress of Berlin: 41, 46, 63
Constantinople: 32, 38 ff., 52, 58 ff., 160, 195
Courcel, Baron Alphonse de: 59, 62, 66
Crete: 53–55
Cromer, Lord: 32, 86
Crowe, Eyre: 121
Cruppi, Jean: 135
Culottes: 81–82
Currie, Sir Philip: 48 f.
Curzon, Lord: 95, 193 ff.

Darmstadt: 198–99
Delcassé, Théophile: 59 f., 62, 64 ff., 70, 74, 75, 78 ff., 85 ff., 92, 94, 117, 147, 154, 155, 203; visit to London, 81–83; biography, 96–97; first Moroccan crisis, 97–105; analysis of fall, 107–108; comment on Treaty of London (1915), 184
Develle, Jules: 58 f.
Diarbekir: 50
Disraeli, Benjamin: 63
Dogger Bank Incident: 91–94, 124
Doumergue, Gaston: 164 ff.
Dreyfus Affair: 98, 107
Dual Alliance: 35, 127
Dufaure, Jules: 12
Dunkerque: 185

Eckardstein, Baron von: 70, 76
Edward VII: 76 f., 131; state visit to France, 80–81; state visit of Loubet, 81–82; German influence in Spain, 110; funeral, 132–33
Egypt: 38, 60 ff., 70 ff.; Egyptian question, 18–19, 41–45, 83–88
England: (see Great Britain)
English Channel: 179
Entente Cordiale: 90, 92, 96 ff., 100, 103 ff., 108 ff., 124 ff., 133, 135, 140, 144 ff.; 154 f., 181, 194, 205; negotiations, 83–87; provisions, 87–88; analysis, 88–89; effect of Mediterranean Agreement of 1907, 122–23
Erzurum: 48
Esher, Viscount: 201
Ethiopia: 61
Ethiopian Agreement: 117–21
Europe: 163

Fashoda Incident: 61–62, 65–67, 72, 145, 183, 199
Faure, Felix: 58, 64
Ferry, Charles: 4, 7 ff.
Ferry, Jules: 4 ff., 12 f., 15, 22 ff., 26; escaped from Hôtel de Ville, 6–7; escaped from Paris, 8–10
Fez: 75, 135 f.
Figaro: 132
Fisher, Sir John: 148, 150
Fleuriau, Aimé de: 170
Foch, Marshal Ferdinand: 186
Foreign Office: 63, 74, 92, 178 f.

217

France: 3, 5, 10, 13, 15, 18 ff., 26, 36 ff., 41, 43 ff., 48, 50, 56–58, 60, 62, 64 ff., 72, 77, 88, 96, 105, 144, 165, 202
Francis Ferdinand, Archduke: 167–68
Franco-German Accord over Morocco (1909): 134–35
Franco-Prussian War: 5, 10, 157, 200
Franco-Prussian Alliance: 44, 53, 103, 117
Frankfort: 198–99
French Congo: 32, 61, 137, 141
French Guinea: 87
French Somaliland: 117
French, General: 95
Freycinet, Charles: 14 f., 28 ff., 41–42

Gallipoli: 186
Gambia: 84 f., 88
George V: 165, 188, 199
Germany: 35 ff., 50, 69, 78, 80, 88, 97, 105, 114, 121, 127, 172 ff., 188, 202
Giers, Nicholas: 43
Gooch, G. P.: 106–107, 207
Great Britain: 18 ff., 37 ff., 50, 53, 57–58, 60, 62, 64, 67 ff., 88, 114, 117, 127, 153–54, 167, 194
Greece: 54 f., 156, 160
Green, W.: 62
Grévy, Jules: 28
Grey, Sir Edward: 110, 115, 124, 126 f., 137 ff., 157 ff., 168, 171, 182, 205, 207, 209; personality, 109; Cambon's request for British aid, 110–14; signed Ethiopian Agreement, 119–20; signed Mediterranean Agreement (1907), 121–23; pledged support to France (1907), 125; Franco-German accord over Morocco (1909), 134–35; Anglo-French Naval Agreement, 147–51; Grey-Cambon letters, 152–55; opinions of Cambon, 163, 201; talks with Cambon during July-August crisis, 169–76, 178, 180–81; signed alliance, 183; signed Treaty of London, 184
Grey-Cambon Letters: 144, 152–56; analysis, 153–56, 176

Hafid, Moulay: 135
Haig, Field Marshal Douglas: 187
Haldane, R. B.: 112
Hanotaux, Gabriel: 48, 50 ff.
Hardinge, Sir Charles: 92, 134, 195–96
Harrington, Sir John: 117–18
Harris, Walter B.: 75 ff.
Herbert, Michael: 52
Herbette, Jules: 13
Hirondelle: 15, 17
Holstein, Baron Friedrich von: 89, 97, 107–108
Homberg, Octave: 201–202
Hôtel de Ville: 5 ff.
House of Commons: 180
Huguet, Major: 112 n.
Hyde Park: 63

Imperiali, Guglielmo: 158, 199
Indo-China: 32
Isvolsky, Alexander: 126 ff., 158
Italo-Turkish War: 143–44, 147–48, 154
Italy: 35 ff., 50, 64 n., 117, 143–44, 161, 194

Japan: 69; *see also* Anglo-Japanese Alliance, Russo-Japanese War
Jullien, E. L.: 200
Journal Officiel: 13
Jusserand, J. J.: 108, 203

Kapp, Wolfgang: 198–99
Kiderlen-Wächter, Alfred von: 136 ff.
Kitchener, Lord: 61 f.
Kühlmann, Richard von: 209
Kurds: 46 f.

La Goulette: 17
Lake Tchad: 87
La Lanterne: 29 f.

INDEX

La Marsa Convention: 21
Lamsdorff, Vladimir: 123
Lansdowne, Lord: 68, 70–72, 79, 96, 111 f., 118–19, 121, 147, 151, 155, 177, 205, 209; discussions with Cambon over Morocco, 73–78; talk with Delcassé, 82–83; negotiations over Entente Cordiale, 83–87; quarrels with Benckendorff, 90–91; Dogger Bank Incident, 91–94; first Moroccan crisis, 99–102; statement of May 17, 1905, 100–101, 207–208
Larue Abbé: 11
League of Nations: 192, 194
Leandre Cartoon: 67–68
Leygues, Georges: 199
Libya: 143
Lichnowsky, Prince Karl Max: 158, 171 f., 178
Lloyd, Lord George: 176–77
Lloyd George, David: 138, 147, 187 f., 195
London: 59 f., 75 f., 81, 91, 99, 104, 111, 129, 167, 170 f., 186, 197, 199, 205
Los Islands: 87 f.
Loti, Pierre: 129–32
Loubet, Émile: 81–83, 99
Louis XIV: 64, 86, 193
Louis, George: 104
Louis Phillipe: 3, 187
Luxembourg: 178

McKenna, Reginald: 148
Maclean, Harry: 73 ff.
MacMahon, Marshal: 5, 12
Madagascar: 32, 71 f., 83, 88
Madrid: 34 f., 73, 121
Mahdi: 61 f.
Marcère, Émile: 12
Marchand, Captain Jean: 61 ff., 81
Marconi, Guglielmo: 95
Maria, Queen regent: 34
Mary, Queen: 165
Maxse, Leo: 176
Mediterranean Agreements of 1887: 64

Mediterranean Agreement of 1907: 121–23
Mediterranean Sea: 72, 144, 148 ff.
Meline: 8
Menelik, emperor: 117–18
Mensdorff, Count Albert von: 127, 158 ff.
Metternich, Count Paul von: 70, 112, 125, 138, 145 f.
Millerand, Alexandre: 197
Molacca: 91
Monson, Sir Edmund: 62, 67 f., 76
Montebello, Count de: 38
Montenegro: 39, 156, 160
Moret, Sigismund: 34 f.
Morocco: 32 ff., 70–80, 82–88; first Moroccan crisis, 96–108; Moroccan question, 133–36; Agadir crisis, 136–42
Mussolini, Benito: 20

Napoleon III: 3 f.
National Guard: 5 ff.
Nazi Germany: 121, 190
Nelidov, Alexander: 43, 48 ff., 58
"New Diplomacy": 203–204
Newfoundland: 66, 71–72, 83 ff.
New Hebrides: 71 f., 83, 88
Nicholas, King of Montenegro: 160
Nicolson, Sir Arthur: 75, 76 n., 77, 114, 124, 135, 146 ff., 152 170., 174 ff., 177–78
Niger River: 85
Nigeria: 83, 86, 88
Nile River: 61 f., 66
North Sea: 91, 94, 179

Oriel College: 95 f.
Ottoman Empire: 39–40, 42, 46, 53 ff., 144, 156; evaluation of Cambon's work, 204–205
Oxford University: 94–95, 130

Pact of Halepa: 54 f.
Pansa, Alberto: 118 f.
Panther: 137 f.

Paris: 3 ff., 10, 13 ff., 18, 20 ff., 38 ff., 60, 67, 81, 87, 92, 104, 125, 139 ff., 170, 192, 199
Paris Commune: 6–10
Paris Peace Conference: 191–95
Persia: 124, 164, 166, 195–96
Pichon, Stephan: 122, 128, 133 ff., 190
Picot, Georges: 195
Poincaré, Raymond: 146, 151 ff., 165; personality, 157–58
Poland: 194, 204
Pontois, Judge: 28 f.
Princip, Gavrilo: 168

Radolin, Hugo von: 97, 102, 104 f., 107 n.
Repington, Colonel: 112 n.
Révoil, Paul: 115
Ribot, Alexandre: 38 f., 187
Richardson, Major: 185
Roberts, Lord: 76
Rome: 31, 122
Roosevelt, Theodore: 105, 133, 167
Roustan, Theodore: 13, 29
Rouvier, Maurice: 97 ff., 101–102, 104 f., 111, 113, 115, 155; Cambon's opinion of, 103
Rumania: 39, 194
Russia: 37 ff., 44, 47 ff., 50, 53, 56–58, 60, 69, 127 f., 184, 188
Russo-Japanese War: 86–88, 90, 128
Russo-Turkish War: 41

Sadok, Mohammed es: 13, 16, 19 f.
Sagasta, Práxedes: 34 f.
Saint-Germain-l'Auxerois, church of: 8 f.
Saint Petersburg: 38, 44, 91, 122, 174
Salisbury, Lord: 66, 67, 69, 72 f., 209; personality, 63–64; reception for Cambon, 64–65; retirement, 70–71
Salonica: 186
Sanderson, Sir Thomas: 76, 199, 207
San Guiliamo: 184
Sans-culottes: 81–82
Sarajevo: 167

Sargent, John Singer: 95
Sazonov, Sergei: 164, 172, 184
Schleswig-Holstein: 106
Schoen, Baron Wilhelm von: 170, 176
Scutari: 160
"Secret Diplomacy": 203
Selves, Justin de: 136 ff.
Senate: 23, 133
Serbia: 39, 128, 156, 158, 160, 168 ff., 186
Sheldonian Theater: 95
Siam: 71 ff., 88
Sidi Ali: 20 ff.
Simon, Jules: 5, 12
Sixte, Prince of Bourbon-Parma: 187–88
Sokoto: 86 f.
Sophia, consort of Francis Ferdinand: 168
Spain: 35 ff., 88, 115, 136
Spender, J. A.: 201
Spuller, Eugene: 36 ff.
Steed, H. Wickham: 178–79, 185
Straits of the Dardanelles: 39 f., 50, 58, 60, 126
Straits of Gibraltar: 72, 74, 79, 84 f., 121, 148
Sudan: 61, 66, 117
Suez Canal: 19, 41, 72, 200
Sykes-Picot Agreement: 195
Syria: 195–96

Tangiers: 74 ff., 97, 115
Taylor, A. J. P.: 208
Temperley, Harold: 106–107, 207
Thiers, Adolphe: 4, 7, 10 f.
Tibet: 124
Times, London: 23, 31, 62, 75, 80, 167, 178, 201; Richardson Case, 184–85
Tisi Affair: 27–28
Tittoni, Tomaso: 118 ff.
Tobruk: 143
Torrens Act: 32, 33 n.
Tornielli, Giuseppi: 36
Transvaal: 67
Treaty of Bardo: 13

INDEX

Treaty of Berlin: 42, 46, 126
Treaty of London: 184:
Treaty of San Stephano: 41
Treaty of Sèvres: 197–98
Treaty of Utrecht: 71
Treaty of Versailles: 193–94
Triple Alliance: 35, 42, 64, 160, 164
Triple Entente: 160, 164 ff.
Tsushima: 94
Tunis: 16, 19, 27 ff.
Tunisia: 13 ff., 16 ff., 23, 26 ff., 38, 202; Cambon's work, 32–33, 204–205
Turkey: 197–98; *see also* Ottoman Empire

Uganda: 117

Van, Armenia: 51
Versailles: 9 ff., 193
Victoria, Queen: 3, 62, 67, 68, 132, 136, 188; reception for Cambon, 64–65
Vigo, Spain: 92 f.
Villa-Urrutia: 122
Vigiani, Rene: 170 f., 176

War Office: 73
White, Sir William: 59
Whitehall: 63, 66, 92, 150, 152
William II: 77, 79, 97, 99, 105, 107, 110 f., 115, 203; meetings and conversations with Cambon, 59, 68–69, 136
Wilson, Woodrow: 192 ff., 196
Windsor Castle: 64, 68, 133, 188
Worms, Doctor: 7 f.
Wyndham, George: 95

Zeitoun, Armenia: 51